Breaking with Communism

To Kathryn Feuer
So you won't have
to search for a copy
in your book-filled
house.

Bob Cessen

7/12/91

Bertram D. Wolfe
(1896–1977)

Breaking with Communism

The Intellectual Odyssey of
Bertram D. Wolfe

Edited and with an introduction by
Robert Hessen

Hoover Institution Press

Stanford University   Stanford, California

The Hoover Institution on War, Revolution and Peace, founded at Stanford University in 1919 by the late President Herbert Hoover, is an interdisciplinary research center for advanced study on domestic and international affairs in the twentieth century. The views expressed in its publications are entirely those of the authors and do not necessarily reflect the views of the staff, officers, or Board of Overseers of the Hoover Institution.

Hoover Press Publication 388

First printing, 1990
96 95 94 93 92 91   9 8 7 6 5 4 3 2 1
Simultaneous paperback printing, 1990
96 95 94 93 92 91   9 8 7 6 5 4 3 2 1

Manufactured in the United States of America
Printed on acid-free paper

Library of Congress Cataloging in Publication Data
Wolfe, Bertram David, 1896–1977.
  Breaking with communism : the intellectual odyssey of Bertram D. Wolfe / edited and with an introduction by Robert Hessen.
        p.   cm. — (Hoover archival documentaries)
(Hoover Press publication ; 388)
  Includes bibliographical references.
  ISBN 0-8179-8881-5 (alk. paper)
  ISBN 0-8179-8882-3 (pbk. : alk. paper)
  1. Wolfe, Bertram David, 1896–1977. 2. Ex-communists—United States—Biography. 3. Sovietologists—United States—Biography.
I. Hessen, Robert, 1936–   II. Title. III. Series.
HX84.W64A3 1990
335'.0092—dc20   89-20044
[B]   CIP

What do I do when I discover I am wrong?
I change my mind. What do you do?

attributed to John Maynard Keynes

Contents

Foreword

Bertram D. Wolfe was the foremost U.S. historian of Soviet Russia. He wrote ten books, scores of articles, and more than two hundred reviews of books about the Soviet regime—from Lenin and Stalin to Khrushchev and Brezhnev. His productivity is especially remarkable considering that his first book on Russia, *Three Who Made a Revolution*, was not published until 1948, when he was 52 years old.

Wolfe had not completed his autobiography, *A Life in Two Centuries*, when he died in 1977, at the age of 81. Two months before his death, he told a friend, "I am almost two-thirds finished," but the book (published posthumously) covers only half his life story. Not a strictly chronological narrative, it ends around 1937–1939 after he describes how his opposition to World War I led him to become an early admirer of Lenin and the Bolshevik Revolution; how he helped create the communist party in the United States and Mexico; how he and Jay Lovestone were expelled from the U.S. communist party by Stalin in 1929; how during the next decade, while hoping for a reconciliation with Stalin, he became an expert on Spanish and Latin American literature; and how he reluctantly concluded that Soviet communism, which he had once idealized and defended, would annihilate human liberty if unopposed. For the next four decades, three themes united Wolfe's diverse activities: his struggle to uncover the truth about the history of Soviet Russia, his efforts to organize resistance against Soviet propaganda and imperialism, and his reappraisal of his own earlier allegiances, not only to Lenin but ultimately to Karl Marx as well.

This book is drawn from Wolfe's papers, which occupy 63 linear feet in the Hoover Institution Archives. Consisting chiefly of his letters from 1939 on, along with unpublished speeches and writings, it is a documentary for the second half of his life, the portion he did not live to complete in his autobiography. His letters, however, cannot be a full substitute because some of his most important friendships—with Edmund Wilson, Sidney Hook, and Stalin's daughter, Svetlana Alliluyeva, for example—barely leave a written trace. He talked with them at length on many occasions but kept no diaries or notes. Also, during long stretches of his writing career, Wolfe wrote no letters. If he was immersed in writing and a letter needed to be answered, his wife replied for him but kept no copies. Although Ernest Hemingway wrote, "Any time I can write a good letter it's a sign I'm not working," this was not true for Bert Wolfe. When he took the trouble to write, his letters were carefully crafted and filled with the sardonic wit and playfulness that make them both revealing of his mind and delightful to read.

This book's purpose is to trace Wolfe's ideas and activities from the late 1930s, when he launched his career as an historian and began his break with communism, down to the mid-1970s, when, in disgust at the policies of President Gerald Ford and Secretary of State Henry Kissinger, he became an early and ardent supporter of Ronald Reagan for president. Wolfe believed that Reagan, more than any other U.S. public figure, understood that Soviet communism is inherently imperialistic and that "peaceful coexistence" and "détente" are propaganda slogans, not evidence that the Soviet Union had abandoned its goal of world domination.

Between 1972 and 1977 I often talked with Bert Wolfe but never asked him why he had broken with communism, that is, what specific issue or event caused him to change his mind. Knowing that he was writing his autobiography, I assumed that I would find the answer there. But he died before dealing with that question.

Although the letters and other writings in this volume illustrate the process of his change and describe many of the incidents that precipitated it, they do not indicate the single occurrence that caused him to renounce communism. In search of an answer I asked Sidney Hook, one of Wolfe's oldest and closest friends, "Given how deeply Bert was committed to communism, what made him change his mind? Was there a particular event that marked his turning point?" Hook answered,

> There was no one event that accounts for Bert Wolfe's repudiation
> of communism. After the humiliating experience of being excom-
> municated by Stalin, the onset of the Second World War [1939],
> and the Kremlin's resumption of its expansionist policy, he real-
> ized that what was at stake were the values of liberal civilization.
> Bert chose the West because at heart he was a Son of the Enlighten-
> ment and dedicated to the ideals of human freedom. It was these
> ideals that he mistakenly believed would be furthered by the pro-
> gram of communism, which, as in the case of many others, led
> him initially astray. But in the full maturity of his years, seasoned

by the wisdom of his historical understanding, he became one of the sharpest critics of all varieties of totalitarianism and a redoubtable expositor and champion of democracy.

This book would not have been possible without the energy and support of Ella G. Wolfe, who made the initial selection of letters from her late husband's papers. Throughout their 60-year marriage she was his research assistant, confidant, and intellectual ally. After his death she supervised the publication of his autobiography and two major collections of his unpublished essays, as well as bringing others of his books back into print. No man could have asked for a more devoted life partner.

I am indebted to Dale Reed for preparing an invaluable inventory of Bertram Wolfe's papers. I also want to acknowledge the support of Charles G. Palm, associate director of the Hoover Institution, and Milorad M. Drachkovitch, who created the Archival Documentaries series. Others who helped me include Michael Jakobson, who translated some Russian passages into English; Amy Rose, who deciphered and retyped several Voice of America radio scripts; Craig Grossman, who tracked down many old magazines and books; and Norman Jacobs, a colleague of Wolfe's at the Voice of America who gave me the benefit of his recollections.

I also owe thanks to staff members at the Hoover Institution Press including Ann Wood, the copyeditor; Paula Shuhert, the book designer; and Carol Whiteley, the proofreader. I am grateful to each of them for their professionalism. Finally, I dedicate this book to the memory of my beloved wife, Beatrice, who graced and enriched my life for twenty-seven years.

Introduction

Bertram D. Wolfe, born in Brooklyn in 1896, was a student at the City College of New York and planning to become a teacher of English literature when World War I erupted. Because he believed war barbaric and the modern world too civilized to settle disputes by violent conflict, he expected the fighting to end quickly. Like many of his generation, he was reassured by Woodrow Wilson's 1916 re-election theme, "He kept us out of war," and felt betrayed a few months later when Wilson asked Congress to declare war against Germany. In 1917, a few months after he turned 21, Wolfe married Ella Goldberg, lost his first job teaching English at Boys' High School because he refused to sign the mayor's war loyalty pledge, and became a cofounder of *Facts: The People's Peace Paper.*

Wolfe believed the brightest beacon for peace was shining in Russia. V.I. Lenin, the leader of the Bolsheviks, was challenging the provisional government that had succeeded the Romanoff dynasty. Alexander Kerensky, the prime minister, was committed to continuing the war against Germany, while Lenin was promising Peace, Land and Bread. Wolfe later wrote,

> [W]hile I watched my country entering the war, I became aware that new rulers were seizing power in Russia and proposing to take Russia out of the war. I was, I must admit, completely ignorant of who these new leaders in Russia were and what their program was beyond their opposition to the war. All I knew was that we were entering the war and they were leaving it, and this induced me to open a large credit to the new, "antiwar" Russia. [146]*

---

*To minimize the frequency of footnotes, quotations from Wolfe's autobiography, *A Life in Two Centuries* (New York: Stein and Day, 1981), are cited by page numbers in brackets.

In 1917 Wolfe joined the U.S. Socialist party because it opposed U.S. entry into the war. At an emergency convention in April the party passed the so-called St. Louis resolution, which declared:

> We brand the declaration of war by our Government as a crime against the nations of the world. In all modern history, there has been no war more unjustifiable than the war in which we are about to engage. No greater dishonor has ever been forced upon a people than that which the capitalist class is forcing upon this nation against its will. The workers of all countries [should] refuse to support their governments in their wars. [185–86]

This manifesto, Wolfe recalled, "delighted me, for it fused my half-baked socialism with my deeply rooted opposition to war and, above all, to universal or total war." [186]

When the Socialist party's antiwar unity began to erode, Wolfe joined its left-wing faction. In February 1919, with John Reed, he wrote a Manifesto of the National Council of the Left Wing of the Socialist Party that called for strikes and revolutionary action by laid-off defense workers and returning jobless veterans. It also urged the socialists to support the new Bolshevik regime in Russia. [192–95]

In September 1919 the Socialist party's left wing became the nucleus of the communist party in the United States. Wolfe later said, "I did not join the Communist Party. I was one of its founders, and if we note the date of the founding of the Left Wing and its call for a 'New International,' I can count myself one of the founders of the Communist International."[†] [229]

Every signer of the left-wing manifesto was indicted in 1919 under New York's criminal anarchy law. To escape arrest and prosecution, Wolfe and his wife fled to California, where he grew a beard and assumed an alias. Thus it was as Arthur Albright that he founded the San Francisco Labor College and a journal called *Labor Unity*. Wolfe was indicted a second time after he represented California at a communist party unity convention in Michigan. Once again he changed his name and appearance and fled to Boston, where he became head of the proofroom at Atlantic Press and an organizer for the communist party's New England district.

[†]As originally conceived by Marx, the First International was an organization of workers. The Second (or Socialist) International, an organization of socialist parties, was created in 1889, but its strength was severely eroded by the outbreak of war in 1914. The Third Communist International—the Comintern—was founded by Lenin in 1919.

By 1919 Wolfe was a committed Communist. For the next twenty years his closest friend and political ally was Jay Lovestone (born Jacob Liebstein in Lithuania in 1898), whom he had known as a fellow student at City College. Both men looked up to Lenin as the leader of the international communist movement and were prepared to obey his dictates. They knew that the Comintern, to which the various communist parties of the world sent delegates, was not a parliamentary body of autonomous coequals; rather, as a condition of membership, each party had to promise that it would obey Comintern edicts. This structure of authority had been spelled out in the Twenty-one Points that Lenin set forth in 1919. For the first decade of their relationship with the Comintern, Lovestone and Wolfe had no trouble accepting these terms.

To Wolfe, Soviet Russia seemed to be the first country that would institutionalize the ideals of the eighteenth century:

> [D]reams of cosmopolitanism and internationalism, of free movement of men, goods and ideas in an ever more open society; dreams of a more limited state with increasing controls from below and curbs upon dictatorial power and autocratic power; dreams of the final abolition of serfdom, slavery and all forms of involuntary servitude, of a greater respect for human life and human dignity, of gentler and juster laws, equal for all and binding on all; dreams of liberty, equality and brotherhood and of a new humanity, free in spirit and intelligence, free in critical inquiry, master to an ever greater extent of nature, of man's own nature, and his social institutions.[1]

To Wolfe, then, the path to human betterment ran through Moscow. Wolfe, comparing Lenin's professed ideals with the worst flaws of the United States and believing that Lenin was a committed Marxist, took Marxist ideals—economic equality, the abolition of poverty, the withering away of the state—to be the true animating spirit of Soviet society. By contrast, he viewed U.S. ideals—legal equality, unlimited opportunity for personal advancement, and government of, by, and for the people—as rhetorical pieties masking privilege and exploitation. If Russia fell short of its ideals, if censorship, forced labor, or one-party rule prevailed, these were only emergency measures necessitated by the exigencies of civil war and encirclement by hostile nations. No matter what deviation from eighteenth-century ideals occurred in Russia, Wolfe felt confident that the situation would be righted once the emergency ended and was proud of his association with the communist party. As he explained,

> The Communists were the first organized party to belong to a centralized, disciplined, international organization, attached to, glo-

rying in, commanded and financed by a party that had power over a
great country—the greatest land empire in the world, and in all
history . . . After a century of failures and sacrifices of the radical
movement, most members of the American party gloried in being
"the American section" of a single, unified, worldwide international which had its seat of power and privilege in Moscow. [374]

Bert and Ella Wolfe, then, like thousands of their generation, believed that by devoting their lives to the triumph of communism they
would be promoting the cause of peace and the general betterment of
mankind. Communism offered them a faith into which they could
pour their idealism and their energies. Consciously deciding not to
have children, they stood ready at a moment's notice to heed the call to
armed revolution or any lesser challenge. In 1922 the call was temporar-
ily deflected when they accepted an offer to become English teachers in
a girls' high school in Mexico City. It was not an assignment they
would have chosen had Wolfe not been a fugitive, living under an alias,
because neither of them knew Spanish. But they learned easily, aided
by a self-imposed ordinance that they would speak only Spanish even
to each other and read only Mexican books and newspapers. This em-
barked them on a lifelong love affair with Mexican and Spanish literature and poetry. (Both took master's degrees in Spanish at the University of Mexico in 1925 and at Columbia University in 1931.)

On the strength of his proficiency in compiling data on U.S. investments in Latin America, which appeared to corroborate Lenin's theory
that imperialism was the highest stage of capitalism, Wolfe was elected
to the executive committee of Mexico's communist party. As Mexico's
delegate to the Fifth Congress of the Comintern, he visited Moscow for
the first time in 1924, a few months after Lenin's death. He wrote a 39-
part series, *Rusia en 1924,* that was published in *El Democrata.* The
material, he recalled, "was gleaned largely from handouts from the
agitprop department of the Comintern concerning the wonders of the
socialism they were building." [572]

When he returned to Mexico in 1924, he founded *El Libertador,* a
magazine whose purpose was to alert and mobilize Latin America's
resistance to the baneful influences of U.S. investments. (He later attributed his views to an "uncritical first reading of Lenin's *Imperialism.*" [343]) In 1925 Wolfe was deported from Mexico. The official
charge—selling illegal drugs—sounded so ridiculous to those who
knew him that it was changed to smuggling $50,000 in Russian gold to
foment a railroad strike (a valuable lesson to the future historian about
the unreliability of official government records). [366]

Wolfe then returned to New York, where he became educational director of the Workers' Party of America, the newest name of the communist party, led by Jay Lovestone. From 1919 to 1929 Wolfe edited and wrote for communist newspapers and magazines in the United States and Mexico including *Communist World, El Democrata, El Machete, El Libertador, Workers' Monthly, The Communist, The Daily Worker,* and *Revolutionary Age.* He was a communist candidate for the New York State Assembly in 1919 and for the U.S. Congress in 1920, but the voters of Brooklyn rejected him. He also was a fund-raiser, teacher, and administrator for communist-affiliated schools. He moved away from his goal of teaching English literature and writing books, for his commitment to communism absorbed him totally.

Although by his own words Wolfe was only a lukewarm socialist, he was becoming an ardent Marxist. Socialism assumes that if government owns industry and abolishes private property, the result will be a society of abundance for all and a world without war. But socialism is vulnerable to empirical refutation. Marxism, by contrast, is a faith, more a religion than a secular philosophy. Marx "proved" that the coming of socialism was inevitable because it was the next stage of historical development. Therefore being a Marxist gave Wolfe the certainty he sought about mankind's future. Years later he explained why Marxism had attracted him:

> Its appeal derived in part from the fact that it was an untried ideal and that it was learnedly propounded. It was clever of Marx to marshal all his learning into a critique of capitalism . . . and avoid as "unscientific" any attempt to picture the future society that was to replace the one he was criticizing. . . . For me, as for most sensitive persons, the existing society had many obvious defects, imperfections, things that could be improved, shortcomings from our dreams of perfection. One felt superior when he noted and criticized these imperfections and offered a learned-sounding, never spelled out, untried and untested remedy that cured everything at once by a simple change in property relations . . . How nice to think that one had answers to all problems, cures for all ills, a simple, certain, manifest remedy backed by books of enormous learning. How easy and satisfying to criticize if one had all the solutions in a single doctrine . . . And how wonderful, when one did not understand the past or the present, to be so certain of the future. [175]

After being expelled from Mexico and returning to New York, Wolfe became a full-time Communist, working as publicity director for the Rand School for Social Science, organizing a summer school for party members, lecturing around the country to communist groups dissemi-

nating the latest directives of the Comintern, and actively defending
Sacco and Vanzetti, Tom Mooney, and the Scottsboro Boys. He also
wrote for Inprecorr (the communist international press correspondence
service) and in 1928 became editor of *The Communist.*

In 1928, a decade after Wolfe's pacifist principles had led him to
help create a communist party in the United States, he attacked pacifism. Writing in *The Communist,* Wolfe charged that the Western
governments were plotting war against Russia and were trying to
provoke it into taking military actions that they would construe as
Soviet aggression: "Only the deliberate and energetic peace policy of
the USSR has so far prevented the outbreak of this war of the united
imperialist governments against the working class and oppressed peoples of the world." Wolfe maintained that authentic pacifism was not
necessarily preferable because *some* wars are desirable: "We Communists do not fight against war 'generally' and in the abstract. We fight
against imperialism and counterrevolutionary war but support and
lead revolutionary wars of the proletariat and of the oppressed peoples
against capitalism and imperialism."[2] His aversion to war, his loath-
ing of violence and bloodshed, now took second place to defending the
Soviet Union.

Throughout the 1920s various factions struggled for control of the
U.S. communist party. Late in 1928, when elections were held to select
delegates to the party's forthcoming convention, the Lovestone slate
won 95 of the 104 delegates, putting it firmly in control of the party.
The U.S. Communists led by Lovestone were dutiful defenders of the
Soviet Union and thought that they were properly appreciated in Moscow. They were soon to discover that they were dispensable.

Wolfe headed back to Moscow for the third time in December 1928
to attend a meeting of the Executive Committee of the Comintern (he
had made his second visit earlier in 1928 as a delegate to the Sixth
Congress of the Comintern). When he arrived in early January 1929,
Louis Engdahl, the U.S. party's representative in Moscow, handed him
a draft of an open letter from the Comintern to the convention of the
Workers' Party of America (Communist). The letter condemned the
factionalism of the U.S. party and hinted at Lovestone's imminent
ouster from the party's leadership. Above all it reminded the Americans that they were not an autonomous group but were sworn to respect and obey the Comintern's decisions. The letter stripped the U.S.
party of any illusion of independence or self-direction.[3] Wolfe recalled
his reaction: "I read the letter with utter dismay. Its authors seemed
completely ignorant of the realities of American life, the internal life of
the American Communist Party, the American labor movement, the

nature of the American government, the place of America in the world of the twenties." [447]

When Wolfe threatened to cable Lovestone in New York to advise him to refuse to publish the letter in *The Daily Worker* until it had been suitably revised, he was summoned to the Presidium of the Comintern's Executive Committee. Wolfe argued that the leadership in New York should be free to rely on its unique knowledge of U.S. conditions in choosing the strategy and tactics most likely to transform the United States into a communist society. He did not realize that the open letter was the creation of Joseph Stalin who, even before Lenin's death, had outmaneuvered his three chief rivals, Leon Trotsky, Grigori Zinoviev, and Nikolai Bukharin, and emerged as the undisputed ruler of Russia.

But even after he learned that he was opposing Stalin, Wolfe imagined that the force of argument would decide the question and so cabled home for reinforcements. Lovestone, Benjamin Gitlow, and eight other party leaders sailed immediately for Moscow. At a final confrontation on May 14, the Lovestoneites were required to swear publicly that they would unconditionally obey all directives from the Comintern. When most of them refused Stalin railed, "Who do you think you are? Trotsky defied me. Where is he? Zinoviev defied me. Where is he? Bukharin defied me? Where is he? And you? When you get back to America, nobody will stay with you except your wives."[4] When Lovestone tried to argue that the U.S. party should be independent, Stalin removed him from party leadership. Lovestone, Wolfe, Gitlow, and their delegation were able to leave Russia alive because, as Wolfe later noted, Stalin "had not yet perfected his technique for cutting short discussion." [17, 551]

Comintern officials tried to reassign the three U.S. leaders. Wolfe was summoned to meet with Iosif Piatnitsky, a key figure in the Comintern's Department for International Liaison, which provided political directives and financial assistance to the Comintern's foreign sections. Piatnitsky assured Wolfe that the Comintern still valued his services and that a great future awaited him. Wolfe, who had not lost his sense of humor, asked, "Comrade Piatnitsky, you want to send Gitlow to Mexico because he can speak Yiddish. You want to send me to Korea because I can speak Spanish. But tell me, why are you sending Lovestone to India?"[5] Wolfe insisted on returning home before taking up a new post. When he arrived in Brooklyn he found a summons from the new leaders of the U.S. communist party. To test his loyalty, they ordered him to endorse the Comintern's open letter. When he refused, he was expelled from the party.

In 1929, under Jay Lovestone's leadership, Wolfe helped create the Communist Party of the U.S.A.-Majority Group. (It was renamed the Communist Party of the U.S.A. (Opposition) in 1932, the Independent Communist Labor League in 1937, and the Independent Labor League of America in 1938.) For the next nine years, the leaders of the Lovestone faction expected Stalin to return the U.S. party to their control. Their break with Stalin and the Comintern in 1929 was not a repudiation of Marx, Lenin, or communism or a criticism of how Stalin was ruling Russia; nor did they disagree about Stalin's ultimate goals for the United States. Thus in 1932, when Wolfe wrote the program for the communist opposition, he emphasized the same basic tenets—the need to establish a proletarian dictatorship in America, abolish private property, and protect Soviet Russia against its foreign enemies—as the official party headed by Stalin's minions.

Despite their agreement on basic principles, Stalin condemned the Lovestoneites as "American exceptionalists," an epithet that became a badge of honor to them. In 1932 Wolfe wrote,

> In the queer jargon that takes the place of intelligible English in upper party circles, the American Communist Opposition is denounced as "American Exceptionalists." If we understand what the party leaders are driving at, we plead guilty to the charge. Yes, we consider that conditions in America are different from conditions in Germany or Spain or the Soviet Union. We are more than "American Exceptionalists." We are exceptionalists for every country of the world! And in pleading guilty to considering the conditions of each country different from those of the rest, peculiar, "exceptional," we are in good company—the company of Marx and Lenin.[6]

Then he quoted a passage from Lenin's essay *Left-Wing Communism: An Infantile Disorder* that lent canonical support to the Lovestoneite position. Wolfe's special skill was using quotes from Marx and Lenin to silence critics and vanquish opponents. Years later he described this predilection as a "disease" called "authoritarian quotationitis." [197]

No one's energies equaled Wolfe's in the service of the Lovestoneite cause. Incapable of resting, his idea of a vacation was to work to exhaustion in a new physical setting and he was always ready to take on a new writing assignment or an opportunity to debate. During his decade as a Lovestoneite, Wolfe edited *Workers' Age;* wrote scores of articles on political issues; reviewed novels by writers such as John Dos Passos, John Steinbeck, and Ignazio Silone; and became increasingly active as a teacher and lecturer. At the Rand School and later at the Workers'

School and the New Workers' School (all in New York), he offered courses entitled Marxist Economics, The Economics of Present-Day Capitalism, The Nature of the Capitalist Crisis, and The Law of Revolution: A Critical Study of the Central Question of Marxist Strategy. He also taught English and mathematics at the Eron Preparatory School in New York from 1929 to 1934.

Fearing that his endless deadlines as a journalist, editor, lecturer, and administrator would keep him from writing a book, Wolfe eagerly accepted a book-writing assignment from a New York publisher who was planning a book of murals by Mexican artist Diego Rivera. Rivera, who had met Wolfe in Mexico City a decade earlier, insisted that the publisher hire Wolfe to write the annotations. Soon after they met Wolfe convinced Rivera, a committed Marxist, to resign from the Mexican communist party and devote all his energy to his murals, which extolled the working class and depicted the evils of the capitalist system. Rivera and Wolfe signed a contract in December 1933, and the book, *Portrait of America*, was published in 1934. Although Wolfe later called it the worst writing he had ever done, the book sold well. A 1937 sequel, *Portrait of Mexico*, attracted good reviews, but the publisher went bankrupt and the stream of royalties ran dry.

In 1936 while writing *Portrait of Mexico* Wolfe persuaded Rivera to give him unrestricted access to his paintings and papers so he could write his biography. A contract (and an advance) from a major publisher, Alfred A. Knopf, enabled Wolfe to return to Mexico for the first time in twelve years. *Diego Rivera: His Life and Times* was published in 1939 and sold well but far short of Wolfe's expectations. As a change of pace and as a financial potboiler, he wrote a nonpolitical novel, *Deathless Days*. His publisher, fearing a lawsuit from the man to whom the book had been dedicated without permission, burned all but two copies. Summing up his situation at the close of the 1930s, Wolfe later wrote, "For all practical purposes as a means of income, free-lance writing for the first quarter of a century was a flop . . . I was virtually bookless and penniless, and my half-decade of writing had left me where I started—with nothing." [713]

But his disappointments as a writer were not the heaviest burdens on his mind, for recent events had pushed him toward a further break with Joseph Stalin and Soviet Russia. In 1951 Wolfe explained why his break with communism had taken so long and had occurred in stages:

> Both disillusionment with one's cherished beliefs, and positive rethinking of one's views are a process rather than a single instantaneous act . . . I did not lightly assume the task of communist orga-

nizer and educator, nor lightly throw it off. I do not change opinions as I do a shirt. The process was thoughtful, painful and difficult . . . I longed to retain some shred of my old ideals and beliefs, longed to believe that I did not have to write off the spiritual investment of *a decade* as a total loss.[7] [italics added]

In fact, his spiritual investment in communism lasted at least two decades, but if any one event could be said to have precipitated the next stage of his break, it was the purge trial of Nikolai Bukharin in March 1938.

Wolfe's decision to denounce Bukharin's frame-up would have been hard to predict. For nearly twenty years Wolfe had faithfully defended the Soviet system. He did not speak out in 1928 when Stalin banished Leon Trotsky to Alma-Ata and later expelled him from the Soviet Union. He never voiced doubts about the trials of "wreckers" and "saboteurs" that ran from 1928 to 1933. He did not investigate or take seriously reports that Stalin had used mass starvation to wipe out the Ukrainian kulaks in 1932–1933, and if Wolfe suspected that Stalin had masterminded the murder in December 1934 of Sergei Kirov, the leader of the communist party in Leningrad, he kept his suspicions to himself. He even ridiculed the idea that the 104 men executed for Kirov's murder might have been innocent. No proof of their guilt did not mean they were innocent and unfairly convicted, as Wolfe explained in *Workers' Age*,

> [N]ot every plotter is foolish enough to carry around documents, just so that uninformed or prejudiced foreign opinion may be satisfied that he was really guilty . . . In the last analysis, any proofs published by any government must depend, in large measure for their credibility, on the questioner's trust in the good faith and justice of that government. If you lack that, what is to prevent you from saying that any and all documents and proofs are forgeries?[8]

Nor did Wolfe voice any criticism in 1936 when Grigori Zinoviev, Lev Kamenev, and fourteen other veteran Bolshevik leaders were executed for allegedly being traitors, saboteurs, and agents of foreign powers. But his trust in the "good faith and justice" of Russia's judicial system was sorely tested when Bukharin's name was raised during the trial of Karl Radek and sixteen others in January 1937. When Bukharin was arrested a month later, it was clear that Stalin was setting the stage for yet another trial.

Two events in 1937 foreshadowed Wolfe's impending break with Stalin. First, he was distressed to learn that the Comintern had instructed the Spanish communist party to oppose nationalization of industry and to nationalize factories only if they belonged to those who supported Franco's rebellion against the Republican government of Spain. The Comintern's instruction to guard and protect "the property rights of small and middle owners" was, in Wolfe's eyes, an unprincipled compromise of communist principles.[9] Worse still, when he visited Spain in March 1937, he learned that the Communists, on orders from Moscow, were disarming, arresting, and sometimes murdering the anarchists, anarcho-syndicalists, and POUM—dissident Communists who were defending the Republican government against the fascist insurrection.

The second foreshadowing of a break came in the form of a book review Wolfe wrote for *The New Republic* in November 1937. Malcolm Cowley, the literary editor, asked him to review *The Case of Leon Trotsky*, a transcript of the hearings of the Preliminary Commission of Inquiry, headed by philosopher John Dewey, which had recently met in Mexico City to question Trotsky about the charges leveled against him in the second purge trial. Living in Mexico and tried in absentia, Trotsky was accused of making a treaty with Hitler and Hirohito to topple Stalin; promising to dismember the Soviet Union by giving the Ukraine to Germany; masterminding industrial sabotage in factories, railways, and coal mines throughout Russia; and plotting to murder Stalin and other Politburo members.

The Dewey commission elicited overwhelming proof that the evidence against Trotsky was fabricated and the testimony perjured or coerced. But Cowley, a loyal Stalinist, apparently felt confident that Wolfe would denounce the hearings as a whitewash—a cover-up of Trotsky's actual guilt. A few months earlier in a review of Trotsky's latest book, *The Revolution Betrayed*, Wolfe rejected Trotsky's claim that Stalin had betrayed the Russian Revolution: "we can only state on the basis of the evidence introduced by the prosecution [Trotsky] and without even asking the defense [Stalin] to open its rebuttal: 'Charges not proved. Case dismissed.' "[10]

Five months later, however, Wolfe began distancing himself from Stalin and Soviet Russia. His review of the Dewey commission hearings focused on the deficiencies in Trotsky's theory of revolutions, the commission's undistinguished membership, and the superficiality of some of the questions the commissioners posed to Trotsky in Mexico City. But although he concluded that Trotsky was not guilty of the crimes of which he had been accused, it was nonetheless difficult for Wolfe to side with Trotsky against Stalin:

> No matter which "verdict" one pronounces in the end, there are painful and intolerable dilemmas to be faced. If it is hard to believe

that Trotsky could conspire with Germany and Japan, desire to
hasten war, hope for the defeat of the Soviet Union, work for the
restoration of capitalism; it is also hard to believe that the leader
[Stalin] of the Communist Party and the Comintern is capable of
framing all these accusations and executing innocent men who . . .
were but yesterday the chief pillars of his regime. Yet one of these
two series of monstrous and discreditable hypotheses must be
true.[11]

When a friend expressed amazement and anger that Wolfe's review
seemed more intent on discrediting the Dewey commission than on
proclaiming Trotsky's innocence, Wolfe explained the anguish he had
endured:

To those revolutionists who have followed from the very beginning
in 1917 the fortunes of the proletarian revolution and have devoted
to it their enthusiasm and love, the idea that any section of its
leadership could so far degenerate as to betray it, represents an
intolerable idea. And when one is forced to choose between two
sections of the leadership, it becomes an intolerable dilemma. I
cannot be indifferent nor can the revolutionary movement remain
unhurt regardless of which of the two we are forced to accept. Do
you begrudge me the anguish? I am amazed that you do not seem to
share it.[12]

Wolfe, who agonized over whether Trotsky was guilty or innocent,
had no such difficulty when Bukharin became the chief defendant in
the purge trial that opened on March 2, 1938. Wolfe could not believe
Bukharin capable of the crimes he was accused of, least of all plotting
to murder Lenin. Wolfe, who had seen Bukharin in Moscow, knew him
to be an intellectual, a gifted painter and caricaturist, and a man who
wept when, on Stalin's orders, the Comintern voted to expel Trotsky
from Russia. [469–74]*

Above all Wolfe knew that Bukharin had loved Lenin and served him
loyally, which meant that this trial was a frame-up, a mockery of justice. Wolfe had reached a breaking point. If he was to salvage his self-
respect, he could neither defend the trial of Bukharin nor condone it by
silence. He felt he had no choice but to speak out. When he announced

---

*Wolfe's final assessment of Bukharin, written years afterward, was, "he still comes out
as the best, the most human, the gentlest, the worthiest of the Bolsheviks I have
known," despite Bukharin's remark, "Of course we should have two parties, one in
power, the other in prison." [pp. 474, 471]

his decision, several friends urged him to reconsider. Why get involved in Russia's internal political conflicts? Why lend support to Trotsky or anti-Soviet critics? And why ruin any chance that Stalin would restore control of America's communist party to the Lovestoneites? But his decision was firm.

On March 9, 1938, speaking under the auspices of the Trotsky Defense Committee, Wolfe called Bukharin's trial an "infamous and murderous farce." He regretted that his appearance on a Trotskyist platform might give "the impression that the issue is Trotsky versus Stalin, or that our protest is primarily for the defense of Leon Trotsky." In the handwritten notes he prepared for the talk, Wolfe wrote, "Well-meaning people . . . have urged me to silence—[but the] whole world knows and recoils in horror. Anyone who fails to raise his voice [is] a guilty accomplice by his silence; he who calls this [justice], slanders communism . . . He who justifies it, bathes his hands in Blood."[13] Later in his talk he said,

> And that blood is the best blood of our generation, the blood . . . of the men who led in the making of the Russian Revolution, of the men who led in the building of the Communist International, of the men who risked their lives in the Czarist underground, who exhausted themselves in the civil war and the famine, who performed miracles of socialist reconstruction, who led the Soviet Union in all of its achievements. If one word of these charges is credited as true, then the Russian Revolution must have been made by traitors, bandits, imperialist spies, provocateurs, murderers, and counter-revolutionaries.[14]

Bukharin was convicted on March 13, 1938. Within 36 hours the customary NKVD execution—a bullet at the back of the neck—was carried out in the dark recesses of Lubyanka prison in Moscow. Stalin, in total command of Soviet society, allowed no time for an appeal or a plea for clemency.

The bullet that killed Bukharin shattered Bertram Wolfe's illusions about Soviet justice and forced him to begin reassessing his two decades of support for the Soviet Union. He began to question why the Soviet experiment had gone wrong and when the process of deterioration had begun. Had Stalin usurped Lenin's legacy or was Lenin's legacy a brutal dictatorship? Rejecting the Marxist view of history, which minimized the influence of individuals on the course of events, Wolfe considered what role men like Lenin, Trotsky, and Stalin had played in Russia's recent history. The idea for a book was taking shape in his mind. Among the questions Wolfe posed were,

Would the October Revolution have taken place at all if Lenin had failed to get across Germany in 1917 in a sealed train or if Kerensky had succeeded in laying hands on him in July of that year? Would the fate of the Soviet state have been different if he [Lenin] had not become paralyzed and died in the early twenties? [What would have happened] if he could have been given a decade to carry out his plan to combat bureaucracy, and incidentally, to remove Stalin as general secretary? . . . How far did Trotsky's personality prevent him from winning the "mantle of Lenin" that most people thought would be his when [Lenin] died in 1924? To what extent would a Trotsky dictatorship differ from, to what extent resemble that of Stalin? . . . How far is the rule of Stalin a continuation of the tradition of Ivan the Terrible and Peter the Great, both of whom Stalin admires, and to what extent does it represent a complete break with Russia's past? . . . How far would Lenin approve of his two self-confessed "best disciples," and to what extent does the Soviet land correspond to the new world he dreamed of building?[15]

Wolfe also asked, "What is the future of the Soviet system and the Russian Revolution? What are the chances of the proud and lonely Mexican exile [Trotsky] staging a 'comeback'? How long can Stalin continue his ever-widening purge which creates a social vacuum around him? After Stalin what?"

By November 1938 Wolfe had completed a prospectus for *Three Who Made a Revolution*. Nominally a triple biography of Lenin, Trotsky, and Stalin, it was an even more ambitious work—a history of the Russian revolutionary tradition, culminating in the careers of these historic figures. He sent his prospectus to Alfred A. Knopf, asking for a $100-per-month advance on royalties for the twelve to fifteen months he thought he would need to write the book. When Knopf failed to reply, Wolfe sent a similar proposal to Viking Press. Perhaps neither publisher thought Wolfe's timetable was realistic, or perhaps they suspected he was planning to write an anti-Stalin tract. In any case, Wolfe signed a contract in 1939 with Dial Press, receiving only a small lump sum advance.

Originally, Wolfe had intended to include the purge trials of the 1930s but decided to end with the October Revolution in 1917 because of the enormity of the assignment. He began work believing he already had mastered the sources and merely had to transform his knowledge into a readable narrative. But on closer examination, he found that the sources were so unreliable, so laced with errors or deliberate lies and exaggerations, that he had to be skeptical about every document and memoir. Before he could write an historical narrative, he had to sift evidence and weigh competing claims to discover what had actually happened in Russia decades earlier. He persevered until the book met the high standards he set for himself, but it took him nearly a decade. *Three Who Made a Revolution* was published in October 1948.

If the truth about events in prerevolutionary Russia was difficult to discern, events in Russia in 1939 were all too clear. Any lingering illusions Wolfe may have had about Stalin, or about Soviet Russia as a force for world peace, were shattered on August 23, 1939, when Joachim von Ribbentrop (representing Hitler) and V.M. Molotov (Stalin's deputy) signed the Treaty of Friendship and Agreement on Frontiers. In reaction, Wolfe wrote "Thoughts on the Stalin-Hitler Pact":

> We [the Lovestone group] have never regretted our break with the degenerating Comintern in 1929. We have had cause to regret the lateness of that break and to marvel at the blindness . . . which prevented our breaking earlier. We have had cause, too, to kick ourselves for so long thereafter striving to believe in the possibility of communist unity and for trying to persuade ourselves that the first frame-up trials had some core of truth in their shell of fabrication. There was more goodwill than good sense in our unwillingness to recognize the painful truth.[16]

Once again Wolfe was not repudiating communism, only its perversion by Stalin. For another decade he would continue to praise Marx, regard himself as a socialist, and call *The Communist Manifesto* the highest expression of his ideals.

Nonetheless, even before the Hitler-Stalin pact was signed, Wolfe had begun to distance himself from Lenin, the architect of Soviet communism. He spent most of the summer of 1939 translating an essay on the Russian Revolution by Rosa Luxemburg, a Marxist theorist, written shortly before she was murdered by German monarchists in January 1919. Wolfe wanted to publicize her thesis that Russia's flaws and failures were caused by Lenin's rejection of democratic institutions. In his introductory essay, Wolfe wrote,

> How profoundly right she was in her democratic faith and in her fear of bureaucracy, of one-party dictatorship, clique rule, and domination by a handful of leaders, of the attempt to solve all problems by decree and universal terror—the intervening years in Russia have amply demonstrated. Today, her warning sounds like the words of a gifted prophecy.[17]

He quoted her words that reflected his own views:

> Freedom only for the supporters of the government, only for the members of one party—however numerous they may be—is no

freedom at all. Freedom is always and exclusively freedom for the one who thinks differently . . . Without general elections, without unrestricted freedom of press and assembly, without a free struggle of opinions, life dies out in every public institution, becomes a mere semblance of life, in which only the bureaucracy remains as the active element.[18]

To Luxemburg's words, Wolfe added, "Alas, her warning went unheeded and a quarter century of uninterrupted terror has made her worst fear more than justified. The *initial deficiencies of Lenin* were magnified by his successor, and his sporadic efforts at correction were abandoned. The result is the bloody monstrosity of the personal dictatorship of Stalin."[19] It was the first time that he openly assigned any blame to Lenin for what Russia had become, but it would not be the last. Once Wolfe permitted himself to place Lenin under critical scrutiny, Lenin ceased to be a heroic figure. By the early 1950s Wolfe had come to view Lenin as the architect of twentieth-century totalitarianism.*

After Hitler invaded Poland on September 1, 1939, England and France responded by declaring war against Germany. Earlier Wolfe, socialist leader Norman Thomas, and other socialists had helped organize the Keep America Out of War Congress; now they made a last-ditch effort to shore up antiwar opinion in the United States. In less than six weeks they wrote a short book, *Keep America Out of War*, which made a case for nonintervention. Wolfe and Thomas argued that the United States had no vital interests at stake in the European war. The new war, they said, was merely a continuation of World War I, which in turn was part of the age-old struggle between European nations for territorial acquisitions. They believed that if the United States allowed itself to become embroiled in Europe's power politics, civil liberties would be annihilated and the nation's economic strength dissipated.

---

*The painful process of reassessment eventually led Wolfe to reject Marxism and to trace the roots of Lenin's totalitarianism back to Marx's dogmatism. "Marx's merit," he wrote in 1965, "was to ask large questions, and sociology and economics are the richer for his having asked them. His defect was to give shallow, oversimplified, dogmatic answers, to advance them not tentatively as his own provisional answers, but categorically as the answers of History and Science to man's questions concerning his society. This it was that gave Lenin the illusion that he could not be wrong." *Marxism: 100 Years in the Life of a Doctrine* (New York: Dial Press, 1965), p. 380.

As a practical course of action they wanted the United States to restore an arms embargo and forbid the exporting of munitions. For nonmilitary products they urged strict enforcement of a cash-and-carry policy: extending credit might tempt the United States to intervene to protect its creditors. Echoing the "merchants of death" idea that modern wars are fomented by profit-hungry munition makers, they argued that all munitions plants should be government owned. To discourage war profiteers, they proposed a heavy tax on all profits derived from war trade. They also called for reducing the military budget and ending U.S. "thinly veiled" imperialism in the Far East and Latin America. At minimum they sought a national referendum before the United States could declare war. Despite the energy Wolfe poured into this book (he wrote most of it himself, working around the clock) and despite Norman Thomas's national reputation (he had been the socialist candidate for president in every election since 1928), their book made no perceptible impact on public opinion.

If Wolfe could not sway the country to his position, at least he expected that his views would prevail within the Independent Labor League of America (ILLA), the Lovestoneite group. Instead, he and Jay Lovestone quarreled with increasing frequency, which further fractured the already small group. Fearing a repeat of the process by which the United States became embroiled in World War I, Wolfe opposed U.S. aid to Great Britain. Lovestone, however, thought that the United States could aid the British without risking war and that it was proper to do so. Lovestone and Wolfe grew increasingly impatient with what each perceived as the other's obstinacy. After a year of escalating disagreements, the ILLA was dissolved and *Workers' Age* (a major outlet for Wolfe's ideas since 1932) ceased publication.

After Hitler broke his pact with Stalin by invading the Soviet Union on June 22, 1941, Wolfe was more certain than ever that nonintervention was the only proper policy for the United States to pursue. He hoped that the two dictatorships would destroy each other, after which the United States could finance the rebuilding of war-torn Europe. But after Japan attacked Pearl Harbor on December 7, 1941, and the United States entered the war, Wolfe realized the futility of trying to keep out of the war in Europe. Fearing that the war against Hitler would unwittingly benefit Stalin—the United States' new wartime ally—Wolfe set out to warn Americans that Stalin's appetite for new territories had not been sated by absorbing half of Poland; annexing Latvia, Lithuania, and Estonia; or forcing Finland to cede the Karelian Isthmus to Russia. Wolfe's goal was to alert U.S. political leaders to the fact that, after Hitler's defeat, the Soviet Union would be the pre-eminent power in

Europe and that while England and the United States were distracted by their war against Japan, Stalin would try to extend Soviet control over many countries, including Yugoslavia, Czechoslovakia, the Balkans, Persia, Turkey, and China. Wolfe believed that if Stalin's territorial ambitions went unchecked, World War III would be inevitable.

Wolfe contacted many groups that had been his best lecture audiences but was unable to secure a single engagement for this topic. He wrote an article, but none of the magazine editors who previously had published his work showed any enthusiasm for promoting his pessimistic, but prescient, viewpoint. Their attitude was "We're not talking about the making of the peace. We're talking about winning the war." [19] But Wolfe never gave up the idea of publishing his warning about Stalin's territorial designs.

In 1943 after he became friends with Richard Rovere, the editor of *Common Sense*, a new monthly magazine, Wolfe implored him to publish his article. Rovere read it, disagreed with its message, and declined. But after Wolfe complained that the press had censored him, Rovere relented. The article, "Stalin at the Peace Table," which was published in May 1943, sounded a warning that few were ready to hear. Wolfe later said he experienced "the anguish of Cassandra, who knew the double misfortune of foreseeing the future and not being believed." [20]

Yet the article did impress one reader, Edward Duckles, a Quaker from North Carolina, who agreed with Wolfe's thesis that the end of World War II would lead to new subjugations of peoples and nations, thereby creating conditions for World War III. Duckles, a southern field-worker for the American Friends Service Committee (AFSC), invited Wolfe to lecture for a week at a Quaker-sponsored foreign affairs seminar at Guilford College in North Carolina during the summer of 1943. The next year the AFSC arranged for him to lecture in seven West Coast cities. Until the end of World War II, only Quaker-sponsored audiences were receptive to his message, causing him to remark that he "became unwittingly a fellow traveler of the Quakers for the duration of the war."

In June 1944, before Wolfe arrived in Seattle to participate in a ten-day seminar, a well-orchestrated campaign was under way to silence him. The Communist Political Association charged that Wolfe's anti-Soviet views were lending support to Hitler. His appearance, it warned, would be "a sickening and shameful spectacle—a blot on the patriotism of the Northwest." During his speech on June 21 Wolfe was repeatedly interrupted by hecklers accusing him and the other speakers of being seditionists, Fascists, Trotskyites, and advocates of a Peace Now plan. Wolfe asked each heckler to identify himself and his affiliation. The next day the *Seattle Post-Intelligencer* published a list of self-identified Communists and, in its lead editorial, equated their disruptive tactics with those of "Hitler's brown-shirted storm troopers" who had undermined free speech in the Weimar Republic.[20]

In his speech elaborating on the theme he had presented in *Common Sense* a year earlier, Wolfe identified seven trump cards that Russia's representatives would hold at the peace table: "The first and best is a moral claim, namely, that with the possible exception of China, Russia has given more in human life, of her treasure, in her effort toward the war. She has lost more, suffered more, and sacrificed more than any other power involved." Second, to secure Russia's entry into the war against Japan, the United States and England probably would have made territorial concessions in Europe and perhaps in Asia as well. Third, Russia would be the greatest power on the continents of Europe and Asia because France, Germany, and Japan would be crippled for years to come. Fourth, Russia's representative would speak with a single voice. "There are no rival parties in the Soviet Union. There is no unstable coalition government. There are no Congressional hurdles . . . There is no independent press." Fifth, Soviet demands would be supported by a "devoted, even fanatical, band of adherents and defenders and admirers" in England and the United States. Sixth, Russia would have the option of unleashing or stifling revolutions in Europe at any time. Seventh, at the conclusion of the war the Red Army would occupy many areas in Europe on which Stalin had set his sights, and their occupation might be viewed as a fait accompli. In contrast Wolfe saw the United States as possessing only one strong trump: its immense riches that could be used to rebuild Europe. Therefore, he recommended that the United States should insist, in return for its aid, that the territorial settlements be "democratic settlements . . . that may contribute to a more durable and lasting peace."[21]

Before Wolfe came to speak in San Francisco, a communist group—the local chapter of the National Maritime Union—tried to block his appearance. The group passed a unanimous resolution denouncing Wolfe as "a known Trotskyite, [who] had made slanderous statements against the heroic Soviet peoples." Wolfe, a seasoned veteran of political hardball, seized the initiative by putting his views on the record in an interview with the *San Francisco Chronicle:*

> I am not now, nor have I ever been a Trotskyite. I have never written or uttered a slanderous statement concerning the Soviet peoples. What they mean is that I have been critical of Stalin. I am

not connected with, nor have I ever had any connection with, the Peace Now movement nor do I favor a peace with Hitler or the present regimes in Germany or Japan.

The campaign of opposition backfired: instead of a boycott, it produced an overflow crowd, with hundreds turned away. The next day an editorial in the *San Francisco Chronicle* with the headline "No Thunderbolts" declared,

> Bertram D. Wolfe, writer and lecturer, spoke as scheduled . . . over the protest of the CIO National Maritime Union that he is a Trotskyite and his appearance would offend our Russian allies and hurt the war effort. Wolfe spoke; Moscow has not withdrawn from the war; the Red Army continues to chase the Germans across Poland. Locally, we have noted no visible damage from this exercise of free speech in San Francisco.[22]

Wolfe's repeated confrontations with communist hecklers and fellow travelers assured him that he had something unique to contribute in the struggle against Stalinism. Although he believed the printed word to have the most enduring impact, he increasingly welcomed opportunities for lectures, debates, and appearances on radio public affairs shows because they enabled him to reach audiences who might never read his articles in small-circulation magazines.

❖　　　❖　　　❖

As World War II progressed Wolfe became reconciled to a longer timetable for completing *Three Who Made a Revolution.* When time and funds permitted, he visited East Coast libraries to examine pamphlets and newspapers that dealt with the events he was trying to reconstruct and interviewed eyewitnesses to the Bolshevik Revolution. His West Coast trip in 1944, although taking two months away from his writing, gave him his first opportunity to visit the Hoover War Library at Stanford University, a repository of rare books and archival collections that he wanted to study.

Despite his slow progress in completing *Three Who Made a Revolution,* Wolfe refused to take shortcuts. He continued to examine documents and compare successive editions of books looking for telling clues and discrepancies as if he possessed limitless time. But realism again forced him to scale back the scope of his book, ending it in 1914 at the outbreak of World War I rather than in 1917 at the start of the Bolshevik Revolution.

When the book rolled off the press during the summer of 1948, the publisher sent advance copies to a select list of reviewers. One of the first reactions came from Samuel Putnam, a former Communist, who wrote that *Three Who Made a Revolution* had liberated him psychologically and praised it for

> the cold, cruel but reinvigorating clarity it brings to one who (an intellectual worker) like myself knows what it is to have floundered for a decade and more in the Machiavellian mazes of the party line—a line that, beneath all its moralistic assumptions and posturings, is in reality ruthless, unscrupulous, unprincipled—only to be bitterly disillusioned in the end. Disillusioned and more than a little ashamed . . . The value of your book for one like me lies in the fact that, by showing us the historical basis of our error, it restores something of our self-respect and at the same time affords the basis for a new orientation.[23]

The first reviews were unanimously favorable. Arthur M. Schlesinger, Jr., wrote in *The Nation*, "You have the sense of a historian so long immersed in the material that his mastery of it is always fluent and expert. The result is clearly the best available study on the prelude to the ten days that shook the world." Crane Brinton praised Wolfe not only for his scholarship and narrative skills but for his objectivity: "It is . . . the book of a man who must be classed as an anti-Stalinist. Yet it has none of the sourness, the disillusion [or] the cynical revulsion . . . one so often notes among American liberals who have finally decided that Stalin Is A Bad Thing." Edmund Wilson wrote in the *New Yorker*, "*Three Who Made a Revolution* is, I believe, at the present time the best book in its field in any language."[24]

After a decade of eking out an income by writing book reviews about Spanish and Mexican literature and history and lecturing to pacifist audiences, Wolfe at age 52 was suddenly in great demand. Writing to a friend, he described his new life:

> Now that my book is out, I have been called upon to do a lot of lecturing: in churches, to high officials of the Army, Navy and State Department in Washington, to Men's Clubs and Women's Clubs, and in all sorts of expected and unexpected places. The reviews of my book have been uniformly favorable and the book promises to be a success in everything but sales. After all, one can't have everything. The State Department bought 100 copies and sent them to

its European desks to contribute to their education on Russia. If the masses do not rush to read a difficult book, the classes do.[25]

Although it was not a best-seller (it sold only a thousand copies the first year), the book sold steadily. By 1970, more than three hundred thousand copies had been sold in English and the book had been translated into seventeen languages.[26]

The critical success of his book enabled Wolfe to gain access to foundations and research fellowships that had been closed to him because he had no doctorate or academic affiliation. Writing to another friend in April 1949, Wolfe was exultant:

> I have just won a Senior Fellowship in Slavic Research at the Hoover Library, Stanford, with no duties but to work on my second volume (*The Uses of Power*). But this belongs to the it-never-rains-but-it-pours department: I have just gotten word . . . that I am also being awarded a Guggenheim. I don't know whether Fortune has at last begun to smile on me or is laughing.[27]

❖   ❖   ❖

Wolfe's progress on the sequel was short-lived. In June 1950, after the outbreak of the Korean War, he was invited to apply for a job with the U.S. State Department. Foy Kohler, head of the Voice of America's International Broadcasting Division, was looking for someone who could counteract communist propaganda and expose the imperialist goals of Soviet foreign policy—to create an Ideological Advisory Unit. The unit's chief responsibility would be to produce radio scripts to be broadcast by the Voice of America in 46 languages worldwide.

Wolfe felt strongly that the State Department under Dean Acheson had been waging a weak and ineffective campaign against Soviet propaganda, reacting to Soviet initiatives but never taking the ideological offensive. He agreed to apply for the job because he knew it would make good use of his talents and experiences. He could take all the knowledge he had gained as an advocate for communism and turn it against Stalin and his apologists in the West and his puppet regime in North Korea.

Wolfe's willingness to work for Voice of America did not ensure that he would be hired. His former association with the communist party required that the Federal Bureau of Investigation explore his past activities and current allegiances. He had to go through the same scrutiny again because the job was a civil service position. Before the questioning began, Norman Thomas and Sidney Hook submitted affidavits to the U.S. Civil Service attesting to Wolfe's loyalty to the United States. Hook wrote,

> [Wolfe] has taken a leading role in formulating the strategy and tactics of democratic defense and offense against communist duplicity and terror in the field of culture . . . He has helped educate a generation about the meaning of communism. He is no timeserver whose views change with every new current in the climate of opinion, but a man of deep conviction who recognized and denounced the Soviet regime of terror and its imperialistic expansion when such judgments were unfashionable and unpopular.[28]

At his civil service hearing in February 1951, Wolfe said that his past communist affiliation was valuable experience for the new job. He pointed out that his predictions about Stalin's postwar intentions had been accurate and cited his writings and lectures as needed ideological and psychological warfare to stop the spread of Soviet influence. Once Wolfe received his security clearance he hired two writers and a small support staff, but he wrote nearly two hundred scripts between 1951 and 1954, nineteen of which are being published in this book for the first time.

Wolfe's overriding goal in his Voice of America scripts was to strip the Soviet Union of any pretense of legitimacy by showing that its constitution was a sham, that its democratic elections were bogus, that there was no mechanism for a peaceful succession when the reigning dictator died, and that the use of censorship, forced labor, one-party rule, and periodic purges were not Stalinist aberrations but essential and ineradicable features of the communist regime. The Voice of America scripts reflect the most fundamental change in Wolfe's thinking—the realization that means and ends are inextricably linked, that one cannot achieve noble aims by despicable methods. He had become convinced that a temporary reign of terror would last as long as the ruler could justify his policies in the name of an exalted ideal such as ending poverty, creating a classless society, or eradicating inequality.

Wolfe opposed authoritarian regimes because they suppressed dissent in the name of maintaining themselves in power. But a *totalitarian* regime is much worse, he believed, for once it begins to cloak its terror in a *moral* mantle, nothing can contain its brutality. As one of his favorite aphorisms states, "Man needs an ideal in order to be able to torture and kill with a clear conscience."

❖   ❖   ❖

In November 1951 Senator Pat A. McCarran, an outspoken anticommunist, criticized the idea that former Communists are not trustworthy and cannot be valuable allies in defending the West against Soviet imperialism and communist propaganda.

> I am convinced that the ex-Communists can be our most potent allies in the battle against communism at home and abroad . . . I would urge both the public and the government to abandon the belief that the communist stain is ineradicable. It is an attitude which makes a mockery of repentance and, in addition, deprives the country of the special knowledge only former Communists possess.[29]

McCarran's premise was not universally accepted. Fred E. Busbey, a Republican congressman from Illinois, sharply criticized Wolfe's selection to head the Ideological Advisory Unit. On July 5, 1952, Busbey rose on the floor of the House of Representatives to defend Ruth B. Shipley, the head of the State Department's Passport Division. Shipley had been criticized for refusing to grant passports to individuals she deemed security risks to the United States. (These included two writers for *The Daily Worker*, singer Paul Robeson, novelist Howard Fast, artist Rockwell Kent, scientist Linus Pauling, and historian W. E. B. DuBois.) After praising Shipley's vigilance, Busbey suddenly shifted into an attack on Wolfe:

> I say, Mr. Speaker, that if the State Department and other government agencies were as careful in screening their employees as Mrs. Shipley has been in screening applicants for passports, then there would be less ado about the pinkos, Communists, fellow travelers, and radicals in the government service. Bear with me while I give you an example of what I have in mind.

Busbey quoted Wolfe's 1933 essay *What Is the Communist Opposition?* as proof that Wolfe had remained a dedicated communist after he was expelled from the communist party in 1929. "Instead of concern-[ing] ourselves as to why a mere handful of rabble-rousers are denied the privilege of traveling in foreign countries," Busbey urged that Congress be given access to the employment files of federal agencies: "We should demand the right to review the file of the likes of Bertram D. Wolfe, and determine who has been asleep while on guard."[30]

Wolfe did not respond to Busbey's attack, for he was told that the State Department wanted to avoid a public confrontation with a congressman. But he did compile and submit copies of his speeches and writings from 1936 to 1951 to show that Busbey's attack was unfair. When Busbey did not press his attack, Wolfe assumed the episode was closed. Thirteen months later, however, Busbey struck again, denouncing Wolfe as a "lifelong Marxian Communist and propagandist of the Communist movement," a "Marxian disciple of proletarian dictatorship," and an "enemy of a free society and republican form of government." He urged that Wolfe be fired immediately.[31]

Wolfe was vacationing in Provincetown, Massachusetts, when a colleague sent him a story from the *Chicago Tribune* headlined "Busbey Names 'Voice' Official as Marxian Red: Bertram Wolfe's Past Revealed in House." In response Wolfe sent Busbey an impassioned defense that shows how Wolfe viewed his own intellectual evolution. (Busbey never replied; instead he mounted a third attack in March 1954 that Wolfe ignored.)[32]

❖   ❖   ❖

Early in 1954 Wolfe resigned from the Voice of America to resume writing *The Uses of Power*, the sequel to *Three Who Made a Revolution*. But, because Wolfe had spent a decade writing the first volume, he felt he could not concentrate all his energies on a single volume that might take as long to complete. Consequently, he adopted a strategy that he described to a friend in 1971:

> [A]s soon as I finished *Three Who Made a Revolution*, I knew that I had an insoluble problem . . . After much thought and inner conflict, I finally decided to undertake larger enterprises as if I might live forever and at the same time to break them into small parts each of which could be published and live a life of its own independently of whether I ever did any further work or not . . . In short, I live each day as if I were to live forever or might wake up tomorrow morning to find myself dead.[33]

Using this writing strategy Bert Wolfe was immensely productive. From 1954 until his death in 1977, he published twelve books, six of which consisted of essays and articles that appeared in magazines and journals as diverse as *Life, The American Mercury, The New Leader, Commentary, Encounter, Antioch Review, Russian Review, Problems of Communism,* and *Foreign Affairs.* Until the end of the 1950s he frequently reviewed books on contemporary Russia for the *New York Herald-Tribune* and the *New York Times.* During these years, however, he was foremost a writer and teacher of Russian history. He spent two years as a research fellow at Columbia University's Russian Institute. He was a visiting professor of Russian history at the University of California at Davis and at the University of Washington. He returned to the Hoover Institution in 1965 and was a senior research fellow there from 1966 on. Each summer he traveled to Boulder, Colorado, to teach at an institute run by Professor Edward J. Rozek. Otherwise, from 1965 on, research and writing were his chief activities. At Hoover, he worked amid thousands of books and his vast research files studying Russia's past.

But he also avidly followed day-to-day events. No matter how busy, he wrote letters whenever someone was being victimized, whether it was Simas Kudirka, the Lithuanian seaman who tried to gain asylum aboard a U.S. ship but was returned to the Russians; Junius Irving Scales, an ex-Communist seeking a presidential pardon for a Smith Act conviction; or Svetlana Alliluyeva, Joseph Stalin's daughter, who sought refuge in the United States and was met with opposition.

Bert Wolfe not only wrote history, he became a historical resource, freely sharing with scholars his memories of deposed Soviet leaders like Bukharin, ex-Communists like Whittaker Chambers and V. F. Calverton, and fellow travelers like Anna Louise Strong and Scott Nearing. (Those portraits are included in this volume.) When asked, he advised colleges how to deal with self-styled communist teachers like Angela Davis and H. Bruce Franklin. But he did not always wait to be asked. Drawing on his lifetime of study of Russia, he initiated long, thoughtful letters to Presidents Richard M. Nixon and Gerald Ford about the proper conduct of U.S. foreign policy, and he encouraged Ronald Reagan to seek the presidency to reverse what Wolfe viewed as the dangerous drift of the Ford–Henry Kissinger years.

As Wolfe grew older he sometimes despaired about the prospects of turning back the tide of communist world domination. But he rallied despondent friends with words of optimism, often his own most recent writings examining the belief—common after Stalin's death in 1953 and Nikita Khrushchev's de-Stalinization speech of 1956—that Soviet

Russia was becoming a more humane and pluralistic society. "Détente," "peaceful coexistence," and the idea of "convergence" between communism and capitalism represented "progressive" thought in Europe and the United States. But Wolfe, emulating the quote of his friend Arthur Koestler—"God only gave us necks so we could stick them out"—stuck his out repeatedly.

❖   ❖   ❖

In December 1975 Wolfe wrote a note indicating what he hoped to cover in the concluding chapter of his autobiography:

> Last chapter: to restore the word freedom and its meaning to the place of honor; to increase once more the trend to democracy, and to weaken, restrain, and lessen the trend to dictatorship, autocracy, tyranny, statism, and totalitarianism; to restore the values that have grown weaker, or been forgotten, and to place the worth of the individual in the center of our consciousness in a mass society. I being now in my eighties shall not live to see them but I hope that on balance my writings shall have contributed in some small measure to the realization of these aims.[34]

This note indicates why he looked forward to Ronald Reagan's election not only as an opportunity to proclaim the moral superiority of democratic ideals and institutions but also for an overdue revision of U.S. policy toward the Soviet Union—a policy he regarded as compounded of naïveté, blunder, and misunderstanding.

Today, more than a decade after his death, Bert Wolfe remains, through his writings, a fighter for the freedom and survival of the West.

Notes

1. Bertram D. Wolfe (hereafter, BDW), "Our Time of Troubles," *Antioch Review,* Summer 1951, p. 131.

2. BDW, "Pacifism and War," *The Communist,* May 1928, pp. 285–96. See also BDW, "What I Will Do When America Goes to War," *Modern Monthly,* September 1935.

3. Historian Theodore Draper explains, "The draft of a Comintern directive, ostensibly sent to permit local leaders to express their opinions before its final adoption, was actually an advance notice for local leaders to change their views immediately in order to qualify as supporters of the Comintern's line before it was officially promulgated." Draper, *American Communism and Soviet Russia: The Formative Period* (New York: Viking Press, 1960), p. 396.

4. Ibid., p. 422 (based on a 1953 interview with BDW).

5. Ibid., p. 527.

6. "Building a Communist Party in the U.S.A.," *Workers' Age,* October 15, 1932.

7. *Interrogatory, Bertram D. Wolfe,* Fourth United States Civil Service Regional Office, Washington D.C., February 1951, pp. 5–6, Box 1, File 17.

8. BDW, *Things We Want to Know,* articles reprinted from *Workers' Age,* Box 25, File 5. The pamphlet contains no copyright page but is dated July 1934 on page 31. This must be an error since it quotes from newspapers of December 1934 and January 1935 (pp. 4, 26, and 28). Isaac Deutscher says the pamphlet was published in 1936, but internal evidence suggests mid-1935. Deutscher, *The Prophet Outcast* (New York: Oxford University Press, 1963), p. 368.

9. Untitled, Box 23, File 24, quoting "Decisions of Presidium of E.C.C.I. on Work of Communist Party in Spain," *The Daily Worker*, January 24, 1937.

10. "Trotsky's Case," *The New Republic*, June 16, 1937, p. 165.

11. "Trotsky's Defense," *The New Republic*, November 24, 1937, p. 79.

12. BDW to Meyer Schapiro, November 25, 1937, replying to Schapiro's letter of November 24; also see Schapiro's reply, November 27, 1937.

13. Notes for speech on the purge trials.

14. Speech on the purge trials, March 9, 1938.

15. Prospectus for *Three Who Made a Revolution*, undated [1938]. BDW often said he decided to write *Three Who Made a Revolution* in reaction to the signing of the Hitler-Stalin Pact on August 23, 1939, but his recollection was in error. See BDW to Alfred A. Knopf, November 18, 1938; BDW to Pascal Covici, Viking Press, December 11, 1938; BDW to George Joel, reporting an error in Dial Press's publicity release on *Three Who Made a Revolution*, April 17, 1939; BDW to Jay Lovestone, "I suppose you know that I signed a contract for *Three Who Made a Revolution*. Will expect help and suggestions, you'll have to read the manuscript, eventually" (May 2, 1939); and BDW to Philip Wittenberg: "advance from Dial Press $600, for which I owe a manuscript which will take another year's work, after I put *more than a year* into it" (May 11, 1940, italics added).

16. Handwritten note, "Thots [*sic*] on the S-H Pact," dated 1939.

17. BDW, introduction to Rosa Luxemburg, *The Russian Revolution* (New York, 1940), pp. viii–ix.

18. Ibid.

19. Ibid., p. ix, italics added. For Wolfe's continuing appreciation of Rosa Luxemburg, see his essay "Rosa Luxemburg and V.I. Lenin: The Opposite Poles of Revolutionary Socialism," *Antioch Review*, Summer 1961, pp. 209–26; reprinted as introduction in Rosa Luxemburg, *The Russian Revolution and Leninism or Marxism?* (Ann Arbor: University of Michigan Press, 1961). Also see profile of her in BDW, "The Last Man in the German Social

Democratic Party," in his book *Strange Communists I Have Known* (New York: Stein and Day, 1965), pp. 117–37.

20. Arthur G. Barnett and Donald W. Calhoun, preface to *Russia at the Peace Table*, an address by BDW (Seattle: Institute of International Relations, 1944); BDW, "Hire a Hall: Some Adventure on a Lecture Tour Through the Land of Free Speech," *The New Leader*, October 7, 1944.

21. BDW, *Russia at the Peace Table*.

22. BDW, "The Battle of San Francisco: Further Adventure on a Lecture Tour Through the Land of Free Speech," *The New Leader*, October 14, 1944.

23. Samuel Putnam to BDW, September 22, 1948. Other appreciative letters came from Adolf A. Berle, Jr., and Oswald Garrison Villard. See Berle to Sol Levitas, September 23, 1948, and Villard to BDW, October 6, 1948.

24. Arthur M. Schlesinger, Jr., *The Nation*, November 6, 1948, p. 525; Crane Brinton, *New York Herald-Tribune Weekly Book Review*, October 17, 1948, p. 5; Edmund Wilson, *New Yorker*, December 18, 1948, p. 104. Reviews in the scholarly journals were equally laudatory. See, for example, Isaiah Berlin, "Three Who Made a Revolution: A Review Essay," *American Historical Review*, October 1949, pp. 86–92.

25. BDW to Lu Geissler, October 27, 1948.

26. BDW to Ewan Clague, October 22, 1970; see also Sol Stein, "Full Circle: A Foreword" in *Three Who Made a Revolution* (New York: Stein and Day, 1984), pp. ix–xiv.

27. BDW to Melvin J. Lasky, April 5, 1949.

28. Deposition of Sidney Hook, February 5, 1951.

29. Pat A. McCarran, "The Value of the Ex-Communist," *American Mercury*, November 1951, p. 9.

30. *Congressional Record*, 82nd Cong., 2d sess., Appendix, vol. 98, part 11, July 5, 1952, pp. A4868–88.

31. *Congressional Record*, 83rd Cong., 1st sess., August 3, 1953, pp. 11120–23.

32. *Congressional Record,* 83rd Cong., 2d sess., March 4, 1954, pp. 2544–50.

33. BDW to Joseph Davis, November 8, 1971.

34. "Notes for Last Chapter," [December 1975].

Breaking with Communism

Bertram and Ella Wolfe
(ca. 1924)

Editor's Note

The letters and other writings in this volume conform as closely as possible to the originals, with two exceptions. First, I have corrected inconsequential errors of spelling and standardized punctuation and capitalization for the sake of clarity. Second, I have deleted passages that are purely personal (health problems or finances, for example), have no historical significance, or would lengthen the text by needless repetition. Every omission is indicated by an ellipsis; the original documents are available in the Hoover Institution Archives for those who wish to consult them.

Letters

1938–1953

Speech on the Moscow purge trials, under the auspices of the Trotsky Defense Committee, New York

March 9, 1938

I want to begin by thanking the Trotsky Defense Committee for inviting me to participate in this meeting. I regret that it is not being held under much broader auspices. I believe that all labor organizations have been derelict in their duty in not arranging the broadest mass protest meeting under the broadest possible auspices, to show that the entire labor movement protests against this infamous and murderous farce. So far we have had only a meeting under the auspices of the Trotskyists, and this one, with invitation to spokesmen of other organizations, but under the Trotsky Defense Committee. This is unfortunate, in my opinion, because it gives the impression that the issue is Trotsky versus Stalin, or that our protest is primarily for the defense of Leon Trotsky. Nor is that sufficiently offset by the fact that my own organization [Independent Labor League of America] is holding a meeting of its own on the issues involved in this same hall next Wednesday night. I want to pledge my organization to work for the calling of a meeting adequate to the issues involved, under the joint auspices of every organization that is interested in the question. The Socialist Party has pledged itself to the same end, and leading figures in the Social Democratic Federation and the Socialist Workers' Party and Anarchists have given similar assurances. To my mind the issues are broader than the controversy between Trotsky and Stalin, or Bukharin and Stalin, broader than the defense of Leon Trotsky, or of all the defendants now on trial, or the thousands and hundred thousands crowding the jails of the Soviet Union, broader than the redemption of the good name of those who have already met death without trial at Stalin's hands, or at the hands of his henchmen such as Yezhov.

The Russian purge and the methods it employs concern the very life of the labor movement in the Soviet Union and, by extension, in all the lands of the earth. Any one who fails to raise his voice unequivocally on this question makes himself a guilty accomplice by his silence. He who is indifferent we must brand for his indifference; he who excuses this accuses himself of being willing to introduce the same methods into our own labor movement; he who justifies it has bathed his hands, as did the conspirators in Shakespeare's play, in the blood of the innocent victims. And that blood is the best blood of our generation, the blood of the men who led the opposition to the world war, of the men who led in the making of the Russian Revolution, of the men who led in the building of the Communist International, of the men who risked their lives in the tsarist underground, who exhausted themselves in the civil war and the famine, who performed miracles of socialist reconstruction, who led the Soviet Union in all of its achievements.

If one word of these charges is credited as true, then the Russian Revolution must have been made by traitors, bandits, imperialist spies, provocateurs, murderers, and counterrevolutionaries. If Trotsky was a spy since 1921, then he was conspiring to overthrow himself while he was the leader of the Red Army. If Bukharin was guilty of conspiring to kill Lenin in 1918, then Lenin was a dupe and a moron to have praised him before his death as the "darling of the party," and the program of the Communist International is the program of a traitor. The rewriting of history has gone so far that Trotsky's heroic efforts to build up a Red Army, drive out foreign intervention, and crush counterrevolution were all expended and, successfully mind you, at the orders of a Germany that was not yet Fascist, a Japan that was not yet through with its twenty-one points, an England that bribed these men to build up a mighty Soviet power so that they might later have more work and more fun trying to crush it.

These mad charges have at last gone so far that Lenin himself is on trial in Moscow. How else shall we interpret the charge that his closest associates were the agents of foreign governments? Is not the charge of German spy levied against the then commissar of war [Trotsky] but a revival of a charge levied in those days against all the Bolsheviks, and first of all against Lenin? Was it not Lenin who passed through Germany in a sealed train? Lenin who was most insistent of all on a separate peace with Germany? Lenin who insisted on the signing of the Brest Litovsk peace while the accused Bukharin and the accused in absentia, Trotsky, were still hesitant?

This trial and this purge involve issues, it seems to me, that are even broader than the labor movement and the issue of honesty and democracy within it. Precisely because the working class is the most

significant class in modern society, precisely because it is the main
bearer of social progress, destined by its position in society, and its
own class needs, to be in the vanguard of every forward-looking
movement, therefore must we recognize that if it is lacking in respect for human life and human integrity, then humanity itself is
doomed to retrogression, rebarbarization, degeneracy and self-
destruction. When Robert Minor [editor of *The Liberator* and *The
Daily Worker*, communist periodicals] delivered himself of his famous declaration, "Honesty is a bourgeois virtue," thereby he calum-
niated the labor movement, slandered the working class, gave the
bourgeoisie—whose rule is based upon devices of hypocrisy—an
honor they did not deserve, and by his attack upon the working
class, he read himself and the party he speaks for out of its ranks,
out of the ranks too of decent human beings of any class whatsoever.

Stalin's bloody deeds against the Communist Party, the Soviet
State Apparatus, the Red Army, the Political Police, the Party Press,
the Planning Commission, the leaders of industry and agriculture,
and the Soviet peoples serve to complement the fearful crimes he
committed against the Communist International and the labor movements in all other countries. Public trials have been mostly directed
against those who were former oppositionists. But he uses the men
whose names he has already blackened and continues to blacken, the
Trotskys and Bukharins, chiefly to frame up those who but yesterday
were his closest associates and the leaders of literally every branch
of Soviet life: the entire general staff, the admiralty of the navy, the
GPU [political police]—all the apparatus of defense internal and external; the premiers and presidents of every autonomous soviet republic and region, excepting only three; the party secretaries of every
district but two; 90 percent of the editors of party papers—all the
apparatus of political leadership of the country; already more than a
third of the central committee and two members of the Politburo
have been included; two vice-commissars of foreign affairs and all
ambassadors but two—virtually the entire apparatus of diplomacy;
the authors of the five-year plans, heads of ten departments of the
Planning Commission, and a score of state trusts—all the apparatus
of leadership of industry and agriculture; even doctors, inventors, poets, dramatists, composers, sociologists—the apparatus of cultural
life is wrecked by Stalin the arch-wrecker.

He has made infinitely harder the task of those of us who love the
Soviet Union and would make the world understand its wonders of
achievement, of those who would defend it against attack from the
ruling class of all lands. He has murdered his comrades in arms,

spewed such filth upon their names and on the fair name of the Russian Revolution that all of us feel unclean even to have to discuss this vileness. Today we can only help the Soviet Union if we succeed in making clear that Stalinism is the very opposite of what we are aiming at and defending. Only by exposing Stalinism, only by wiping out its foul influences, can we redeem the honor of the Russian Revolution and of our class whose greatest effort in history it so far represents.

Time will not permit me to attempt tonight to give a positive exposition of the causes of this frightful phenomenon, or the prospects of overcoming it. Our organization is more convinced than ever that we were right in making, as we did, a clean break with the growing system of corruption in the Communist International. In retrospect it is clear that we should have done it earlier. We are more convinced than ever that we were right in denouncing and breaking with the system that made a world party a tail to a faction in the Russian party. Even the best of the Russians after Lenin's death, men like Trotsky, Zinoviev, and Bukharin, failed to understand that. Our organization is more convinced than ever that today the Soviet Union can go forward only if the Russian Communists and the Russian working class throw off the monstrous yoke of Stalinism, that the labor movement elsewhere can flourish only if it repudiates as vile and obscene the gangster methods and the traitorous policies of Stalinism.

If I am asked, "Can Stalinism be overthrown?" I answer: "How can Stalinism possibly continue in power? Has it not taken a path which leads from arrest to arrest, from forgery to forgery, from murder to murder? Is not the Soviet Union for the first time in a decade without a five-year plan? Is not Stalin forced by his policies to destroy his own tools? Has he not been obliged to purge a second layer which replaced the first, and a third replacing the second? Is he not destroying his very base for existence?"

Our task is to make clear what is happening, to redeem the Russian Revolution from its destroyer, to defend and spread what was positive and heroic and progressive, and still is so, in the Russian Revolution, to clean out the seepage of filth that threatens to infect the movement, and to deal with scrupulous cleanliness, clarity, decency, and honesty, and maximum working class democracy, with the problems of our own working class.

———————◆•◆———————

Wolfe devoted many months in 1939 to translat-
ing Rosa Luxemburg's 1918 essay, The Russian
Revolution. *When it was advertised, he received a*
stinging letter from E. V. Walker, who had been
translating the same essay for another publisher.
After defending himself against the charge that he
had undercut the other translator, Wolfe focused
on the bitter factionalism that was splitting the
socialist camp.

December 1939

To: E. V. Walker

Your strange letter of December 12 was shown to me, and since I am
the translator of Rosa Luxemburg's *The Russian Revolution*, I have
undertaken to answer it . . .

There is a broader matter involved, which I hope, for the sake of
the future of our movement, you will give some thought to. Is it not a
matter of grave concern, which should cause us to do some thinking,
that comrades who have so much in common that they both admire
this great work of Rosa Luxemburg should be alienated from each
other by such bitterness and suspicion as would permit you to make
such conjectures—rather than comradely inquiry—and to write such a
letter? I assume that your publication of the pamphlet, like mine or
ours, is not a commercial venture but recognition of its essential
greatness as a guide to a revaluation of the Russian Revolution and a
reconstruction of our badly damaged and divided and demoralized
revolutionary movement. I did it as a labor of love, and received no
compensation, though I could ill afford the time, not being a paid
functionary but a volunteer worker in our movement who earns an
inadequate living (even more inadequate than that of our paid workers!) by writing. I assume your motives and interests are not dissimilar and since you have selected the pamphlet, your outlook must be
not dissimilar to ours and that of Rosa Luxemburg herself. This little
episode, therefore, becomes symptomatic of the atmosphere that sur-

rounds our movement as a whole—an atmosphere of suspicion, distrust, cherishing of old hates and prejudices and factional reactions—an atmosphere which leads to the unwholesome conclusion that one and one's little group of intimates and coreligionists has a monopoly of all virtue and clarity and desire for a better world, and that everybody else is continuing the unequal battle at such cost out of motives of trickery and what not. This attitude, if it ever achieves power, makes for one-party or one-clique dictatorship and purge. If, as is only too likely, it does not come to power, it condemns our movement to remain divided into sterile, mutually embittered sects, fit only to render impotent the movement that needs above all reunification, reconstruction, cleansing of the very air we breathe, rebuilding of an atmosphere of comradeship and trust without which we can never face a world of genuine enemies and enormous tasks.

As for the fact that we now have two translations of this pamphlet, I do not think it is a bad thing. You will doubtless reach some people with it that we cannot, and we some people that you cannot. The main thing is to get it read and studied and understood. And despite this unpleasant episode, it is good to know that you and Travers Clement [national secretary of the Socialist Party] and we all value the same pamphlet so highly as to put so much effort into it. It shows that despite the weight of the old heritage of suspicion, the movement is really groping its way towards reunification of thought and outlook which is a prerequisite for its reconstruction as a whole . . .

<hr>

The following is an excerpt from Wolfe's introduction to Rosa Luxemburg's essay, The Russian Revolution *(1939).*

II. APPRAISAL OF THE RUSSIAN REVOLUTION

Others might regard the Russian Revolution with blind idolatry or blind hatred. But this clear-eyed, courageous woman, watching in the darkness of her prison cell, in a land made doubly dark by military dictatorship and socialist betrayal, did not let the promise in the eastern sky blind her to the new problems of the new day she had worked for and longed for.

The great service of the Bolsheviks, she explained, was to put socialism on the order of the day, to save the Russian Revolution from extinction, to begin the proletarian way out of the shambles of war, to redeem the tarnished honor of the Socialist International.

But the revolution was no model revolution carried on under model laboratory conditions. It had occurred in a backward land, cursed with poverty, lacking in a democratic tradition, ill-equipped economically and culturally for the building of a model socialist order. It had occurred in the midst of war and economic chaos, under the advancing bayonets of the German military machine, at a moment when the working class elsewhere had failed in its duty. How could it be a model revolution occurring thus under the hardest conceivable conditions? What right had we to reproach it for its failings for which our own dereliction was so largely responsible? And would it not be dangerous to try to make virtues of its hard necessities, and saddle other movements with the obligation of worshipping and imitating its weaknesses, in place of assimilating the essence of its mighty example?

"It would be a crazy idea," she wrote, "to think that every last thing done and left undone in an experience with the dictatorship of the proletariat under such abnormal conditions should represent the very pinnacle of perfection."

But it was this crazy idea which formed the foundation of the Communist International from the outset and ultimately caused its destruction! That is why Rosa Luxemburg opposed its formation, for she saw the inevitable defect in the foundation . . .

She did not shrink from recognizing that violence might have to be employed to prevent the violence of those who would drown the revolution in its own blood. But even there it was but a poor auxiliary weapon to the far mightier and more effective one of enlightening and stirring into activity the millions who could thus reduce the active counterrevolutionists to an important handful. All other problems—the checking of corruption and bureaucratism, the combating of ignorance and degeneracy, the improvisation of new economic, social, and cultural forms—could only be solved by the broadest possible initiative, enlightenment, and self-activity of the masses. No party, she knew, had a monopoly of wisdom nor a filing cabinet full of ready-made solutions to the thousands of new problems to be presented each day in the course of building a new social order. At best, the socialist program had a few negative recipes—a little knowledge of what had to be eliminated in the old order, and a few general indications as to the direction in which to look for the solution of the first questions presenting themselves. The actual solutions were neither a matter of authority nor prescription but of endless experiment, of tentative trial and fruitful untrammelled suggestion and invention. "Socialism, by its very nature, cannot be introduced by ukase . . . Only unobstructed, effervescing life falls into a thousand new forms and improvisations, brings to light creative force, itself corrects all mistaken attempts."

Such is the core of Rosa Luxemburg's teachings, which her opponents so scornfully referred to as her "theory of spontaneity" and "underestimation of the role of the party." She would have limited that role to stimulation of the masses into democratic self-activity, not domination and substitution of itself for the masses. How profoundly right she was in her democratic faith and in her fear of bureaucracy, of one-party dictatorship, clique rule, and domination by a handful of leaders, of the attempt to solve all problems by decree and universal terror—the intervening years in Russia have amply demonstrated. Today, her warning sounds like the words of a gifted prophecy.

> With the repression of political life in the land as a whole, life in the soviets must also become more and more crippled. Without general elections, without unrestricted freedom of press and assembly, without a free struggle of opinions, life dies out in every public institution, becomes a mere semblance of life, in which only the bureaucracy remains as the active element. Public life gradually falls asleep, a few dozen party leaders of inexhaustible energy and boundless experience direct and rule. Among them, in reality, only a dozen outstanding heads do the leading and an elite of the working class is invited from time to time to meetings where they are to applaud the speeches of the leaders, and to approve proposed resolutions unanimously—at bottom then, a clique affair—a dictatorship to be sure not of the proletariat, however, but only of a handful of politicians . . . Such conditions must inevitably cause a brutalization of public life: attempted assassinations, shooting of hostages, etc.

Alas, her warning went unheeded and a quarter century of uninterrupted terror has made her worst fears more than justified. The initial deficiencies of Lenin were endlessly magnified by his successor, and his sporadic efforts at correction were abandoned. The result is the bloody monstrosity of the personal dictatorship of Stalin. If the test of a scientific theory is its ability to diagnose and predict, surely the soundness of Rosa Luxemburg's estimate of the relation of democracy and dictatorship has been fully verified. How far she is superior to those critics of Stalinism who, out of false pride or autocratic temperament, reject her views is revealed by the fact that Leon Trotsky, who has had more than a decade in which to re-examine his own conceptions in deportation and exile, has not to this day attained to her clear and simple vision of the initial defects in the Russian Revolution and its political system.

———————————◆•◆———————————

This excerpt from Wolfe's speech to the Keep America Out of War Congress urges U.S. Jews to oppose U.S. entry into a European war.

April 6, 1939

WAR AGAINST WAR-MAKERS!

. . . Now a word as to the deluded. I want to say a word of, and to, the most justifiably deluded, the element that makes the war party so much larger in New York than elsewhere in this country, those whose anguish blinds their visions as each day their spirits are bruised and shocked afresh by the daily budget of news of Jewish persecutions thruout the world. Profiting by their anguish which amounts to hysteria, there are those who would sell them the coming war as a war against anti-Semitism. And this is the more dangerous delusion because the growth of militarism and reaction in this country is bringing with it the growth of anti-Semitism.

To you I say there is no way of putting an end to your endless torture except by putting an end to militarism, reaction, war, and capitalist imperialism which begets them all.

Are you so blind as to ignore the connection between the rise of modern imperialism with its theories of superior and inferior races, and anti-Semitism?

Are you so ignorant of the history of the suffering of your own people as to have failed to see a connection between militarism and reaction, between reaction and persecution?

Do you see no significance in these dates?

1870: Franco-Prussian War, followed by two decades of anti-Semitism in both Germany and France, culminating in the Dreyfus case?

1905: Russo-Japanese War, followed by reaction and anti-Semitism culminating in the Kishinev massacre. [Kishinev, a city in Bessarabia in what is now the Moldavian republic, was the scene of an anti-Semitic pogrom in which several hundred Jews were murdered. The massacre actually occurred in 1903, before the Russo-Japanese War.]

1914–18: World war, followed by worldwide reaction and worldwide anti-Semitism on a scale never known before in history.

You, of all people, should be among the last to desire another war. Take care, I beg you, lest not only the reactionaries and militarists of this country should grind you and the Negro people under the iron heel, take care a thousand times more lest those who desire to keep this country out of war should get the idea that you are working to put America into it. When you lose the sympathies of the masses who have nothing to expect from war but misery, then you will be lost indeed.

*The next three letters were written to Kenneth
Rexroth, the San Francisco poet and literary critic
who headed the Randolph Bourne Council, an
antiwar group. Bourne (1886–1918) was a literary
critic and radical who opposed U.S. entry into
World War I.*

October 23, 1939

To: Kenneth Rexroth

I am sorry I could not answer your airmail letters earlier, but they
had to fall into a folder with scores of others, while I was doing a
rush job with Norman Thomas of a book [*Keep America Out of War*]
elaborating the program and outlook of the KAOWC [Keep America
Out of War Congress].... The ms finished yesterday, I am starting
to ... answer a month's back mail. Spurred on by your third airmail
letter which arrived today, yours is the first letter to be answered ...

First, let me say that you, like all of us who have been through
the terrific period of disintegration and disillusion in the radical
movement between the First World War and the Second, give me the
impression of harboring too many subjective reactions to those you
fought with. If Lillian Symes, for example, is running the KAOW too
narrowly, some fresh blood and a little patience should broaden it
out to what it should be, a genuine common front of all those who
are opposed to America's entrance into the present war and willing
to fight it. I don't think the Trotskyists, in so far as they follow their
peerless leader, will be in it or can be, not on a priori grounds, but
because (1) they believe and insist on preaching to the masses that
our entrance is inevitable, which is a paralyzing idea tending to
make impossible any mass struggle against war; (2) they are committed to "expose" and destroy the KAOW; (3) their leader recently
stated in so many words that not only must America enter but America should enter as the only way of freeing Stalin from Hitler ...

The FOR [Fellowship of Reconciliation] is as you have discovered
a Christian pacifist group. It is working loyally with the KAOW but,

obviously, is not suited to your group. If you cannot disarm Lillian Symes's reported antipathy to you and tendency to run her organization too much as an S.P. [Socialist Party] auxiliary—the impression I get from your letters—or if you cannot disarm your own suspicions of her, it is perfectly simple for you to form your own KAOW group, separately from the one she is in. Of course, the two groups, and others, could then cooperate on certain joint efforts like big mass meetings, etc. There's room enough for all. Naturally, Trotskyists who want to work—not bore from within (and I mean bore in both senses) or capture or blow up—should be as welcome as any one else. It's an antiwar movement and there should be no faith tests, blood tests, background tests, or any other, except genuine determination to work together on the limited and urgent program of the KAOW, and not turn each "joint" effort into a wrangle and free-for-all. We cannot admit loyal Stalinists at present, even though some of their programatic statements on war sound like ours, any more than we can Bundists [German-American supporters of Nazi Germany], because these two groups are not honestly and reliably antiwar, but oppose America's entrance because they favor a war victory of the other side, the Stalin-Hitler bloc . . .

November 9, 1939

To: Kenneth Rexroth

. . . The Manifesto of the Randolph Bourne Council is excellent, as is the whole idea. Naturally, that doesn't mean I agree with every last word . . . [ellipses in original] I can't even say that for the Communist Manifesto!
    . . . More serious is the decision to leave your manifesto unsigned. By their very nature writers and artists are publicists, public men. There is no point in a special grouping of them if they are going to take shelter behind anonymity. What is sometimes prudence in a revolutionary mass organization—even then not always—becomes self-negation in a writer or group of writers. As writers our business is to give our views as publicly as we know how, and face

the music. That has made up the great service and the greatness, for shorter or longer periods dependent upon their consistency and courage, of all the writers of the past two or three decades whose names we respect or have respected—the [Ignazio] Silones and [André] Gides and [Jean] Gionos [French novelist jailed in 1939 for his pacifist views] and the rest. We will of course publish your good manifesto with the note that it has been adopted by a number of California's leading artists and writers, but no one has any obligation to believe us or be impressed without the names. A writer who conceals his views on the war ceases to be a writer and "thinker" so far as his influence and activity is concerned, for the duration. I deeply hope that you fellows will reconsider your decision on the matter. Randolph Bourne's name should serve as reminder.

———————◆·◆———————

When Rexroth told Wolfe he was hoping to compile an antiwar anthology, Wolfe recounted the reception given to his recent book Keep America Out of War.

January 16, 1940

To: Kenneth Rexroth

. . . As to the antiwar anthology, I should be glad to see one gathered and printed, but the publishing world is likely to be wary here [New York]. There is a deliberate press conspiracy against any straightforward antiwar stuff, especially if it is recognizably socialist. The Thomas-Wolfe book, for instance, was not reviewed by a single New York paper or book reviewer. It's three months now since it was issued, and not one word in the press. It was refused by the department stores, not displayed by other booksellers, and refused by most of them. Stokes, who published it, says he feels as if he had thrown three hundred review copies into the middle of the Atlantic Ocean and then thrown in 1,500 dollars in advertising after them—*spurlos versenkt* [sunk without a trace]. If it is selling at all, it is by word of mouth, with few mouths to give the word, and through organizations like the KAOW [Keep America Out of War]. Yet my last book [*Diego Rivera: His Life and Times*, Knopf, 1939] got a splendid press, and Norman Thomas can usually get his share of publicity here. Other antiwar books have not been treated much better. Therefore, the problem would be finding another publisher willing to bite . . . I should be glad to help in seeing the manuscript around New York if it ever got that far.

———————◆•◆———————

Writing to Jay Lovestone, Wolfe criticizes President Franklin Roosevelt's recent efforts to enter the war on England's side and explains why U.S. aid to England is undesirable.

Provincetown, July 13, 1940

To: Jay Lovestone

Your letter dated the 12th is of the kind which makes one despair of ever communicating thoughts or entering into discussions. No discussions can be carried on if one party to them concentrates on externals, and picks up some tag which leads to the closing of the mind and the cessation of examination. How far can we get if you persist in calling a position which challenges yours not a position but a moral lecture. Obviously, that gets nowhere. It disposes of, but doesn't analyze, accept, refute, learn from, teach . . .

On the main question I do not think we will get very far by such a route. I have made no moral judgments, only political ones, whether sound or mistaken remains to be seen. I have given no moral lectures. If I feared "grimaces," that was a cautious word for what actually happened while I was speaking at the last meeting.

Such phrases as "moral lecture" is one of the things I heard then and fear as calculated to embitter and shut off discussion, not help it.

I do not say merely that the new position of "quarantine," "aid," "support for England," etc., is unintentional aid for Roosevelt. It is actually the position he has been pushing for two years. That does not necessarily make it wrong. You and the other comrades do make important reservations concerning keeping out of war and concerning independence, and important strictures on his actions. But we are not strong enough to put "conditions" to him and make them stick. We are deluding ourselves if we pretend that we can change his aid to "conditional aid." Our job, as Will [Herberg] has rightly pointed out also, is to expose his fraudulent aid slogan. That is the best we can hope for exerting our little strength on a national governmental scale. And that holds our forces independent in practice as well as theory. Our positive aid job is to give such aid and secure such aid as we can for the labor and independent forces. That has nothing to do with morals, and it is the heart of my position.

Against it you allege that it is not new. Newness is not in itself a virtue. The new experience with France teaches us precisely the unreliability of the Churchills et al. The new, i.e., recent, progress of Roosevelt in putting through his fraudulent involvement under the guise of aid and preparation for offense under the guise of defense, his war of hysteria and ten billion dollar budget and the rest, leads me to the conclusion that we were right, are in more danger now, and should fight him harder than ever if we really mean to accomplish our keep-out-of-war and independent, fight-American-totalitarianism position.

"Are you prepared to write in the *Workers' Age*," you ask, "that you are against even conditional aid to Britain." My answer is clear. If not, I will repeat and clarify further in the *Age*. Our little group and all its following is not strong enough to impose conditions on the aid being given. It may be effective in exposing the war drive hiding under the aid slogan, and to some small extent in giving aid to our own camp in Britain. For that reason I have emphasized that we must know our strength, where to apply it, and what traps to guard against. You want me to say, "Yes, I Bert Wolfe am opposed to giving such assistance." That's a false dilemma. I have stated, and repeat, that if aid could be separated from the war drive which hides under it, I would favor it. Since it cannot be so separated, the slogan can only serve to confuse and demoralize our forces and weaken our independence and struggle against Roosevelt. If it makes you happy to retort that that is "appeasement" or "unintentional aid for Hitler," you yourself know better, and shut off all possibility of really examining the question of what our actual forces must accomplish and where they should actually be applied.

"Sterile isolationism," like "old stuff," is another mind-closing formula. Fighting Roosevelt, exposing the frauds under aid and defense, believing that we can best help the world by keeping out and giving such direct aid as we can muster to independent forces like the ILP [Independent Labour Party of Great Britain] and the PSOP [Worker and Peasant Socialist Party of France] is not isolationism, nor has anything in common with it. We have had that word tossed at us enough by our enemies. There are quarters from which we have a right not to expect it. The same goes for "appeasement" and "objective aid to Hitler." . . .

Well, this is the last time I shall pester you with a letter on this question since your manner of replying leads me to despair of making myself understood—lord knows I tried—or getting anywhere. Yes, the discussion will be a long one, and I shall be on deck on Labor Day. Perhaps [face to face] we will have less misunderstanding and more clarity.

As to the rest you've been so kindly prescribing, I am out here to work, and because Ella is out here to rest, and two can live cheaper and better as one than as two. But I work daily until four, spend from four to five at the beach, then dine and work til bedtime. I am way behind on my Russian book, and it is beginning to torture me with its unfinished tasks and unsaid thoughts and unmanageable burdens. I bit off an awful lot. However, the hour or so at the beach and the little errands about town are lovely and help keep me in trim for the work. As for giving my mind a rest, I could think of no greater torture.

———————◆———————

*William Edgerton, a professor from North Carolina
whom Wolfe met when he lectured at Guilford
College, raised several questions about New York
intellectuals and their attitudes toward the Soviet
Union. Wolfe replied as follows:*

February 29, 1944

To: William Edgerton

Your letter of the 26th with its confident promise to talk many interesting things out with me this summer gave me a little jolt, for I
opened and read it just two minutes after I finished a phone conversation with Ray Newton settling the fact that I am to spend an entire
summer on the Pacific Coast. It was my desire since I have long
been looking for some way to get to the Hoover Library at Palo Alto
to do some research needed for my book and since my wife and I
have long looked forward to spending a summer once more in California where we spent three happy years from 1919 to 1922. The
only drawback is that I shall miss seeing you and [Edward] Duckles
this year, something which I had been looking forward to.

Letters are a poor substitute for afternoons and evenings of
friendly talk and we are both too busy to thrash out all the interesting questions you raise by mail. Does not your life ever bring you to
New York? If so, please let me know in advance and arrange to have
dinner at my home or to meet me wherever the exigencies of your
trip permit.

As to the answerable items in your note: *The New Leader* is one
of the most interesting and informative weeklies procurable today, as
you suggest, immeasurably superior to the *Call*. It is worthwhile sub-
scribing to. The Social Democratic Federation [S.D.F.] consists of old
time "right-wing" Socialists who are today far to the "left" of the
communist party which, for the sake of service to the interests of
the Russian state as it conceives such service and for the sake of
gaining power through maneuver and adoption of false colors, has
dumped all its basic principles overboard. The Norman Thomas So-

cialists and the S.D.F. group are now quite close to each other in
platform and are thinking of reuniting, but the differences in sophistication and approach to fresh problems are likely to hold them apart.
The chief difference in the two papers is that the *Call* appeals to
"the sticks" while *The New Leader* is essentially a New York paper
with a background of European Marxist sophistication and some energetic young men on its staff who do not share the old-fashioned
Social Democratic credo at all.

As to attitudes toward Russia among the dissimilar and incom-
mensurable persons you list as "intelligent and well-informed," it is
surprising to note how much of what passes for intelligence is emotion and how "information" may be colored by the will-to-believe
and the unwillingness or incapacity to face facts. My generation in-
vested a tremendous amount of spiritual capital and hope in the Russian Revolution ([William Henry] Chamberlin and I not less—rather
more—than some of the others you mention) and it is not easy to
see the "capital-investment" of a lifetime written off as a bad investment. [Jawaharlal] Nehru's attitude is colored by the fact that the
Soviet Union at its best has represented a banner raised against imperialism and for socialism and that Russia has always appeared as a
counterpoise to Britain in India. Being in jail does not help one to
gain access to correct facts. Louis Adamic is a good man but was
never a well-informed one or a man who could harness his emotions
to his intellect. I know him well and have always thought of him as
a sort of peasant with a pen in his hand, full of fine feelings which
are sometimes used, by those who know his weaknesses, for sinister
purposes. The Yugoslav situation is the prism through which he
views the world and all things are distorted therein . . .

[Malcolm] Muggeridge, writing on worshipful pilgrims to Russia,
once said:

> Their delight in all they saw and were told constitutes one of the
> wonders of the age. There were earnest advocates of the humane
> killing of cattle who looked up at the massive headquarters of
> the OGPU with tears of gratitude in their eyes, earnest advocates
> of proportional representation who eagerly assented when the ne-
> cessity of a one-party dictatorship was explained to them, earnest
> clergymen who walked reverently through anti-God museums
> and reverently turned the pages of atheistic literature, earnest
> pacifists who watched delightedly tanks rattle across the Red
> Square and bombing planes darken the sky, earnest town-
> planning specialists who stood outside overcrowded ramshackle

tenements and muttered: "If only we had something like this in England!" [*Winter in Moscow*, Eerdmans, 1987]

And now he might add: earnest advocates of the right of self-determination and honest plebiscites who cheered when the Baltic countries were overrun; earnest and irreconcilable opponents of Hitler who burned the palms of their hands applauding when the Stalin-Hitler pact was signed which unleashed the Second World War. The will to believe is a strange distorter of the vision, and we are apt to approach the things on which we have charted our hopes in a misty aura of our own preconceptions.

As to your question concerning why Russia is moving away from communism and not toward it and what alternatives are involved, that is such a small matter that it is the subject on which I am doing my book.

Asked for his opinion of journalist Dorothy Thompson, Wolfe replied as follows:

May 17, 1944

To: William Edgerton

. . . I am also reminded that I did not answer your last note which contained an inquiry concerning Dorothy Thompson. I do not read her column except irregularly and accidentally and have always thought of her as a girl with a good heart but not too good a head. She is apt to give as her opinion that of the last convincing person she interviewed, although, if things stir her long enough she is likely to hammer out an opinion of her own. The few things of hers I have seen on Russia have been neither brilliant nor evidence of the fact that she has taken any real trouble to master the complicated materials involved . . .

In short, Bill, what I am driving at is that we live in a frightfully complicated world and one in which intrigue has developed to a pitch that makes the E. Phillips Oppenheim mystery thrillers look amateurish. In such a world, good intentions are not enough; intellectual persistence, hard-headedness, alertness, and detective powers which make Sherlock Holmes always so wise do not even always suffice.

Although Wolfe described himself as a "fellow traveler of the Quakers" during World War II, he wrote some of his harshest letters to Quakers he believed were unwitting communist fellow travelers. One such occasion arose when Anna Melissa Graves, a Quaker from Maryland, sent him the manuscript of her book about Russia.

November 5, 1944

To: Anna Melissa Graves

I must ask your pardon for having kept your manuscript so long. I really have been over my ears and topknot in work. Besides, I must own to you frankly that I had a psychological obstacle—grave misgivings as to your ability to face the truth fully and freely on Russia . . . To me people who out of noble motives or ignoble refuse to face the facts and build upon them are worthless to and destructive of the causes they wish to serve, for they alienate where they would enlighten and persuade. Having got that off my chest, I turn to your manuscript.

. . . Twice you speak of open churches and freedom to worship as you observed it and deprecate the idea that there was genuine religious persecution. Again you are generalizing and leading the incautious reader to generalize too far from your own limited experience. There were periods of ebb and flow in the degree of religious persecution. There are definite figures now available for all periods as to the number of priests imprisoned and executed and the number that have survived . . . If you are interested, the best source in English, the work of a man frankly religious and frankly hostile to Bolshevism in its earlier and later forms (less to the later), in a work based chiefly on Soviet records, is N.S. Timasheff: *Religion in the Soviet Union* (Sheed and Ward, 1942). My only suggestion is that you tone down the implication that, because you saw no persecution at a given time, all accounts of such persecution are sheer invention . . .

My only larger differences are two: (1) you speak repeatedly as if the USSR of today were not an imperialist country . . . What one woman thinks or knows does not matter, but only if you recognize that Russia in foreign policy is becoming one great power among other great powers (more strategically situated on the continent of Europe than others) pursuing by violence, bullying, and deceits its own self-interest, only then can you accomplish your major objective: understanding as a means of preventing or heading off, as far as lies in your power, a future war . . .

(2) Of the same order is your statement that "of all the great countries the USSR is least bad." I haven't time, nor scarcely capacity— nor, I doubt, have you—to argue or prove or disprove this kind of statement. I am convinced that this is a statement you have no right to make, nor to make its opposite . . . Actually Russia is better in some respects than other lands and worse in others. You do better when you measure it in terms of its own ideals. To make the evils of your own land always worse . . . than the evils of other lands is but the reverse by inversion of the perverted standards of the chauvinist who makes his own land always in all things better and the evils of the other land always worse and omnipresent. Do you really have to work yourself up into believing that everything at home is the worst in order to fight against domestic evils . . ? I don't think so . . .

Anyhow, let me congratulate you on the general promise of your Russian book. Its chief contribution will be to remind readers that Russians are human beings and that, besides a regime and an army and a physical weight among great powers, there is a vast land full of human beings, fallible, lovable, capable of joy and sorrow, like Americans and Englishmen and Germans and Italians, human, perhaps all too human, beings. When all the others are treating Russia as purely dehumanized politics and making pro-Russian equal pro-regime and anti-regime equal anti-Russian people, it is a relief to see a work that takes your approach. If I have ventured to suggest what I thought is so often weak and wrongheaded in your approach, it is always because I have been aware of what is so worthwhile in it too.

———————————◆•◆———————————

Wolfe wrote a follow-up letter to Anna Melissa Graves about her book on Russia.

November 8, 1944

To: Anna Melissa Graves

I swore that I should say no more on the subject of my last letter, but your rejoinder, both by its content and by its appreciation of my true intent, compels me to yet one last attempt to clarify the issue.

You are not a private person, merely trying to save your own soul, but you have assumed the grave responsibility of writing and speaking, of multiplying your views in hundreds, thousands, you hope hundreds of thousands of copies. You are trying to tell others what the facts are, what their attitudes should be. Under those circumstances you have no right to evade the responsibility of ascertaining the facts concerning which you speak. If you have money to publish a book, time to write it, you must have money and time to read the *New York Times,* and the patience to sift truth from falsehood. Again and again your writings betray the fact that you are repeating analogies learned from quite different situations, attitudes adopted twenty years ago, without taking the real trouble to see how much the new historical situation differs to be revised. Because Shakespeare was a poacher or De Quincey took opium or Anatole France took many young girls to his bed in his old age, not every writer who poaches, takes opium, or has many lovers is therefore a genius. Each must be examined on his own merits. Because newspapers lied about the

blowing up of the *Maine,* not every report of an attack is thereby
settled. Each has to be examined afresh, and the one who is too set,
or sure, or lazy or busy to examine the new case in its own terms (of
course keeping in mind the old experience as a possibly, but by no
means a certain, guide or a complete answer to all new questions),
such a person has the right to his or her prejudices (for that is what
judgments in advance of examination of the facts are), but not the
right to tell others in print.

Thus you assume, wrongly I am sure, that Stalin is to the Russian
Revolution what Napoleon was to the French. Had you been ear-
nestly, prayerfully I might almost say, reading and studying all reports, in the daily press, the Russian press, reading between the
lines, difficult but necessary, these last twenty years and especially
the last half dozen, you would know that Stalin corresponds (and
then only very loosely) to the corrupt figures of the Directory, but
not to Napoleon, and that Russia under his recent leadership stops
revolutions where they are developing, is able to bolster reaction as
conservatives in origin cannot, because he pretends to represent and
trades on the name of the Revolution. Churchill or Roosevelt would
not have dared to murder the leaders of the Polish socialist and Jewish trade union movement as Stalin did . . . You are not excused
from analyzing the statistics of the purges, who and how many and
what kind of victims, merely because they are hard to get, and hard
to analyze and because others can lay cuckoo eggs of false interpretation into the statistical nest. Statistics, like daily events of an historical character, must be mastered by those who would try to tell others either "the facts" or what to think, or a proper attitude. But
deeper than that responsibility is the other question you raise. The
real trouble, I have come to feel, is that you are not opposed to evil
on principle, but only to evil when it comes from your pet source of
grievance, the peculiar inverted nationalism which sees the evil
thing only when your own country does it, . . . When you start with
the foundation of principle, let us say, imperialism is evil regardless
of which country practices it, then, and only then, have you the
right to be heard on a sober comparison of Japan's power to practice
the evil it is bent on, versus England's power to practice it. Only
when you start with principle, the principle that the murder of revolutionists in the name of the revolution is evil, have you the right to
be heard on the question of which country, which army, which police force, is the most effective and energetic enemy of revolution or
progress at present. And even then, we get back to the first issue:

nobody has the right to tell others, to write for others, without pains-
takingly acquiring all the available facts and sifting them. "I think it
must be so" may be all right, though I doubt it, when talking to
yourself; it is irresponsible and lacks regard for truth and for your
audience when you are talking to others. . .

I did not have this "on my chest" in any personal sense, but only
in the sense that I felt, and feel, that there is something gravely
wrong with your approach to truth and evil which in the end will
render worthless or at least gravely vitiate the efforts on which you
have spent a quarter of a century and for which I have only good
wishes.

Friendly discourse is always possible because I have always liked
you and admired your intentions even where I disagreed with their
execution.

Thanks for seeing through the "scolding" to the intentions.

---

*In 1944 Wolfe explained to Norman Thomas why
he opposed a negotiated peace with Germany or
Japan if the present rulers were not deposed.*

May 2, 1944

To: Norman Thomas

. . . Democratic, humane and progressive and socialist elements cannot now propose that our governments should sign any kind of peace
with the present rulers of Germany or Japan (or Italy). Our only
hope, and the only hope of the German people, once the cruel war
already exists, is that it end with the maximum results for social
progress possible and the maximum guarantees against evasion, re-
gression, and renewal of the evils that brought it on. Every criticism
of a deal with [Pietro] Badoglio [Italian premier who succeeded Mussolini in 1943] applies with immeasurably greater force to a deal

with Hitler. It would salvage reaction in Germany and strengthen it here at home. There are conditions under which our government may prefer it, none conceivable under which you could.

I have never believed that countries should go to war to dictate to the governments of other countries. But we are at war and in a position, for better or worse, to decide with what elements in Italy or Germany or elsewhere to sign a peace, and cooperate in its realization. The last man in the world with which they could be done beneficially would be Hitler.

In the same sense, I would be energetically anti-war if there were an attempt to make a war to dictate to Russia its system or government or ruler. But if the conditions in Europe you describe should lead to a war between England and the United States on one side and Russia on the other, I should certainly hope to see the peoples of all the countries involved determining their own destinies and working together for the permanence and fruitfulness of the peace which would ensue, and Stalin and what he represents would certainly not be the most desirable ruler and regime for that purpose.

One more matter: What do you think of asking A. Philip Randolph [U.S. labor leader, founder of the all-black Brotherhood of Sleeping Car Porters] to accept the presidential nomination of your party [Socialist]. Not as a picturesque gesture but because he would dramatize the suppressed issue of the war—the equality of peoples and races, and freedom of the colored and colonial peoples, the rights of minorities in Europe and here at home, the impossibility of dictating to Germany how it should treat Jews or what racial laws it should have, if we are unwilling to permit the same determination by public opinion . . . of our treatment of minorities here at home.

---

*Wolfe favored independence for all colonial na-
tions, regardless of whether they were dominated
by England, the United States, or Russia. In support of India's release from British rule, he sent
this message to novelist Pearl S. Buck, chairman
of the India League of America's dinner honoring
Madame Pandit, Nehru's sister.*

January 24, 1945

To: Pearl S. Buck

As the center of war shifts to the Far East, the recognition of the
independence of India, like the recognition of the integrity and sovereignty of China, are decisive for the shortening of the war and the
decency of the peace. British temporizing on the independence of
India, Russian suggestions for a new partition of China, American
flirtation with the idea of bases which spell continued colonial status elsewhere, and the failure of the United States to throw its full
weight into the scales for giving Asia back to the Asiatics, is Japan's
strongest weapon today. To save the lives of millions of soldiers, to
build a world in which the white minority can live in peace and
brotherhood with the awakening millions of colored peoples, to give
the Atlantic Charter meaning in the Pacific, the United Nations
should recognize the independence of India at once.

---

*In a speech in New York on May 20, 1945, protest-
ing Russia's arrest of sixteen Polish leaders, Wolfe
identified the futility of appeasing Russia.*

The issue we are met to discuss here today transcends the fate of the
sixteen anti-Nazi leaders whose arrest we protest. It transcends the
fate of Poland whose mutilation was sanctioned at Yalta. It even transcends the fate of the Baltic nations which have been engulfed in a
total silence. It transcends the blackout of news which shrouds the
whole of Europe from the Elbe River to the Adriatic Sea.

There is no geographical limit to the principle of Justice. If peace
is indivisible, if there is One World, then Justice is indivisible, and if
we renounce our ideals east of the Elbe River or the Adriatic Sea, we
undermine them everywhere . . .

If we concede Russia's right to arrest and hold the members of the
Polish Home Army, recognized officially as Allied soldiers not only
by Britain and America but even by Germany, then it is no wonder
that Russia dares to hold even our American prisoners captured from
the Germans—*as she is doing today*. Drew Pearson [a Washington
journalist] reveals that our American prisoners have been turned
over to the Lublin puppet government to be held as hostages. We
must negotiate with Lublin and so recognize Lublin if we want them
released.

If we recognized Russia's right to violate her treaties of friendship
and nonaggression with Poland and the Baltic states, why are we
surprised when she violates her Yalta agreements with us over Aus-
tria, Romania, Yugoslavia, or Poland?

All these acts are the very policies and aggressions which we
fought this war to prevent.

Russia gave us fair warning of everything she is doing today when,
in January 1943, she admitted the execution of the Polish Jewish
patriots [Victor] Ehrlich and [Henryk] Alter. Like the sixteen, they
went to Russia in order to cooperate. There were brief protests in
America at that time. Enthusiastic friends of Russia, like Eleanor
Roosevelt and Wendell Willkie [defeated Republican presidential
nominee, 1940], even joined in them, but those protests were a nine-

day newspaper wonder and were soon forgotten. Evidently our government learned nothing from them.

The appeasement and the lying about Russia as a democratic, freedom-loving nation went on as though nothing had happened. That policy reached its climax at Yalta. There the British and American governments abandoned the principles and promises they had proclaimed in regard to Poland throughout the war. Before Yalta they had demanded, at least they had *publicly* demanded, that any Russian claims on Poland must be postponed until after the war, so as not to interfere with the common war effort; that the settlement between Poland and Russia be arrived at by arbitration; that *all* the United Nations have a voice in settling it; and that it be not imposed by force, unilaterally by the greater upon the lesser power.

Until Yalta, the American government still publicly maintained the principles of the Atlantic Charter, which had been the promise which encouraged the Poles and others to continue resistance at whatever cost. According to the charter, the people living in the disputed area must have the final voice in settling their fate. We could not in honor be a party to a scheme in which millions of men and women are handed around as if they were bundles of fagots or bundles of coal. Nor could we ask the Polish government to consent to the loss of nearly one-half of her territory and one-third of her population *before* they had the opportunity to consult the Polish people and get a mandate. We could not do any of these things, and yet we did them at Yalta.

If the Polish government in London had yielded to Russian, British, and American pressure, it would have been forever disgraced. It would have become a puppet, too, bearing the same brand on its forehead that has marked the Lublin puppet government from the day of its birth. And now that the Yalta agreement regarding Poland has collapsed, in spite of the fact that we went to fantastic lengths to keep our part of the bargain, the American and British governments are at least free from the commitments which they should never have made.

I want to say a final word about the special significance of what is happening in Europe for minority groups in America. There has been a widespread attempt by communist propaganda to depict Russia as a protector of the Jews, and Poland as the enemy of the Jews. But the totalitarian state itself is the greatest enemy of the Jews and of every other minority group.

One of the greatest of Jewish relief organizations, the Joint Distribution Committee, has estimated that 600,000 Polish Jews were deported by Russia in 1939 and 1940. In a book published by the International Labor Office of the League of Nations, written by Professor [Abraham] Kulisher, the same figure is given, and that figure is also accepted by the Institute of Jewish Affairs. These facts dispose completely of the argument that only ethnic Poles failed to welcome the seizure of eastern Poland.

The Jews, like all minority groups, have a supreme interest in the establishment of civil liberties and the protection of human rights throughout the world. And may I express the hope that you here in this hall who are rightly sensitive to these injustices committed against minorities abroad will be equally sensitive to injustices committed at home. For we must learn that Justice is indivisible.

In 1946 when Wolfe was asked for biographical data about himself for inclusion in a book about prominent American Jews, he offered the following reflections about his Jewish identity:

January 5, 1946

To: Abraham W. Scheinberg

Your letter, asking for biographical data, raises a question which has been raised for me a number of times by Jewish encyclopedias and *Who's Who* publications, a question which I find difficult to answer.

Your letter sets me down as one of the "Jewish people of distinction in the United States." Whether I possess "distinction" is a matter which you have determined by your own standards of classification, and I have no responsibility therefore. But am I Jewish? That is a problem in which I must make some decision and in which you too shall have to decide.

Certainly my parents were both Jewish. They accounted themselves Americans by nationality, held no concept of a Jewish race, but held themselves to be Jews by religion. But personally I am not religious in any exact sense of the word, although I possess an ethical code largely founded on the Jewish, Christian, and humanitarian heritage to which I am intellectual heir.

Hitherto I have always failed to answer such questionnaires. But because Jews are so persecuted today, I would gladly proclaim myself a Jew if that would help this persecuted people in the slightest. Yet, by the same token, I should gladly proclaim myself a Negro if that would be of use to Negroes, a Chinaman or a Korean or a Pole or a member of the defeated German people (my father was born in Germany) if that would help them to build a more decent and secure life than is the promise of their present plight. In the twenties and early thirties I fought more for Latin American rights and the equality of the Negro people with the Whites in this country than for the Jew. Latterly I have done more on behalf of the Jew, but only because his plight was the most acute in recent times. I have little of the special Jewish heritage (knowing neither Yiddish nor Hebrew nor Ladino); I account English my mother tongue and Spanish my second language. I do not believe in Jewish nationality for myself, though since nationality is primarily a matter of feeling, I would defend the right of self-determination for those Jews who possess a feeling of nationality, as for the awakening nationality of the Arabs and the submerged nationality of the Lithuanians and Catalonians, and so on throughout. Nor am I a Jew by religion. But while Jews suffer as Jews (or while any race or color or creed or nationality or religion is condemned to less than full human estate), I would gladly accept fellowship in their suffering if that is of the slightest use to them or of the slightest force in compelling me to more active struggle on their behalf.

If with these limitations you care to list me in your publication, I shall be glad to be included. The question for you to determine is whether under these circumstances you care to list me among "Jewish people of distinction in the United States."

Writing to Arthur H. Vandenberg, the ranking Re-
publican on the Senate Foreign Relations Commit-
tee, Wolfe urged that no Marshall Plan aid should
go to Spain as long as Francisco Franco ruled it.

March 31, 1948

To: Senator Arthur H. Vandenberg

I hope you will use your influence in the Senate and in the Republican party to undo as speedily as possible the damage done by yesterday's action in the House aimed at the inclusion of Spain in the list
of "democratic" powers to be helped by the European Recovery Plan
[ERP].

That action, even if reversed, gives the strongest talking point to
Messrs. [V.M.] Molotov and [Andrei] Gromyko [Soviet diplomats]
that they have had for a long time, and quite undoes the good effect
of our having taken the initiative in Trieste. It will be difficult indeed for the friends of democracy in Italy and France to explain the
position of the United States on this matter. I can imagine the embarrassment of the representative of the American Federation of Labor in Europe, Irving Brown, when he tries to explain it to the Force
Ouvriere, and the embarrassment of Sforza or Sarragat in Italy.

By no stretch of the imagination or of terminology is the Franco
government one of the United Nations or one of the democracies,
any more than the governments of Mussolini, Hitler, or Stalin. It did
not come to power by democratic process, but by military conspiracy
against the legally elected government. It holds its power by total
dictatorship. It owes its victory to our "non-intervention" and to the
direct intervention of Germany and Italy. The notion that the United
States is willing to help Franco to continue his undemocratic domination of his own people hurts us immeasurably in Latin America,
where Franco's emissaries have been the chief propagandists of anti-
American and antidemocratic influence; in Italy, where it will
strengthen communist propaganda and weaken the democratic parties; in France, where it will be deeply embarrassing to the Force

Ouvriere. And above all, it will help revive the largely broken pres-
tige of the Communists in Spain. They have been claiming all along
that only Russia supports the democratic forces and that the United
States is pro-Franco. Now they will have the evidence. And the British government will have a no less difficult task in explaining it to
its own people.

I hope, Mr. Senator, that you will not limit yourself to having the
action reversed, but will take the occasion to make a clear statement
to the effect that only governments genuinely democratic or striving
towards democracy can merit and expect ERP help.

Wolfe received many fan letters after Three Who
Made a Revolution *was published in 1948. Here
he replies to novelist James T. Farrell, a former
Communist and author of the* Studs Lonigan *tril-
ogy.*

November 7, 1948

To: James T. Farrell

We writers work so much in solitary isolation that it is most encouraging to get comment from a fellow writer who has also immersed
himself deeply in the same field. Our loneliness is the greater since
we have ceased to be parts of a common movement, or since that
movement has so far disintegrated as no longer to offer a sense of
solidarity or a decent meeting place for the exchange of ideas and
opinions. I especially value your favorable opinion since I know that
you too have been engaging in a similar process of re-evaluation
which involves both re-examination of the facts and re-examination
of one's self and one's beliefs.

I have taken a long time on the book, something like ten years in
all, letting its structure grow slowly and organically, taking nothing

for granted, and continually surprising myself with my own discoveries and conclusions. I was most of all surprised when the facts forced me to take the side of the Russian Populists or Social Revolutionaries in many fundamental questions as against the Russian Marxist Social Democrats.

As to the peculiarly Russian nature of all Russian movements (even the doctrinaire zealous extremism of the Westernizers in their Westernism), on which you comment questioningly, it is one of the things that simply grew upon me as I studied these men and their controversies. When I finish my second volume (when and if) I am strongly attracted by the idea of making a special study of the Russian intelligentsia as a whole—their formation, their psychology, their role, their leading ideas, and their fate . . . As in the writing of my book, I got the peculiar sensation that my material took possession of me instead of vice versa, moved me deeply, forced me to conclusions I had not altogether anticipated, and made me listen to myself with something bordering on astonishment. I suppose novelists must often get that sensation about their work, but I had never imagined that what is generally regarded as noncreative writing would develop so much of an inner organic force and appear so much to the writer's consciousness as partially determined by forces which do not seem to be in one's consciousness at all until they well up from what is fashionably and inadequately called the region of depth psychology, or still worse, the unconscious.

After World War II Wolfe's days were numbered as
a fellow traveler of the Quakers as he increasingly
came to view them as apologists for Stalin and So-
viet imperialism. In July 1948, when he lectured
again under Quaker auspices in California, he was
paired with "peace evangelist" Kirby Page. On
July 10 he wrote to his wife: "I did the best job I
have ever done—under the most difficult circum-
stances. In the end the issue was between Kirby
Page's appeasement because God wants you to
love your enemies and my reminder that Czechs
and Russian common people and Poles . . . were
also entitled to concern and love. It was the
mushymindedest crowd I ever met, but my last
talk (entirely new and adapted to their mentality)
really went home." Three months later he wrote
to Kirby Page explaining why his pacifist views
would lead to war and needless suffering.

October 26, 1948

To: Kirby Page

I have been trying to find time to write you ever since I heard you
speak in Whittier and end with God's name and a prayer. Frankly, I
was deeply shocked by that prayer and that invocation of God's
name to justify a talk which identified the Russian people with the
Kremlin and ignored all the lesser neighbor nations and their fate.
Surely your God who watches the sparrow fall is as much concerned
with the 10,000,000 or more in concentration camps as he is with
the nine or eleven men in the seats of power. It is much as if a man
had used prayer ("What does God want us to do about America") to
silence a criticism of American justice in the Sacco-Vanzetti case or
the Mooney case. Moreover, the pretense that there are only two
great powers to consider (if I may be permitted some more theology,

that is the unconscious sin of pride), and that the fate of the little peoples does not matter, is not the way to peace, but the way to making war in the long run inevitable. If there is one chance of avoiding war today, it is that of telling the truth, which maketh free, and distinguishing between the Russian people and their oppressive rulers, and giving support to the Russian people by word and act, as well as to the peoples under the iron heel, just as American imperialism can only be curbed, as you and I helped to curb it, by giving support to Nicaragua, Haiti, Santo Domingo, etc., when they demanded the withdrawal of the American marines. I saw peace lovers make the same mistake with Hitler that you are now making with Stalin, to hush 6,000,000 cremated Jews, a spread of German tyranny to neighbor lands, and war made inevitable instead of conceivably avoidable.

I beg you to rethink your views on this subject, and to be charier of implying that you are voicing the will of God when you are urging a program which smoothes the way for the will of Stalin and the spread of spheres of influence until they overlap and war becomes inevitable. At best, that is but your fallible judgment of how to keep the peace, to be matched with my fallible judgment in equal debate and not to be reinforced with prayer and God's name.

Believe me, Kirby, I write this so frankly and sharply out of old friendship and a sense of shared values and hopes. Similarly, if I were in Europe today, in Russia, say, and men criticized our Jim Crow [segregationist policies], I would not tell them to cease lest they bring on hatred and war, but would urge them to multiply their pressure upon the United States for abolition of Jim Crow. That is not hatred of the American people, but love of them. And so when the Kremlin makes unremitting war on its own people and lynches them by tens of thousands in purges and condemns millions of them not to Jim Crow but to slavery, I am sure that the Christian tradition and the Quaker tradition particularly, that fought slavery in the United States must fight slavery today in Russia. The war of nerves that Stalin wages against other peoples in order to justify his state of emergency dictatorship is but a faint echo of the actual war he wages on his own people. In all your prayers, Kirby, remember the Russian people, and the neighbor peoples. Therein, and therein alone, lies the hope of peace. If the peace lovers do not tell the truth about these things and genuinely oppose them, the warmongers will in the end misuse them, even as they did the evils of the Hitler regime in its day.

*During the Chinese civil war, Wolfe favored U.S.
aid to the Nationalists, led by Chiang Kai-shek.
He believed that if the Communists, led by Mao
Tse-tung, won control, China would become a Soviet satellite. In 1949, when Norman Thomas
asked him to present his China policy to a meeting of the Post-War World Council, Wolfe was unable to attend but sent the following letter outlining his views:*

January 4, 1949

To: Norman Thomas

Sorry I will not be able to make the meeting. But my position on
China can be briefly stated:

1. Most attitudes and judgments overlook the central fact that Chinese communism is a new postrevolutionary form of Russian imperialism. Witness its sanctioning of the annexation of Mongolia,
   the return [of] Port Arthur and Dairen, the approval during the
   Stalin-Matsuoko pact period of Japan's seizure of Manchukuo
   (Manchuria), and the annexation of Tannu Tuva.

2. The hope of preventing World War III lies in the restoration of
   Chinese independence and territorial integrity, no less than in the
   restoration of Western Europe. The two power vacuums are the
   two temptations to Stalin and the two dangers to the world. If
   ever he should feel his rear secure and the 450,000,000 manpower
   of China under his control, he will be doubly tempted to roll over
   Europe to the Atlantic (what can stop him) in order to combine
   the manpower of Asia and Russia with the industry of Russia and
   Western Europe in what will seem to him an unbeatable combination for the "final conflict" and the seizure of power on a Eurasian and world scale.

3. The central government has the deficiencies that one must expect
   of a government not yet formed, born in a civil war which has

run since 1910, or, counting the Boxer Rebellion, since the last century, and has been complicated and made infinitely more terrible and difficult by attacks on China by Japan, Russia, and other European powers. How can there not be inflation mounting steadily as long as the struggle continues? How can the struggle be short when it seeks to transform in 35 years or so what has existed for 35 centuries? The so-called corruption is as old as China, exists on both sides, will be as hard to eradicate as it has been, still is, and will be for the rest of the century in Mexico. In its present specific form it is the work of Sun [Yat-sen], rather than Chiang. He it was that married into and received the support of the Soong family, he who retained the old "war lords" or royal provincial governors, because he thought they would eventually die out, and much bloodshed could be spared by keeping them. Chiang cannot undertake a real war on this heritage as long as he must combine all possible forces against extinction of the republic and the nation. (You have been in faction fights and know how it forces you to put some issues to the fore and ignore others until those have been won or lost.)

4. Whatever the defects of the central government, and I am willing to ignore the remarkable propaganda job that historically ignorant and fellow traveler–touched and communist Americans have done on the Chiang government—admitting them to be then as vast as the smear campaign suggests, I still point out that the central government is the only one which struggles for the independence and territorial integrity of China, the only one out of which democratization can come once the civil war grinds to an end. Therefore, I would support it if it loses the North (we get the credit for that outflanking operation through Manchuria and northern Korea). I would support it if it has to retreat to Canton, as it has done several times under Sun and Chiang, or if it retreats to Formosa (more than once Sun and Chiang have had to offer their resignations and flee). Or if it retreats abroad and becomes a tiny government-in-exile of the devoted few who will still wish to fight for territorial integrity, independence, and a nontotalitarian, i.e., potentially democratic regime. The war lords will not retreat abroad but will go over to the Communists on the best terms they can make. Many are with them now. If Chiang falls, I would support whoever succeeds him. If the Kuomintang breaks up, I would support whatever fragments reassemble anywhere in the world to renew the effort. For there is no

other party that has emerged out of Chinese history, and no Mar-
shalls [General George C. Marshall, sent to China by President
Truman to negotiate between the Communists and Chiang Kai-
shek to end the Chinese civil war (1945–47)] can conjure Chinese
parties out of their bureaucratic or brass hats. If China is lost to
totalitarianism, then Western Europe becomes but the perilous
edge of the great totalitarian Eurasian continent, a tip of a penin-
sula, and World War III becomes inevitable and its very outcome
uncertain for civilization. I do not think, however, that the last
act of the Chinese drama will be played out in our time. We are
too headline and Winchell-Pearson conscious [Walter Winchell
(1897–1972), syndicated columnist, whose opinionated radio news
show attracted a large audience; Drew Pearson (1897–1969), con-
troversial journalist whose column, "Washington Merry-Go-
Round," had an estimated readership of 50 million], and fail to
note that the rhythm of Chinese life is slow and secular and different from the swift vibration of French uprisings or American
prairie fire crazes. I tried in vain to tell people that Franco would
not fall when Hitler and Mussolini did, for, though he was helped
by them, he arose out of a Spanish struggle that began in 1808
and has gone in long cycles of three-, seven-, and fourteen-year
struggles followed by periods of exhaustion, in which, in the
course of perhaps two centuries, Spain will eventually show a majority for a republic and liberalism (actually, in 1936, the land was
just about divided 50-50 after more than a century of prolonged,
bloody, intermittent civil war). Chinese history has a slow
rhythm that makes Spain's look like a metronome. Be that as it
may, not only the fate of China, but the fate of Asia and Europe
at least, is being fought on in Chinese exhausted overpopulated
fields. The issues: shall China be annexed or absorbed by Russia
(the other powers are no longer serious threats at present)? Shall
it go totalitarian insofar as a nonindustrialized state can enter
into that postindustrial form of slavery without ever having
known any of the freedoms of the democratic age? Or shall its
integrity be preserved as a culture and a nation, so that modern
industry may some day irrigate its fields, improve its transporta-
tion, war on its millennial famine, and lay foundations for something better than a subhuman life and for the beginnings of democratic freedoms and respect for individual life and dignity? To
"support" with our tongues imaginary parties is an evasion.
There are only two real parties: the Kuomintang, democratic in
aspiration and loyal to the Chinese nation as a potential entity,

and the communist party, Russian formed, Russian dominated, totalitarian in aspiration, and ready to unite or divide China as Stalin wills. While it wins and while it loses, the Kuomintang de-
serves our support until something better appears. To withdraw
support is to guarantee something worse. I would have American
aid set conditions, but only such as are compatible with the dignity and sovereignty of a government that has withstood invasions and internal attacks, and in one form or another will with-
stand many more.

------

*Replying to Professor Solomon Bloom of Brooklyn
College, Wolfe explains why, in* Three Who Made a
Revolution, *he portrayed Lenin as a democrat in
view of his later totalitarian behavior.*

March 2, 1949

To: Solomon F. Bloom

. . . As to the interpretation of Lenin as democrat, there is really no
difference between us. My method of writing, deliberately chosen, is
not to force my conclusions upon the reader but to let them grow
out of the evidence as it accumulates. Hence my book returns again
and again to the same problems at various stages of the story, each
time presenting the problem more amply as choices are made by my
personages and as more ample consequences flow from those
choices. Thus, *so far* in my story, Lenin remains in his own mind a
democrat. That is to say, by purely intellectual, or perhaps, ritually
formularistic conviction, he believes himself to be a democrat,
though it must be clear to the discerning reader that in temperament, in passion, and in a number of decisive actions he has already
unconsciously rejected or acted against those outwardly held democratic doctrines. In my second volume, to be called *The Uses of
Power*, his temperament and power-centered convictions, and tacti-

cal and organization methods, will come into open conflict with his democratic formulae. But the fact that I realize it now does not seem to me to justify my running ahead of my historical story and obliging my reader to accept my word for it, until it flows overwhelmingly from the evidence of action in living situations. And even then it will be useful to judge Lenin's actions of 1917 in the light of his own earlier theories and, at least intellectually held, value judgments, on the nature of socialism and the social process. It goes without saying that it will be even more useful to examine the work of his "best disciple" [Stalin] in the light of both the earlier and later Leninism. Even as late as summer 1917, I find Lenin (before he takes power) advancing many democratic views. It is the moment of taking power, the method of holding power, and other subsequent choices that finally determine the character of his regime and the sum of his own character.

There is, in fact, a peculiar symmetrical reversal in the attitudes of Marx and Lenin toward democracy and decentralization. Marx begins as a strong authoritarian centralist and, whatever his temperament may have remained, after the Paris Commune, his writings become definitely more decentralist, antiauthoritarian, and democratic. This arises primarily as a by-product of his examination and defense of the Paris Commune, and his defensive reactions to Bakuninism. But Lenin reverses the process. His early writings, even until late 1917 (*State and Revolution*) all emphasize the later, decentralist, more or less democratic Marx. But as soon as he takes power, he begins to quote only from the earlier Marx. Thus are the two Marxes matched in reverse by the two Lenins.

Finally, I might add, I am not only not forcing conclusions upon the reader, but not even upon myself. From the outset, after a few initial shocks and surprises which the research gave me, I decided not to anticipate any conclusion, but to examine the facts of each period as they then existed *and then looked to the participants*. Of course, I have the long-range development in the back of my mind, so that little episodes often take on big meanings not in virtue of what they are but in virtue of what they are likely to become. At such points I have sometimes asked the reader to think ahead, but have tried not to do the thinking for him. If my book merits any of the kind things you have said about it, I think it is in part due to that deliberate choice of method and structure.

———————◆◆———————

In the postwar years, Wolfe played a major role in organizing opposition to Soviet propaganda offenses in the United States. In the following letter he asks Ray Murphy of the U.S. State Department to expedite a visa for Pavel Lysenko (brother of Stalin's favorite biologist, Trofim D. Lysenko) so he could come to New York and address a Freedom House rally about the suppression of civil liberties and the lack of cultural freedom in Russia.

March 20, 1949

To: Ray Murphy

I am writing to you to urge that you do all in your power to see that the appropriate government departments cut through any red tape and expedite the trip of Pavel Lysenko to the United States in time to speak at our freedom rally at Freedom House on Saturday night, March 26. Herewith a few reasons:

1. The State Department, by issuing visas to Communists coming here for anticultural freedom and pro-Soviet imperialist propaganda, has put itself in debt to the American people. It owes it to its own people to permit guests invited by the Americans for Intellectual Freedom to get visas on time.

2. It will not be a government responsibility since Lysenko is already an IRRC [International Refugee Relief Committee] case. All we ask from the government is the cutting of red tape, and the expedition of visa and travel *in time* for the appropriate rally, made necessary by a prior government action in favor of the delegates to a communist conference.

3. The world does not know how many men of science and letters have perished in purges or have fled to secure cultural and other human freedoms. If Pavel Lysenko can get to our meeting and say but these few words in Russian: "The Oparins, Shostakoviches,

etc. sent here by the Kremlin for the purposes of its war on its own people and other peoples, represent neither Russian science, nor Russian culture nor the Russian people" that will make the headlines, and blanket the Kremlin's conference in America with real news of the fight for peace and freedom. I have spoken to many newspapermen and intellectuals here since I got the idea of inviting Lysenko, and all are agreed that it would be a huge story and would make main headlines on the decisive day of the Kremlin's American propaganda conference. Yet when I asked people here to phone and visit Washington, they got cold water thrown on the suggestion in the name of red tape and other reservations. If red tape could be cut, and our very laws violated to admit these communist spokesmen, it can also be done for one victim of cultural tyranny who is also a spokesman for cultural freedom. The other speakers at our freedom rally will all be American scholars, but we want this one spokesman for the real feelings of the silenced and tyrannized-over Russian people to get a chance to say his say in good time.

------◆·◆------

In 1952 the American Jewish Committee Yearbook was considering whether to reprint and distribute Loyalty in a Democracy, *a pamphlet by Maxwell Stewart, and asked Wolfe to evaluate it for them. Sharply critical, he pointed to his own recent loyalty investigation as a fair and proper procedure. An excerpt from his report follows:*

May 1, 1952

To: Morris Fine

The whole pamphlet has an exaggerated tone and the cartoons are hysterical in their implications concerning the actual state of civil liberties and the actual nature of government loyalty investigations.

It says: "The security and loyalty programs as they have been inter-preted, put a premium on mediocrity. They have led to a debasement and a degradation of the whole civil service with disastrous effect on the calibre of men and women who enter government service."

This is a slander both on our civil service loyalty boards and on the men who work in the government. Actually I have gone through a loyalty investigation myself, have put a number of State Depart-ment employees through such investigations in the sense that I spon-sored their employment, and have testified on behalf of a number of people under investigation. I was impressed by the fairness and de-cency of the process. There was no atmosphere of a trial. There was no "presumption of guilt." I was informed of all the allegations against me in writing and given time to answer them in writing. I was told that I had the right to a hearing, but I was not obliged to have a hearing; that I had a right to be represented by counsel; that I had the right to call witnesses or present affidavits. It is perfectly true that I was not given the source of allegations against me, but I was given the exact wording of those allegations. The investigators could not conceivably get some people to tell what they think if they did not guarantee that the information would be kept confiden-tial, just as an employer asking previous employers about a worker or asking his teacher about him gives assurance that "this will be kept confidential as to source." This is proper in questions of em-ployment but in questions of crime, the courts have really held that the FBI has had to subject its informers to public appearances and cross-questioning. There are few governments in the entire world in which the police would have been compelled by the courts to render useless all their agents who had been inside the communist move-ment by compelling them to testify publicly, or else have their testi-mony rejected. One of the remarkable things about the United States in this hour of difficulty is that in the [Judith] Coplon case, the case of an undoubted breach of trust and betrayal of secrets to a foreign power, Miss Coplon was properly protected by the judge against FBI testimony until the FBI consented to call its witnesses into open court. The same has been true of all the communist trials. I do not believe we can keep our freedoms alive if we do not show our under-standing of how they actually operate and do not show the same warmth in pointing out where they continue to operate as in point-ing out where they are under strain or in question.

———————————◆◆———————————

*Norman Thomas asked Wolfe to comment on a
pamphlet by Paul Cadbury, a member of a recent
British Quaker mission to Moscow and Kiev.
Cadbury reported that "people in Moscow seem
happy," that "real freedom to worship [exists] in
Russia today," and that "the people in Russia
want peace desperately" [N. Thomas to BDW, February 7, 1952; Paul S. Cadbury,* Quaker Mission to
Moscow *(Philadelphia: American Friends Service
Committee, 1951), pp. 5–7]. Wolfe, increasingly
estranged from the Quakers, wrote the following
reply:*

February 12, 1952

To: Norman Thomas

The Cadbury pamphlet is staggering. It ignores the fact that Moscow
and Kiev are both capitals and showplaces, that when one asks to
see "a coal mine" one is shown the model coal mine. Similarly there
is a show prison in Russia. [Alexander] Weissberg in his book *The
Accused* [1951] tells how he was brought there to be fattened up
before being delivered to the Gestapo and makes it seem like heaven
after the other prisons. And even Weissberg was never in a provincial
prison.

Mr. Cadbury is slandering the Russian people by saying that they
are "content" with the way in which they live. The hundreds of
thousands that have died in purges, including the flower of the communist movement itself and the over ten millions who have been
sent to concentration camps demonstrate that the Russian people are
not the ignorant cattle that Mr. Cadbury suggests they are. So do the
hundreds of thousands of nonreturners and escapees testify to the
fact that this people like any great people knows what freedom is
and what slavery is.

On the standard of living issue, words fail me. When a man is determined to see good where there is evil, there is no telling what he will see. I am sending you herewith some sober Voice of America scripts which tell with great restraint the big lie concerning the Soviet standard of living. They are based upon Soviet statistics and United Nations statistics. Besides, Mr. Cadbury leaves out the fact that the largest single section of the Soviet working class, the ten millions plus, are working at forced labor in freezing barracks, dressed in rags and literally starving to death. Are these people no longer laborers because they labor in slavery? No one can prove except the Soviet leaders whether there are ten or twenty million, but even the lowest estimate is three times as large as the entire industrial working class of Russia in the year 1917 which the Russian Revolution was supposed to "liberate." In any measure of the standard of living so vast a category would certainly have to be included.

What can I say about Stalin's mendacious "peace" propaganda? It is meant to take in the Cadburys, and it does. In general, as Stalin himself has more than once pointed out, he talks peace most energetically when his actual movements are most warlike . . .

Mr. Cadbury reduces such monstrous things as the extinction of the freedom of Poland, Lithuania, Latvia, Estonia, Hungary, Romania, Bulgaria, etc. and the starting of war in Korea under the general phrase "again and again the Russians seem to have done the wrong thing at the wrong moment."

The extermination of the liberty of an entire people, and the introduction of the police and concentration camp system and the purge even of communists in Iron Curtain countries is called "clumsy." Mr. Cadbury believes that we have "a duty to be forgiving and understanding." I do not know what has gotten into the Quakers. Certainly this is not the old Quaker tradition toward evil. The Quaker in the great day of his church resisted evil, called evil by its right name, but regarded the bearing of arms as one evil among others. In nineteenth-century America, the Quaker refused to bear arms in the Civil War, but they did not condone slavery, nor seek to regard it as "clumsy," nor urge "understanding" of the slave owner in place of understanding the plight of the slave.

What has happened to the Quaker tradition that built the underground railway to aid slaves in their escape and surrounded the slaves with love and sympathy and support? The great Quakers of the nineteenth century would be shocked beyond measure that one who spoke in their name could lecture on the Soviet Union without saying one word on the new slavery or the ruthless blood purges. A group worthy of the Quaker tradition would be publicizing throughout the world the terrible revelations of the Gliksmans [Jerzy Gliksman, *Tell the West* (New York: Grisham Press, 1948)], Lippers [Elinor Lipper, *Eleven Years in a Soviet Prison Camp* (Chicago: Regnery Press, 1951)], Weissbergs, Compesinos, and the nameless millions represented in such works as *I Speak for the Silent* [Vladimir Tchernavin, *I Speak for the Silent Prisoners of the Soviets* (Boston: Hale, Cushman and Flint, 1935)] and *The Dark Side of the Moon* [*The Dark Side of the Moon*, preface by T. S. Eliot (London: Faber and Faber, 1946)]. One Quaker leader of our day, Roy McCorkle, having witnessed the human detritus spilled back into Germany from Soviet concentration camps, after it had been worked to exhaustion, said to me: "If I have not looked upon the satanic face of evil when I witnessed that, then I do not know what evil is." He also said to me: "Bert, the day that you cannot bring your testimony to my people, I will no longer be director of the Peace Section of the American Friends Service Committee." Roy is no longer director of the Peace Section which suggests that satanic evil has scored a victory inside the upper echelons of the American Friends Service Committee. Mr. Cadbury's address is a sample of the gentle-seeming Quaker apologetics for monstrous evils. It is a determined "Christian" attempt to "understand" the rulers and not the ruled, the slave drivers and not the slaves . . .

I hope these few off-the-cuff remarks and enclosures will help you in the Cadbury matter.

———————————◆•◆———————————

Wolfe protests to Senator Robert A. Taft [R-Ohio]
about his attack on the Voice of America.

March 16, 1953

To: Senator Robert A. Taft

It is possible that you may remember me since in 1945 when few could be found to stand up for Poland against the Soviet Union, you and I appeared together under the auspices of the United Association of Polish Americans to defend Poland's right to be free. So much by way of identification.

I was shocked beyond measure by your address on television yesterday in which you said that the working force of the Voice of America, of which I am one, is "full of fellow travelers." Do you really think that the Kremlin would be spending so much money and effort in jamming us if that were so? Have you not noticed that *The Daily Worker,* which has been yapping endlessly about "McCarthyism" has become delightedly silent since Senator [Joseph R.] McCarthy began his attacks upon the Voice and its work? Do you really have enough names, or any names to cite, that would justify you in saying "full of fellow travelers"?

Senator, I want to assure you that I am as sensitive as you or Senator McCarthy to fellow travelers and Communists. I know their line and their language and their way of reacting. In the two years that I have worked for the Voice I have neither been hampered in my plans nor run up against any evidence which would justify your words.

Voice of America Scripts

1951–1954

The Death of General Ulrich

Officially Moscow is mourning today for the death of General Vasily Vasilevich Ulrich, who, according to *Red Star* "devoted all his conscious life to the cause of the party of Lenin and Stalin." But countless Soviet citizens will have quite other feelings at the passing of this man who presided at the bloody trials which destroyed the leading cadres of the army, the Soviet state, the communist party, and Soviet industry and agriculture. After Stalin himself, and his agents [Andrei] Vyshinsky and [Nikolai] Yezhov, no other figure so completely symbolizes and embodies the bloody purges than does Col. Gen. Ulrich.

Beginning as a devoted member of that band of Lettish [Latvian] sharpshooters who helped Lenin and Trotsky and their associates to shoot their way to power, Vasily Vasilevich Ulrich at first had nothing to do with the administration of justice. He was a military man pure and simple. As long as Bolshevism dreamt of humanizing its penal code and bringing it into line with enlightened modern ideas on jurisprudence, what could a purely military figure have to do with justice?

But the bright dreams of the twenties progressively yielded to the harsh, relentless, and increasingly bloody counterrevolution of the thirties. It is hard to remember now that Lenin once favored—before he came to power—the resolution of the Socialist International for the abolition of capital punishment. Hard to believe in the present day of ferocious punishment of crimes against state property that Stalin's party once believed that crimes against property were not crimes at all, that when a man stole it was a testimonial to the existence of poverty and misery and want, and an indictment of the regime and social system that made theft possible and necessary, rather than an indictment of the poor victim of society, the thief himself.

It is hard to believe now that the Soviet government in the early twenties adopted an enlightened penal code protecting prisoners against exploitation, guaranteeing that they should be treated politely, not be addressed with the insulting *ty* but with the polite *vy*, guaranteeing cigarettes, mail, visits, and work at trade union wages. The dream was never more than a dream, but even the very traces of the dream disappeared from the statute books with the rise of camps, summary executions, and bloody purges.

General Ulrich attracted the notice of Joseph Stalin, who had need of such men, by taking charge of one of the earliest frame-ups, that of the trial of six British and various Soviet citizens in 1933, on the accusation of spying. The Britons were condemned to death, yet when the British government protested at the frame-up, they were released. But General Ulrich's reputation was made. He became judge president of the Military Collegium of the Supreme Court: fitting symbol of the fact that ordinary justice was being converted into the brutality of martial law. What other land, the Soviet citizen asks himself in secret, what other land could possibly have a military collegium on its supreme court for civil justice?

General Ulrich presided over the trial of the seventeen Bolshevik leaders in 1936, with the old Menshevik Andrei Vyshinsky as their prosecutor. He became adept at staging the monotonous series of confessions of impossible crimes. Yezhov or [Lavrenti] Beria softened them up in the torture chambers of the Lubyanka and taught them the lines they were to say. Vyshinsky rehearsed them. And Judge President General Ulrich presided over the staged play with savage and relentless skill.

If an actor forgot his piece or, before the microphone, tried to withdraw his extorted confession and proclaim the truth, it was Ulrich who had to know when to adjourn the court sessions (as in the case of [Nikolai] Krestinsky [1938]) so that the victim could be led back to the torture chambers and schooled to retract his retraction.

It was Ulrich who took special relish in mocking the victim and pronouncing the death sentence. All his military colleagues, from [General Mikhail] Tukhachevsky down—70 percent of the entire officer corps—perished in the purges. All communist party secretaries of autonomous republics and regions—except two. All chairmen of Soviet republics. Aided by such executioner judges as Ulrich, the general secretary [Stalin] of the Central Committee—its supposed servant—eliminated 50 out of 71 members of the Central Committee elected in 1934, and all the old associates of Lenin.

This was the coup d'état, the political expression of the counterrevolution. In property relations this counterrevolution was represented by the expropriation of the land which the revolution had given the peasants and now took away from them as it turned them into state serfs of state-controlled collectives. Naturally, with such a system of justice General Ulrich could become, and did become, the "teacher of young Soviet jurists" in the ways of court martial, purge, confession, concentration camps, and executions that represent the counterrevolution in Soviet penal procedure.

Now General Ulrich is dead, and the Stalinist machine mourns, for it has risen to power by treading upon the bodies of the old Bolsheviks and the other victims of Stalin's arbitrary cruelty and Ulrich's ruthless inventions in the field of jurisprudence. Stalin, no doubt, mourns, too, for it is not easy to forge such instruments of brutal terror.

But the millions in concentration camps—more than twice as many millions as there are members in the Komsomol [Young Communist League] and the communist party together—what do they think on this day of official mourning? And those other millions, who have a parent, a son, a relative, a friend in a concentration camp, what do they think of this man's passing? If they mourn at all, it is because as *Red Star* says, "General Ulrich's spirit and work lives on." If they mourn at all, they mourn that with the death of this sinister figure, the bloody system of vengeance, torture, and total state brutality which he symbolized, has not yet passed away.

May 12, 1951

Russo-Polish Relations and the Murders in the Katyn Forest

This week, in the quiet sanctuary of the spirit which no police inquisitor can enter, the Polish people are observing a gloomy anniversary. They are remembering that fateful moment, on April 26, 1943,
when the Kremlin suddenly broke off all relations with the Polish
government in exile, giving as pretext the fact that the government
had ventured to ask for an impartial commission of inquiry of the
International Red Cross to find out how 4,000-odd Polish officers
had died in the Katyn forest, and what had happened to an additional
11,000-odd who had vanished without a trace. Because the Kremlin
blocked an impartial inquiry, the name of the Soviet government has
not been cleared to this day, and the mystery of the death and disappearance of 15,000 Polish officers has remained unsolved. Private
committees have since been set up, notable among them being the
American Committee for the Investigation of the Katyn Massacre,
whose chairman, Arthur Bliss Lane, was formerly America's ambassador in Poland. That committee has been gathering evidence for
years: the official Soviet government report, the official German government report, the official Polish government report, testimony
from medical doctors from many lands who examined the rotting
corpses in the Katyn forest, testimony from Polish army officers who
survived the holocaust, testimony from all who have evidence to
offer. Today, on the eighth anniversary of the rupture of Soviet-
Polish relations, and approximately a decade after the murders in the
Katyn forest occurred, the American committee announced that it is
setting up a commission of jurists and lawyers to examine all the
accumulated evidence, and establish the ascertainable facts for all
the world to pronounce judgment.

The Polish government with which Stalin broke off relations on
April 26, 1943, was the Polish government in exile, with public headquarters in London, and underground headquarters inside Poland. It
was this Polish government which had preserved Poland from col-

laboration with Hitler, which had resisted Hitler even in those terrible days of 1939, when Stalin was allied with Hitler in the partition of Poland. It was this government which, as soon as Hitler attacked Stalin, generously agreed to forgive and forget the Russian aggression. It was this government whose underground forces had unceasingly harried the German lines of communication that ran through Poland into the Soviet Union. It was this government which had led the two heroic insurrections in Warsaw which will go down in history as two of the brightest pages in man's long struggle against tyranny. But, by 1943, the tide of battle was turning in Russia, and Stalin was already laying the plans for the annexation of all his neighbor states through Soviet puppet governments. For the Poles he had set up a puppet council at Lublin, and was seeking for a pretext to break off relations with the Polish government in exile and the Polish underground army. The pretext he chose was as sinister as the act of rupture itself.

The London Polish government had for some time been pursuing its simple duty of trying to learn the whereabouts and fate of some 15,000 Polish officers of all ranks, from general to noncoms, who had been taken prisoner by the Red Army when it attacked Poland from the east in 1939. These officers had originally numbered 15,400, but for eighteen months now only 400 continued to communicate with their families, while 15,000 had disappeared without a trace. General Sikorski, General Anders, General Berling [senior Polish military officers], and Ambassador Cziechanowski had repeatedly inquired about their whereabouts and repeatedly asked for their release to officer the new Polish army being built up under the Stalin-Sikorski agreement. Repeatedly Stalin, Molotov, Vyshinsky, had answered that these men had been released, that they were on their way to the recruiting centers, that they had crossed some remote frontier, that they would soon turn up. The answers were contradictory, but always agreed that the men had all been released. Finally, on April 13, 1943, the German government announced that it had uncovered the corpses of 11,000 Polish officers, buried in the Katyn forest on the east bank of the Dnieper, ten miles from Smolensk in the German-occupied area of the USSR. Stalin, who had all along been reporting that all Polish officers had been released, now accepted the German figure of 11,000 corpses, but reported that they had been abandoned in a Russian retreat, and captured and killed by the Germans.

The world did not know what to think. Among the United Nations there was an inclination to believe the statement of the Ally,

Stalin, and to regard the whole exhumation of bodies as a trick of Hitler to sow dissension among the Allies. The Polish government, pursuing an elementary duty of any government to its citizens, asked for an impartial inquiry into the fate of these men by the International Red Cross. Instead of readily agreeing, in order to remove a horrible suspicion and brand the true perpetrator of a genocidal crime, Stalin treated the request as a pretext for breaking all relations with the Polish government, and recognizing in its place his future Iron Curtain puppet government which could be counted on to ask no embarrassing questions about the fate of any of its citizens, either in prisoner-of-war camps, concentration camps, or mass graves.

Now, eight years later, many matters still remain unclarified in this fearful episode. But slowly the evidence has accumulated and the outlines have become increasingly clear.

The first startling fact that emerged was that only 4,144 bodies were actually uncovered in the Katyn forest. Yet Generalissimo Stalin, who rejected all other claims, has repeatedly accepted the statement that over 10,000 bodies were exhumed. Only 4,144 bodies have been turned up, and the fate of the remaining 10,000-odd missing Polish officers remains a sealed mystery from that day to this. Somewhere in the Russian land they lie buried, presumably near the other two officer-prisoner camps in the Smolensk region. If the Soviet government were anxious to clear up the mystery, it would not find it hard to locate the rest.

The second piece of evidence comes from twelve international scientists, invited by the German government to visit the mass graves in April 1943. True, some of these scientists were from German-occupied countries like Denmark, Finland, and Belgium and might then have been under duress. But the might of Hitler is broken, and an international court of inquiry could easily get them to talk freely now, if the Kremlin would but consent. And not all of the scientists were from German-occupied countries. For instance, there was Professor Naville of the University of Geneva, whose bona fides no one has called in question.

The third piece of evidence is an array of letters, diaries, newspaper clippings, etc. found on the bodies of corpses, bearing dates only up to April and May 1940, when the Red Army still had possession of Smolensk. No document was found on any corpse bearing a later date than May 1940: that was the month in which each of them was shot, a bullet in the base of the brain. Stalin asserts they were shot by the Germans in August 1941. Yet they were wearing their winter issue clothing, woolen socks, scarves, and in no officer's pocket was there a scrap of paper dating later than early May 1940.

Fourth, there is the testimony of Lieutenant Colonel Van Vliet who was taken to the Katyn forest by his German captors. An American officer, he voluntarily reported to the United States Army that he had seen convincing evidence of the Russian origin of the mass murder. Not wishing to complicate Russo-Polish relations as long as there was any hope that Stalin would permit a free Polish government, the U.S. Army long delayed the release of Van Vliet's report. But it would gladly have permitted Van Vliet to testify at any impartial hearing, if the Soviet government had shown any readiness to have this fearful mystery cleared up. On September 18, 1950, the Department of Defense finally released, or rather declassified, Lieutenant Colonel Van Vliet's report.

Fifth, there is evidence of the Soviet government's strange and contradictory actions at the Nürnberg war crimes trials. Surely, if this was a Nazi crime, Nürnberg was the place to clear it up. The Soviet representative, Colonel Pokrovsky, actually made the charge, and we quote: "In September, 1941, 11,000 Polish officers who were prisoners of war were killed in the Katyn forest by the German Fascist invader."

But when it became apparent that the accused prisoners at Nürnberg would be allowed to summon witnesses and documents in their defense and that a genuine investigation might take place, the Soviet prosecutor once more blocked an all-sided clarification of the mystery, and this point in the indictment was withdrawn.

Thus, eight years have passed. The circumstantial evidence piles up. The government which should be most interested in establishing its innocence, if it is innocent, blocks all impartial international inquiry. The only certain thing that emerges is that on April 26, 1943, the Kremlin broke off its relations with the Polish government in exile for the mere request of an International Red Cross inquiry. Only 4,000-odd bodies have been accounted for and 11,000 Polish officers are still "vanished without a trace." And the setting up of the Polish Lublin puppet government began the procedure of virtual annexation of neighboring countries, "liberated" or Ally, which violated every promise of the Atlantic Charter and which guaranteed that there would be no sound and just peace at the immediate end of World War II.

The rupture of relations with the Polish government was fateful not only for the history of Poland. It was the first huge step in the Kremlin's aggressive expansion by occupation, which the whole world now knows as the "cold war."

January 29, 1952

This script was originally broadcast in April 1951 on the eighth anniversary of Moscow's breaking off relations with the Polish government in exile. This is an updated version.

Who Is the Imperialist?

As a preparation for his party congress, Joseph Stalin today published a statement in the party magazine *Bolshevik* on imperialism, the Iron Curtain, and the division of the world into two economic centers and two parallel world markets.

"The only way to avoid war," the generalissimo declares, "is to abolish imperialism." That is one of the truest things he ever said. But *who* is the imperialist? Where is the aggressive expanding imperialism that threatens the peace of the world? Who set up the barbed wire borders between land and land? Who set up the economic and political Iron Curtain? Who put the Iron Curtain between the Soviet empire and the free world, and with an imposing display of armies, police, and purges stopped the free movement of men, of ideas, and of goods? Who has used force to put an end to the open society toward which the entire modern era has been striving, and put in its place in one-third of the world a totalitarian system and a rigidly regimented and closed society?

Who is the imperialist?

Who sent the ultimatum to Romania in June 1940 which read: "Within four days . . . Soviet troops will occupy Bessarabia and northern Bukovina . . . The Soviet Union insists."

On August 2, 1940, the Soviet army annexed 3,700,000 persons and 50,200 square kilometers of Romanian territory.

Who is the imperialist?

Who annexed the Baltic states in alliance with another aggressive imperialist, Adolf Hitler? Who annexed Lithuania with 55,700 square kilometers? Latvia, with 65,800 square kilometers? And subjugated six million freedom-loving and inoffensive Baltic people?

Who is the imperialist?

Did not England, France, the United States, and the Soviet Union all sign the Atlantic Charter which said: "We seek no aggrandizement, territorial or other?"

And at the end of the war, who seized territory? Who took northern East Prussia with 14,000 square kilometers of land and the populous cities of Königsberg, Tilsit, and Insterburg?

And who seized the province of Carpathian Ruthenia from her friendly ally, Czechoslovakia? Who took 12,700 square kilometers from the little Czechoslovakian nation?

Who is the imperialist?

Who took the Porkkala naval base, the Karelian Isthmus with the great city of Vyborg or Viipuri, the western shore of Lake Ladoga, the Petsamo area, and other pieces from Finland? What imperialist took those 45,600 square kilometers with a half million people from Finland?

Who is the imperialist?

Who took Tannu Tuva with its 165,800 square kilometers, who took Port Arthur and the railroads, who took Outer Mongolia and is now moving in on Inner Mongolia and Singkiang from the supposed friendly ally, the People's Republic of China?

Who is the imperialist?

Who took southern Sakhalin and the Kurils from Japan with 46,400 square kilometers of land and nearly a half million inhabitants? In short, who took over 684,000 square kilometers with 25,000,000 people from all its neighbors on all its borders, from foe and friend, in defiance of the Atlantic Charter and all its friendship and nonaggression pacts?

And then there is this matter of the divided world, the closed markets, the closed imperial economic plan, the Iron Curtain? Who took control by force, purge, police, and occupation armies of Albania (28,000 square kilometers), Bulgaria (110,900), Czechoslovakia (127,700), East Germany (110,100), Hungary (93,000), Poland (311,800), Romania (327,200), China (9,700,300), Outer Mongolia (1,621,100), North Korea, (325,600)? Who dominates this total area of over 13,000,000 square kilometers with over 500,000,000, perhaps over 600,000,000 people? Who has murdered its leaders, noncommunist and even communist? Who is responsible for the death or imprisonment or exile or suicide of Masaryk, Benes, Mushanov, Dmitrov, Petkov, Nagy, Pfeiffer, Mikolajczyk, and the officers in the Katyn forest? Who has purged Rajk, Kostov, Pauker, Gomulka, Slansky, Clementis, and other Soviet empire proconsuls?

And the free world, during this same period while the Soviet imperial juggernaut was running mad over all its neighbors, east, west, north, south, in Europe and in Asia: what was the free world doing about the question of empire?

Voice: The free world was granting independence to India with 3,131,300 square kilometers and 347,300,000 people; Pakistan with 874,200 square kilometers and 73,300,000 people; Indonesia with 1,511,200 square kilometers and 80 million people; Ceylon with 65,600 square kilometers and 7,300,000 people; the Philippines with 296,300 square kilometers and 20,000,000 people; Burma with 677,900 square miles and 18,000,000 people.

Commentator: In short, while the Soviet Union was subjugating over 13 million kilometers of territory with over 575,000,000 people, the free world was liberating over 6,500,000 square kilometers with over 550 million people.

And while the free world was trying to rebuild for peace with UNRWA [United Nations Relief Works Agency] aid and Marshall Plan loans, the Soviet empire was terrorizing and conquering its neighbors on every side of its far-flung frontiers, setting up the planned tyranny of the closed autarchic Soviet imperial economy, breaking the world into two parts, opening war in Korea.

Lenin wrote:

Voice: Imperialism is that state policy which leads to the annexation of territories and to the national oppression of occupied countries.

Commentator: A good definition? Under it, who is the imperialist?

And now Stalin writes in *Bolshevik* that the way to bring peace to a war-weary world is to put an end to imperialism and unify the markets of the world.

We couldn't agree with him more.

October 3, 1952

Stalin Dismisses the Nineteenth Congress

And so, the Nineteenth Congress of the Communist Party of the Soviet Union grinds to an end, and the general secretary, one-time servant, now master of the communist party, did not even deign to report to it. All he gave was a bare ten-minute address, not to the congress itself, but to his obedient fifth column from other countries.

Time was when the communist party congress was the "supreme body" of the communist party. Or as the statutes say: "the supreme organ." In those days it was the congresses that determined policy. The Central Committee was an executive body to carry out the policies determined by the congress. The Politburo was an organ of the Central Committee. And the secretary was the keeper of the minutes, the receiver and answerer of mail, the servant of the Central Committee.

In the days when congresses determined policy, they had to be held not less than once a year. Oftener if a new issue arose requiring a change of line. They represented the collective wisdom of the party. They had stormy debates. As long as Lenin was alive, regular as clockwork or the calendar, every March or April there was a congress. And Lenin really reported to it. If somebody thought differently there was a co-report. Stormy debates. Real votes. Rival resolutions. Majorities. Minorities. Amendments. Discussion. Life!

Slowly the life ebbed out of the party congress. Policies were made elsewhere. The Central Committee took over from the congress. The Politburo replaced the Central Committee. Then the boss replaced the Politburo. The congresses became mere cheering squads. To use Stalin's ugly and inhuman word, they changed from a collection of thinking human beings into a "monolith." A block of granite—a tombstone. Stalin got into the habit of postponing the congresses until he had *settled* the issues they were supposed to examine. He presented them with faits accomplis. Before the Fifteenth

Congress, he ousted Trotsky, Kamenev, and Zinoviev. Not at the congress, but before the congress. Before the Sixteenth Congress he delayed for a year and a half to expel Bukharin, Rykov and Tomsky. Not at the congress, but before the congress.

The Seventeenth Congress was delayed for four years—until 1934—in order to finish off the peasants. Not until the famine was over and the concentration camps bursting with peasants, not until the land the revolution had given them was taken away again and they were returned to state serfdom, did Stalin permit the Seventeenth Congress to assemble and "approve" his actions.

And the Eighteenth Congress was held not within a year, but postponed for five years. From 1934 to 1939 no congress! Why? In 1934 there was nobody at the congress but Stalinists. Stalin personally handpicked a Stalinist Central Committee of 71. Yet, one by one, he removed them. Of the 71 elected in 1934, by 1938 only 21 remained! One, Kirov, was assassinated. Thirty-six simply disappeared. One, Marshal Gamarnik, committed suicide. Nine were announced as shot. Three died that most unnatural of deaths for an old Bolshevik—a natural death. Only after Stalin had murdered the Central Committee elected by the supreme body, only after the blood purges had run their fury to the end, did he call a congress, the Eighteenth, in 1939. But even to that miserable body, cheering the murderer of the majority of the Central Committee it had elected—cheering the coup d'état of the dictator—even to that party he made a pretense of reporting on his stewardship.

The Nineteenth Congress was postponed for thirteen long years. War and peace were decided without a congress. The pact with Hitler, the attack on Poland and Finland and Lithuania, Latvia and Estonia, the pact with the democracies, the subjugation of the Balkans—a score of important matters were decided behind the back of the party and without instructions from a congress. But now, Stalin did not even trouble to report to the Nineteenth Congress on all these matters.

He showed his contempt for the "supreme organ" of the party by publishing what passes as a report in *Bolshevik*, three days before the congress opened. He put in a ceremonial appearance to be cheered, but did not pretend to report on his stewardship.

This marks a new milestone in the degeneration of the once-powerful party congress. Stalin has never in his life reported to a *Soviet* congress. He permits the Soviets to discuss and approve a budget near the end of the fiscal year to which it applies. And he puts in a ceremonial appearance and graciously permits them to cheer him.

But his contempt for the Soviets is dramatized by the fact that he has never troubled to report to them on anything.

Now he treats the party congress with the same contempt he has always displayed toward a Soviet congress. He permits the party congress to approve a five-year plan that has been running for two years. And he puts in a ceremonial appearance to permit the delegates to cheer their gracious sovereign. But he does not report anymore to anybody. The boss is boss. Everybody reports to the boss. The boss reports to nobody. All he does is put in an appearance, accept the plaudits of the congress, short-circuit their debates with an article which turns their reports into footnotes and hallelujahs. And then, when he gets up to speak, it is merely to dismiss the congress and to review the fifth column of communist delegates from other countries.

Such is the fate of the body which is still mockingly called in the statutes, the "supreme organ" of the party. As Hitler called the once-mighty Reichstag and the Nazi party congresses to permit them to cry "Heil Hitler," so Stalin now calls Soviet congresses and party congresses to permit them to cry "Long Live the Great Stalin!"

October 16, 1952

The Rationale of the Purges

Voice 1:   The revolution devours its own children.

Voice 2:   How did Trotsky die?

Voice 1:   How did Zhdanov die?

Voice 2:   How did Zinoviev die?

Voice 1:   How did Kirov die?

Voice 2:   How did Yagoda die?

Voice 1:   How did Rykov? How did Bukharin? How did Tomsky die?

Voice 2:   How did the Men of October die?

Voice 1:   Of the 21 men elected to the Bolshevik Central Committee under Lenin in August 1917, the dedicated Communists who Lenin gathered in the underground and who planned, led, and won the October Revolution, only two are still alive. They are Molotov and Stalin. Eleven were publicly murdered by the government they brought into being. Tomsky committed suicide. Trotsky was exiled in Turkistan, driven into exile, then murdered by an NKVD [People's Commissariat of Internal Affairs] assassin in Mexico. Others disappeared without a trace, purged by the government they brought into being. Or, since everything that government does is credited to Joseph Stalin personally, murdered by Joseph Stalin personally.

Voice 1:   The revolution devours its own children.

Voice 2:   Not only the Men of October died in the purges. The men who killed them died the same miserable death.
Menzhinsky, if we are to believe the Soviet trials, was poisoned. Yagoda, executed. Yezhov, who sentenced Yagoda to death, executed. And now . . .

Voice 1: And now *Pravda* of January 13 attacks Lavrenti Beria.
           Pravda charges:

> Some of our Soviet organs and their leaders have
> lost their watchfulness. The organs of state secu-
> rity did not discover the terrorist organization of
> wrecker doctors in time, although there have al-
> ready been instances when enemies of the people
> like Doctors Levine and Pletnev killed the great
> Russian writer M. [Maxim] A. Gorky, and outstand-
> ing leaders of the Soviet state, Kuibyshev and
> Menzhinsky.

Voice 2: So now Stalin charges Beria—who killed so many—with
           lack of vigilance. Who knows what may happen to Beria?

Voice 1: So now it is the turn of the doctors? The Politburo, which
           decides when one of its members needs to go to a hospital,
           decides when one of its members needs treatment or an
           operation, now tells us that Soviet medicine is not to be
           trusted. Even those who were announced to have died a
           natural death are now exhumed by the NKVD who certifies
           that they were murdered.

Voice 2: Not only old Bolsheviks. Not only doctors. Not only Cen-
           tral Committee members. Under the total state, terror is
           total. Stalin even murders his henchmen. His loyal support-
           ers. The agents who spread his power. He has murdered
           Slansky, Rajk, Kostov. Tomorrow it may be Pauker and
           Patrascanu. What is the rationale of such a purge?

Voice 1: If you want your enemies to fear you, begin by murdering
           your friends. The total state is built on fear, and to sow
           fear, any arbitrary killing is sufficient.

           I remember the sudden waves of terror when Stalin was
           climbing to power. Every time Stalin got ready for some
           new fight in the party he first sowed an atmosphere of gen-
           eral terror by arbitrary raids upon some defenseless layer of
           the population. The purpose was to make everyone feel
           there was danger to the state, to make everyone feel his
           turn might be next, to make the atmosphere tense with
           fear and terror.

           Thus before he moved against the leaders of the unions
           and the state, he made a raid on the dentists, charging
           them with having hidden gold for tooth fillings, on the
           kitchen help in restaurants and the meat experts in the
           commissariat of agriculture, charging them with poisoning

the cattle, poisoning the food. Scapegoats for hunger and fear and terror.

Voice 2: And there was the Shakhty trial, the Razmin trial, the Vickers trial, before the attack on the standards of the working class. And the so-called kulak raids and village murderers trial before they forced collectivization.

Voice 1: Under Stalin purges have diminished and purges have increased but they have never altogether ceased.

Voice 2: The history of mankind reveals no phenomenon quite like these mass purges. Those of 1936 to 1938 embraced high and low, idealists and cynics, old Bolsheviks, Men of October, Red partisan heroes of the civil war, close associates of Lenin, fourteen out of sixteen presidents of Soviet republics, the majority of the secretaries of regional communist parties, veterans of the underground against tsarism, the majority of the Soviet generals, Soviet scientists and intellectuals, "honored guests" who had sought refuge from other lands, German, Polish, and Hungarian Comintern leaders, holders of the Order of Lenin and Order of the Red Banner, then in turn all the high officers of the NKVD who had carried out the executions, along with millions of rank-and-file party members and ordinary workers and peasants, members of national minorities and great Russians, nomadic tribes that would not settle down, and leaders of the nomadic tribes who had settled down.

Voice 1: Could virtually the entire General Staff be traitors? If we believe it, then communism is the most monstrous movement in the whole history of mankind, to have produced so many traitors. Has any other army in history ever accused its entire General Staff, 70 percent of all its officers of the rank of colonel or above, of being traitors? If they were indeed traitors, then communism is a poisonous, corroding, sink of corruption.

Voice 2: And if they were not really traitors, then the regime that framed up loyal adherents, innocent men, is still the most monstrous regime in all human history. What other system of government ever engendered so many spies and traitors? What other movement claiming to be ideological ever corrupted so many of its leaders? What other regime ever found it necessary to murder so many of its citizens?

This is the true face of the total state. It talks peace and wages unending war on its own people. It talks national autonomy and national equality and ends in anti-Semitism and the purge of the leaders of all the nationalities. It talks freedom and ends in terror. It talks about being scientific and ends by purging geneticists and medical doctors. It talks anti-imperialism and subjugates all its neighbors and exports to them its purges, its concentration camps, and its terror.

But such purges make more enemies for the regime than they can possibly remove. Every victim has friends, loved ones, family. And every one who is injured by the total state, according to its totalitarian logic, is thereby rendered suspect.

A regime that wages such a pitiless war on its leaders, its scientists, its generals, its officials, its engineers, its peasants, its workers, a regime which carries on an unending war on its own people cannot endure forever. More than any other regime does the total state contain within itself the seeds of its own destruction.

Voice 2:   The revolution devours its own children.

Voice 1:   And not only its own children. It devours itself . . .

January 14, 1953

There Is No Forced Labor Because the Constitution Forbids It

There is no forced labor in the Soviet Union. There are no concentration camps, no forced labor camps, no correctional labor camps, no barbed wire enclosures, no towers with guards and machine guns, no fierce dogs, no camp prisoners, no millions of rightless slaves. How do we know all this? We have just learned it from a speech delivered by the Soviet representative to the Economic and Social Council of the United Nations, I.V. Chechyotkin. And by what magic did he whisk away overnight all the camps and all the millions of prisoners? Very simple. He said, "There are no concentration camps or forced labor camps in the Soviet Union because such institutions are contrary to the Soviet constitution."

A constitution is a marvelous thing. There are four main types of constitutions. First, there is the British constitution. It is not even a written constitution. It does not exist on paper. It was never adopted by any constituent assembly. It just grew. Out of documents wrested from rulers, like the Magna Charta. Out of laws passed by all the successive parliaments and decisions made by the British courts. Nothing on paper. No single document. Yet there is no country in the world that more faithfully follows its constitution in good times and bad, in war and peace, than does the British people.

Then there is the Constitution of the United States. It is a written document. It was adopted by a constituent assembly or constitutional convention. It provides for legal revolution by providing for its own amendment. And it is also slowly modified, stretched, enriched, and modernized by judicial decisions and interpretations. It, too, is faithfully lived up to. Many countries have such constitutions.

Third, there is a type of constitution adopted by a number of countries which expresses in part what they live up to, and in part what they aspire to be.

Finally, there is the Soviet-type constitution. It is a propaganda constitution, a facade used to conceal the real relation of forces in the Soviet Union and satellites. It bears no relation to reality. Thus, there is not one word in the Soviet constitution about a dictator, *vozhd*, leader or boss. But Stalin was for nearly thirty years dictator, boss, leader and *vozhd*.

The constitution forbids frame-ups and torture and false arrest. But the doctors were framed up under the constitution. We have *Pravda*'s word for that. And during the great blood purges the generals, Politburo and Central Committee members, and millions of party members, officials, and rank-and-file citizens were framed up and sent to concentration camps or executed. But now the purges could not have happened because they are forbidden by the Soviet constitution. And no one is in a concentration camp. And there are no concentration camps. Because they are forbidden by the Soviet constitution.

Simple, isn't it?

Maybe the constitution does forbid camps and forced labor. But we have before us the criminal code published by the Ministry of Justice of the USSR in 1950. And we have the volume of the *Bolshaya Entsiklopedia* dealing with corrective labor. The encyclopedia says, "Forced labor is one of the basic measures of punishment in Soviet socialist criminal law."

You will find that on page 36 of volume 37 of the large Soviet Encyclopedia. And in the criminal code, article 20, section b, you will find, "Deprivation of freedom in corrective-labor camps in remote areas of the USSR is a measure of social defense of a judicial-corrective character."

A footnote to article 20 prescribes that the term *corrective labor* should henceforth be substituted for the previous term *prinuditelny trud*, or forced labor. Same guns, same guards, same dogs, same barbed wire, same misery, but a new name. "A rose by any other name would smell as sweet."

In the collection of laws of the Soviet government there is a passage on the NKVD, now MVD [Ministry of Internal Affairs] and MGB [Ministry of State Security], which sets up the Chief Directorate of Corrective Labor Camps and Labor Settlements.

You will find that in article 283, section 3e. And in section 8 of the same article you will find that the secret police "has the power to apply as an administrative measure [that is, without trial] the deportation, exile, imprisonment in corrective-labor camps for a period up to five years and expulsion beyond the confines of the USSR."

What then was the purpose of Soviet representative Chechyotkin's barefaced denial of the existence of what the Soviet law provides, the

Soviet encyclopedia discusses, the Soviet five-year plans take into account in building canals, roads, etc. and what thousands and millions of Soviet documents, forced labor camp sentences, and forced labor camp releases attest to?

The answer is simple. For nearly two years now, the Economic and Social Council of the United Nations has been investigating forced labor all over the world. Wherever forced labor is used for political oppression or coercion, and wherever forced labor forms an important part of the economy of a country, the special commission of the United Nations has directed its attention. It has gathered law codes, economic plans, copies of books, articles, certificates of commitment and certificates of release, and testimony from hundreds and thousands of former inmates of forced labor camps. This spring or summer it will make its first report. And against this mass of patiently gathered documentary evidence and sworn testimony, Delegate Chechyotkin waves the magic wand of the Soviet constitution and hopes to make the report go up in smoke and the evidence disappear.

Pretty soon, the archprosecutor Vyshinsky, who sent so many men to concentration camps, will make the same speech in the General Assembly. He will prove that he never framed up, never prosecuted, never sent to slave camps, never purged . . . because the constitution forbids it.

"Paper," Joseph Stalin once wrote, "will put up with anything that is printed on it." And his master, Lenin, wrote, "He who believes in words is an idiot." Out of such cynicism come the cynical methods of whisking away unpleasant facts by verbal juggling.

"We have no concentration camps because the constitution forbids it. We have no dictator or *vozhd* because the constitution forbids it." Vyshinsky never sent up any innocent man because the constitution forbids it. There were never any purges because the constitution forbids it.

But the United Nations' investigation goes on. The free world is aroused by the return of slavery in the modern world. It will not rest until the slave laborers are freed. If Delegate Chechyotkin wants to stop the campaign of free labor, of the free world, of the United Nations, of all freedom-loving men everywhere, against this monstrous slavery, there is one simple way. It is not to quote the incredible Soviet constitution, *but to open the camps and make every Soviet slave once more free.*

April 10, 1953

Long Live Karandash

The Soviet people were not consulted when Stalin was made dictator, nor are they consulted as to who should be his successor.

[Georgi] Malenkov becomes premier. Were the people asked? He becomes secretary without their vote; and loses his secretaryship without their vote. Beria returns to the control of the MVD and MGB. Molotov displaces Shvernik as foreign minister. Zhukov is recalled from the remote station where the envy of the dictator had driven him, and returns to Moscow to become deputy war minister. Are any of these changes good or bad for the people? Who can say? Such things are decided by the men in the Kremlin, who eye each other, test each other's strength, and maneuver for position in the muted struggle for leadership. All that the ordinary Soviet citizen knows is that the rulers are a little uncertain of themselves as they prepare to struggle with each other, and a little less arrogant with the people. They proclaim an amnesty, a little amnesty for little people charged with little offenses. That at least is something. Why was it done? How long will it last? Who proclaimed it to undermine whom?

But one concession every Soviet citizen recognizes as genuine. One reappearance every Soviet citizen applauds. Not Beria's return to the police ministries nor Zhukov's to the War Ministry stirred as much excitement. On March 25, three weeks after Stalin's passing, *Soviet Art (Sovetskoye Iskusstvo)* announced, "In the new program of the Moscow circus, Karandash has renewed his appearances after long interruption . . . With the fire of satire, textually not too bright as yet, perhaps, he fights against stuffiness, conceit, and smugness."

Karandash! Karandash was Russia's most famous clown. More than once he made the people laugh too heartily and his program was canceled. Who does not remember his famous gags? His spunk in the face of censorship and terror? Who does not remember the early postwar days when he appeared upon the stage beating a live hen, and explained: "Although the war is over, she still insists on laying powdered eggs!"

Then there was the act in which he dragged out a sack of potatoes and sat on it refusing to say a word. After repeated prodding by his stooge, Karandash finally answered: "All Russia is sitting on a sack of potatoes with its mouth shut."

Then there was the time when Karandash began to describe a wonderful structure he had come upon while traveling over the Russian countryside. It was heavily guarded, he said. It had great wooden towers at intervals. It had barbed wire around it, and was guarded everywhere by fierce dogs and armed men. "And yet, if I wish," Karandash continued, "I can still get in!"

Stalin was reported to have been thrown into a cold rage by that gag, and the brave little man with the shuffling walk, the oversized shoes, and the melancholy visage disappeared from view until three weeks after Stalin's death.

The Soviet people are glad to get their Karandash back, but they ask: for how long? They remember those earlier clowns, Bim and Bom, who made the people laugh at bureaucracy and arrogance and official privilege, until they disappeared forever from view.

They remember the most beloved Soviet humorist [Mikhail] Zoshchenko, whose books outdistanced every other writer but Gorky and Demyan Bedny. Human foibles of all kinds were the object of Zoshchenko's gay and gentle satire: ignorance, pettiness, stupidity, cruelty, greed, bad manners, rudeness, selfishness, lack of culture, the housing shortage, poverty, dirt, the gap between the high-sounding pretensions of propaganda and the painful Soviet reality. He knew the uncertainties of man's life, the weaknesses in high places and low, the tragedy of the human condition which makes men laugh in order that they may not cry. His writings were so popular, one critic wrote, because they provided the reader "with a blissful escape from the loud slogans of the revolution."

During the great speedup of the thirties and forties he proposed to write a scientific treatise on "The Differences between Man and the Beaver." When his critics nagged him to write the same dull propaganda as the rest of them, he wrote: "Let me talk, comrades! Let a man express his ideas at least for the purpose of discussion!"

When they ordered him to write less about weaknesses and sorrows and little comedies of man's life and more about the achievements of the five-year plans, he answered:

> The thing is that my genre, that is the genre of the humorist, is incompatible with description of achievements. That is the concern of writers of another genre. To each his own way: the tragic

actor plays in Hamlet; the comic actor in *Revizor* (*Inspector General*). It seems to me that each of us must follow his own bent.

He wrote of the comedy and timeless tragedy of man's aging—a pseudoscientific treatise on how to renew one's lost youth. His critics told him: One should stay young by working at top speed on the great collective constructions of the five-year plans. But his book *Youth Restored* answered for him:

> I want to be useful in the struggle for socialism by helping people to stay young. Perhaps here and there I have made mistakes—in which case I humbly beg pardon from science. These medical opinions of mine have not been copied from books. I have been the dog on which I have performed all the experiments.

But compassion for their sufferings and help to laugh at the sorrows that are too deep for tears are one of the comforts that the men in the Kremlin deny to Soviet man. So Bim and Bom disappeared. Karandash disappeared. And Zoshchenko was silenced in 1946.

Now Karandash has returned to the Moscow circus. If his jests have the old fire, if Zoshchenko should be permitted to write once more in the old vein that made the printing presses unable to keep up with the demand for his works, if the Soviet people will be permitted to laugh once more at themselves, at their troubles, and at their rulers, this at least will be recognized as a genuine concession from the men in the Kremlin. For as long as laughter is driven underground there is no solace in slavery, and freedom to laugh at fraud and deceit and pompous arrogance is the first step toward the restoration of freedom. As long as laughter is not free, nothing is free. So, while the men in the Kremlin try to decide whether they shall all shout "Long live Beria, or Molotov, or Malenkov, or Khrushchev!" the people of Moscow let out the exultant cry "Karandash is back! Long live Karandash!"

June 24, 1953

The Kremlin Does Another History

For over two decades, Soviet historiography has been in a steadily deepening crisis. Histories succeed each other as if they were being consumed by a giant chain-smoker who lights the first volume of the new edition with the last volume of the old. There was more barbarous defiance about Hitler's book burning, but in the Soviet Union the burning of essential records is more systematic, more thorough, more continuous, and more calculated. One day a given statement of an event, or a given interpretation, is obligatory, and must be repeated, parrotlike, by everybody. The next day it is condemned and it is death to remember it.

The mortality has been particularly high in histories of the communist party, histories of the civil war, histories of the Soviet era. On Sunday, July 26 [1953], *Pravda* devoted 7,500 words to outlining a new history of the last 50 years of the Bolshevik party. It suggests to the faithful that Stalin's *Short Course in the History of the Communist Party*, which has been gospel since 1939 and has been printed in all languages in editions of more than 40,000,000 copies, is now to go the way of all previous party histories. Millions who have struggled to learn by heart its dull and mendacious pages must now forget all they have memorized and start the memorizing of the newest gospel—no less dull, no less mendacious, no less difficult to swallow, but nevertheless, official, until the next version is written with a pistol in place of a pen.

The cemetery of buried books is strewn with the hastily buried corpses of earlier histories. Each of them was in turn official. Each of them in turn became heresy, treason, anathema. In 1923, Zinoviev's *History of the Russian Communist Party* was the official text that all had to master. A few years later, his book was burned. Yet a few more years and a bullet was lodged in the base of his brain to put an end to all inconvenient memories.

In 1926–27, Yaroslavsky's two-volume history was official. He lived to die that most unnatural of all deaths for a Bolshevik historian, a natural death. But his two-volume work died long before him.

In the early 30s the official history was Popov. It too was in two volumes, and went through more than sixteen editions. Yet a few years later it had gone over the cataract with the earlier works in this unending flood of histories.

Next came Knorin's *Short Course*. But in 1939 it was replaced by the *Short Course*—"edited by a commission of the CPSU [Communist Party of the Soviet Union]" and published anonymously. It was full of hundreds and hundreds of references to The Great Stalin, yet a few years later, Joseph Stalin personally claimed to be the author of the self-laudatory volume.

And now, if we are to judge from the shrinking in the number of mentions of Stalin to a mere four in a text of 7,500 words in last Sunday's *Pravda*, Stalin's *Short Course* is doomed to go the way of all histories in the land of permanent book burning. Ominously, for all who have memorized the Stalin glorification, *Pravda* pronounces these words: "Incorrect, non-Marxist expoundings on the role of individuals in this history must be eradicated."

The greatest, dullest, and most mendacious best-seller in the entire history of publishing, with more than 40,000,000 copies in more than 60 languages, is to be burned, and the memory of its dull and revolting formulae of Stalin aggrandizement and Stalin worship "must be eradicated."

Only a few weeks earlier, the great police chief–historian, Lavrenti Beria, passed from the Kremlin palace to the dungeon. He had won Stalin's favor with his *History of the Bolshevik Movement in Transcaucasia*, where he showed how in a total state the pistol guides the pen in writing what passes for history. Now his Transcaucasian history and the *Short Course* will be burned together.

The earlier histories, Yaroslavsky's, Popov's, Knorin's, were factional, one-sided, untruthful in many respects, but they did give fairly complete lists of names of party leaders, delegates to party congresses, members of Central Committees, and Politburos. Gradually, as the blood purges continued, not only the men disappeared, but their very names disappeared from the pages of the new "histories." They became "unpersons," who not only ceased to exist, but whose nonexistence was extended retroactively into the past as if they never had existed. Thus the history of the civil war has been rewritten as if there never had been a commissar of war named Leon Trotsky. The history of the Comintern is rewritten as if its first chairman had not been named Zinoviev or its second chairman, Bukharin.

But the new *Pravda* history has attained the ultimate in bloodless depersonalization. The only safe names to mention are Lenin—many times; Stalin—four times, one of them to praise Lenin; [G.V.] Plekhanov [leading Russian Marxist]—once. These men are safely dead, and their memories not altogether purged. But no living name is mentioned because a struggle goes on for the succession. He who yesterday praised Beria is today a dead duck. He who today praises Malenkov or Molotov or Zhukov may be doomed tomorrow. So the ultimate in the depersonalization of history is the blank space, the anonymous "party and government," the standardized replaceable parts.

The perpetual burning of histories shows more than a contempt for man's historical achievement, the slow painful accumulation of centuries.

This perpetual destruction of men and their very names shows more than a contempt for truth.

For the total state is built upon contempt for mankind itself, contempt for the masses of humanity who have a right to a knowledge of their past as something on which to build the present and the future. As long as men themselves are regarded by a ruthless band of power-hungry tyrants as manipulable material to be used, warped, destroyed, to serve their power hunger, so long will history be clay in the hands of these unskilled potters. Only men who are compelled to account to humanity for their deeds can have any respect for truth, or fact, or history, or humanity.

July 29, 1953

Making Two Bureaucrats Grow Where One Grew Before

In that great masterpiece *Gulliver's Travels*, Jonathan Swift has a wise man say: "Whoever could make two ears of corn or two blades of grass grow upon a spot where only one grew before, would deserve better of mankind and do more essential service to his country than the whole race of politicians put together."

Today, the Soviet government is applying the direct opposite principle. In *Izvestia* of September 15 and *Pravda* of September 15 [1953], the Soviet government announces that it will try to overcome the disastrous cattle and food shortage produced by a third of a century of communist rule and nearly 25 years of forced collectivization. And what is the sovereign remedy for communism's failure in agriculture? The remedy is neither more nor less than to make two politicians grow where one grew before!

Six ministries are to be formed where there were three before. That means not merely six bureaucrats to consume the product of the peasants where only three bureaucrats were a charge upon his productive labor. In the vast Russian land, each ministry has hundreds of officials in the center and in all the regions. And Ivan Ivanovich, bending over his little plot, and tending his chicken or his cow, will have to feed them all, and obey all their conflicting orders, before he can feed himself or the workers in the cities. Such is the logic of bureaucratic communism.

The same issue of *Pravda* and *Izvestia* that carried this curious proposal gave the full text of the Report on Agriculture of the first secretary of the communist party, Nikita Khrushchev. Here are his startling figures on what has happened to the livestock of the Soviet Union in a third of a century of communism and a quarter century of forced collectivization. The figures speak for themselves:

On January 1, 1916, despite the ravages of two-and-one-half years of war, there were 58 million head of cattle of all kinds in the old Russia of the tsars.

With comparative freedom for peasant labor under the NEP [New Economic Policy], the number of head of cattle grew from 58 million in 1916 to 66 million in 1928.

Today, in 1953, after all the annexation of new lands, First Secretary Khrushchev reports that there are only 56 million head of cattle of all kinds—still less than in 1928 under the NEP and less than in 1916 under the tsar.

And what are the remedies which he proposes? They are the time-honored remedies of communism.

1. To make two scapegoats grow where one grew before. Therefore ex–police Chief Beria is now added to the list of scapegoats, along with [A.A.] Andreyev and other ministers and commissars who preceded him. Lavrenti Beria had his faults and they were monstrous and murderous, but he was a murderer of men and not of cattle. He had nothing to do with agriculture. The boss for the last few years, the man responsible for the bankruptcy to which First Secretary Khrushchev referred was none other than First Secretary Khrushchev himself.

2. The second sovereign communist remedy is to change the bureaucratic setup—cut down the number of ministries if they have just been increased, increase them if they have recently been cut down. In this case: make two bureaucrats grow where one grew before.

3. The third sovereign remedy is the most revealing one: it is to admit a tiny little bit of freedom, a touch of the stimulus of free private enterprise, some incentive for the enserfed peasant so that he may feel that in some measure he is once more working for himself.

So it was in Lenin's day. First Lenin tried to collectivize everything. The result was disastrous failure and famine, strikes in the cities, rebellion in Kronstadt, insurrection in the countryside. Lenin retreated from full communism to the comparative freedom of the NEP. The farms prospered. Meat and corn and wheat increased. Heads of cattle increased. The standard of living of the workingmen in the cities increased. Nineteen twenty-eight was the best year that the mass of workers and peasants have ever known under Russian communism. But the Bolsheviks were merely applying an old Russian principle: "Let the wool grow a little so that it can be cut better." In 1929 the great drive for peasant expropriation and forced collectivization began, and they cut not only the wool, but also the hide and much of the flesh.

At least 5,000,000 peasants perished. Famine raged in the cities. The losses in livestock were almost a half of the total number of animals which existed in 1928.

Then once more, the communists decided to retreat—to let the wool grow a little again so that it could be sheared once more. This time they retreated much less than in the NEP, retreated ever so little. But even this retreat was one more confession of the essential bankruptcy of communism in agriculture. Along with the kolkhoz [collective farm] serfdom, the state now permitted each peasant family to own a diminutive private plot. In his free time, after his slavery on the kolkhoz, the peasant could cultivate for himself in a kind of a hole-in-the-corner freedom a tiny little plot of "free" land. In a few years 18,000,000 such tiny private-enterprise farms sprang up with an average of one acre of land, ⅔ of a cow, ⅓ of a pig, 1 and ⅔ of a sheep and a few chickens.

Not much. Only 5 percent of all the arable land in the country, but according to the Soviet government's own startling figures, this 5 percent of the land produced 20 percent of the total agricultural product of the USSR! On this small private plot, without tractor or kolkhoz implements, with only a spade and a watering can and the muscles of his arms and back and the song in his heart when a man works his own land in freedom for himself, the peasant as peasant produced four times as much per acre as on the soulless feudal kolkhoz! The privately tended cows gave more milk and more calves, the chickens more eggs and more chicks. For that which a man does with love and for himself, he does well. And that which a man does in bitterness and for the omnipotent and tyrannical state, he does badly though he have all the tractors in the world, and all the police and bureaucrats on his back and all the slogans of the party in his ears.

Angered and alarmed by this evidence that the tiniest fragment of freedom is better than the sloganized slavery of communism, the party and government once more began a drive in 1939 to "collectivize the cattle." With interruptions for the war, that drive has lasted from that day to this. And now, once more its failure is recognized. Khrushchev makes his terrible statistical confessions. Once more the scapegoats. Once more the bureaucratic shuffles. Once more the minuscule concessions: "Let the wool grow a little so that it can be sheared once more."

Such is the record of a third of a century of communism. Such is the record of a quarter of a century of forced collectivization and kolkhoz-sovkhoz [state-owned farm] slavery. After a third of a century of communism there is no country in the world more badly in need of an agrarian revolution than the Soviet Union. The whole history of communism proves it. And no further round of scapegoats, petty concessions, and bureaucratic shuffles will change the picture. The remedy is not "six ministers where three grew before."

The remedy was known to Tsar Alexander II when he decreed the Emancipation of 1861. The remedy was known to Lincoln when he freed the slaves and signed the Homestead Act giving state lands to any farmer who would till them. The remedy was even known to Lenin when he reluctantly decreed the NEP. The remedy was known too to Dean Swift who was born in 1667 and who wrote in his *Gulliver's Travels:* "Whoever could make two ears of corn or two blades of grass grow upon a spot where only one grew before, would deserve better of mankind and do more essential service to his country than the whole race of politicians put together."

September 15, 1953

Death Comes for the Dictator

Today it is seven short months since Joseph Stalin died. Seven months and already that name which has appeared as many as 121 times in a single day on a single page of *Pravda* has shrunk to the point where one cannot find it mentioned so much as once in a week of *Pravda*s.

Air fleet day passed without Glory to Stalin being spelled by planes upon the sky, and without Vassily Stalin to receive the salutes and credit his father with being the father of all airplane designers and designs. Fleet day passed without sailors jumping into the sea and spelling Great Stalin in the waters as they swam. Army day passed without any more credit to Stalin for being the father of the Soviet armies than to Trotsky, whose role as actual first war commissar and architect of the Red Army has long been buried in slander and oblivion.

April passed this year without the usual spring announcement of Stalin prizes in literature and the arts. Six more months have gone since and still no Stalin laureates, no hail of 100,000-ruble prizes in great Stalin's name. Has the name lost its charm? Has his inspiring genius been buried with him? Are the prizes to be renamed? Or abolished? Or are the survivors and contenders for Stalin's mantle still struggling and haggling behind the scenes each to get the greatest number of henchmen or favorites on the prize-winning list?

And what has happened to the directive "On the Sacred Duties of Writers," published in the *Literary Gazette* twelve days after Stalin's death, which said that the all-important task of Soviet writers was "to portray for future generations the greatest genius of all times and all peoples—the immortal Stalin." Does immortality wear out so soon?

Speaking of "immortality"—what has happened to Dr. [Alexsandr Alexandravich] Bogomolets [1881–1946] and his famous longevity serum, ACS? What a fanfare there was about the great "physiologist-pathologist" of Kiev and his epoch-making discovery! Having shortened the lives of millions and prematurely ended the lives of millions more, Stalin showed intense interest in the problem of the prolongation of life in general, and his own in particular. All the best doctors in the Soviet Union were mobilized for his staff of personal physicians in the Kremlin and for the special experimental laboratory to prolong his life.

But after Bogomolets had assured the world that Stalin could live to 149 or more with the Bogomolets treatment, the great doctor himself died in 1946 at the age of 65. Soviet propaganda agencies were quick to explain that for some reason the serum could not be used on Bogomolets. When [Mikhail Ivanovich] Kalinin [1875–1946, chairman of the USSR Supreme Soviet, 1937–1946] died the same year, Soviet propaganda fell silent. Not a word then about "serum ACS."

But Stalin, having the greatest state in the world as his personal possession, simply mobilized more physicians, more laboratories, more resources. All the best doctors in Russia were called up as his staff of personal physicians in the Kremlin, and as special experimenters to prolong his life.

He used terror to intimidate them, as proved by the famous frame-up of the "doctor-poisoners" made up from the best physicians in his entourage.

The Cominform [Communist Information Bureau, created in 1947 to counter the Truman Doctrine and the Marshall Plan], too, was enlisted in the great work of prolonging the life of the one indispensable man. From Nikos Zahariades, Greek communist leader, came this prayer: "The ordinary women of our country say: 'Let the Lord shorten our lives by years and add minutes to Stalin's life. We are so many that he will live forever.' "

The gods are immortal, and so Stalin was exalted to new heights and from all his subjects were exacted tributes appropriate to the cult of a living god.

"Stalin. Always we hear in our souls his dear name," wrote *Komsomolskaya Pravda*. "And here in the Kremlin, his presence touches us at every step. We walk on stones which he may have trod. Let us fall on our knees and kiss those holy footprints."

Others called him "Beloved father," "The sun shining over our country," "Our bright star," "The wisdom of immortal thought." *Pravda* wrote:

> Oh great Stalin, oh Leader of the peoples,
> Thou hast given life to man
> Thou hast made fruitful the earth

Thou hast rejuvenated the centuries
Thou has made the springtime burst into flowers
Thou hast made the strings vibrate with music
Thou, splendor of my spring, oh Thou,
Sun reflected by millions of hearts.

"There is no fortress," Stalin himself has said, "which Bolshevik determination cannot conquer." He decided to take by storm the power over men of the Angel of Death, and to wrest by force and conjuration from the hand of Heaven the secret of immortality.

But alas, God will not be mocked, and the Angel of Death is no respecter of persons. Death visits alike and with impartial mien the humblest cottage, the prison cell, and the heavily guarded Kremlin fortress towers. He has the password for all sentries, the key to all locked gates, the *propusk* (pass) that will get him into the most heavily guarded hall.

Seven months dead and the name that was to live forever has all but vanished from the Soviet press. His lieutenants eye each other up in fear, wondering who will get whom in the muted struggle for the succession to the post of absolute dictator and living god.

Seven short months, and the name that was to live forever and receive worship as an immortal and living god has shrunk to that of an almost forgotten man. Only one thing still keeps it from total oblivion in the Soviet press: the name of Stalin is needed as a link in the apostolic succession which runs from Marx to Engels to Lenin to Stalin to the man who will yet kill off his comrades and become the next absolute dictator. And some day, when the Russian people and the other peoples of the Soviet Union have once more regained their freedom from all dictators, the name of Stalin will take its place in another context as one in the series with Ivan the Terrible and Genghis Khan. For one thing is certain: in the long run, force is as powerless over the heart and the memory of man as it is powerless to drive off the Angel of Death.

October 5, 1953

Totalitarian Semantics

Every one who reads the Soviet press and satellite press is perturbed by the extent to which it distorts the general human meaning which words have acquired in the course of centuries.

Take the question of heresy for instance. As the modern world moved toward greater tolerance and greater freedom, there were virtually no new words developing for any new heresies, while the old words fell into gradual disuse. But the total state wages war on so many types of "thought-crimes" that recently the United States High Commission in Germany, examining the East German communist press, came up with the following startling crop of thought-crimes or heresies for which people in East Germany were being condemned, threatened, and purged: "Cosmopolitanism, objectivism, bourgeois nationalism, particularism, Titoism, pacifism, warmongering, conciliationism, Trotskyism, Zionism, relativism, factionalism, Social Democratism, trade unionism, equalitarianism, opportunism, reformism, formalism, naturalism, collaborationism, lack of vigilance, diversionism, schematism, careerism, individualism, familyism, kulakism, practicism, nonpartyism."

And there were many more. Behind this sudden spawning of new heresies and thought-crimes lies the tragedy of new persecutions. These are not merely new words, but for every new "ism" there are new victims. Some "isms" count their victims by the tens or hundreds, others by the thousands and tens of thousands. This rash of "deviations" or thought-crimes suggests that a straitjacket is being forced upon the minds of the men who live in the "people's democracies."

The very term *people's democracy* has a new and strange sound. Democracy comes from two Greek words meaning people's rule. What then can be the meaning of "people's people's rule?" Does it not suggest that some violence has been done to the word *democracy* if the word *people* has to be repeated twice? And is it not strange to contemplate that it is precisely the lands in which people are not allowed to form political parties and choose between rival platforms and rival candidates that are the lands called "people's democracies?"

Even more bewildering is the use of the word *peace* in the press of the Soviet Empire. One observer who counted the number of times that the word *peace* was used in special contexts in one week of issues of the press of the Soviet Union and its satellites made the following discoveries:

> To be for "peace" one must harvest crops on time, fulfill and overfulfill one's deliveries to the state, increase the norm, overfulfill the norm, cut the costs and increase the productivity of labor, support the five-year plan, protect state property, study Russian in all the satellites, "volunteer" for extra work, subscribe heavily to government loans, support a five-power conference but oppose a four-power conference, come and vote in an election in which there is no electoral contest, love the Soviet government and hate the free democracies . . .

and a host of other things which men have never before associated with the term *peace*. Peace is thus tied up with so many irrelevant and even hostile things that it begins to lose its original meaning.

Even prelates of the church are expected to join the chorus of hate of the outside world. At the last World Peace Council attended by the Metropolitan [high official of Russian Orthodox church] of Moscow, the Metropolitan spoke of "the bestial Americans, hordes of modern barbarians, gnashing their teeth, like some foul plague." Any one who knows Christianity can only pity a churchman who is forced to use such language in the name of peace.

Thus, the "peace" campaign is at the same time a hate campaign in which peace means preparation for war.

If the free world, shocked by the Soviet postwar conquest of 600,000,000 people blandly called "liberation," begins to plan to defend itself against further aggression, this is called "warmongering." If a citizen of a subjugated country continues to love his country and long for its return to an independent existence, he is called a "traitor." If he betrays his country and becomes a willing puppet of the conqueror, he is called a "patriot." If a Chinese conscript is driven into North Korea to fight against the independence of the Korean republic, he is called a "volunteer."

What is at work here is the fact that totalitarianism mobilized language as it has mobilized everything else in the total state: man, industries, sciences, ideas, emotions, means of communication. The technique of this strange double-talk is as simple as it is upsetting. A well-known word with an appealing meaning is applied to whatever the regime wishes to justify. And a well-known word with a repulsive meaning is applied to whatever the regime wishes to destroy. Dictatorship is called democracy; war, peace; freedom, slavery; and slavery, liberation. Nothing is what it seems. Nothing is called by its right name.

This process is fraught with the greatest dangers. First, there is the danger which we referred to at the outset: it becomes harder and harder for men to communicate with each other and understand each other across frontiers. Then, there is the danger that men with absolute power over the means of communication and all that is said may create a language in which it becomes impossible to tell the truth. Finally, there is the danger that men will lose their ability to think clearly, for men think with words, and if the words themselves are ruined by such power manipulation, then thought is poisoned at its source.

People have long realized that the total state makes unending war on its own people and on its neighbors: a war of propaganda, a war of nerves, and a physical war of concentration camps, purges, outlawry of opposition, a war of internal conquest and foreign conquest. But what men are only beginning to realize is that this system of destroying the meaning of words and using them as if they were their opposites is a war on the very spirit of men, and on one of the powers which distinguishes man most clearly from the other animals—namely, his power of reason.

November 18, 1953

Are All Things Caesar's?

With the arrest of Cardinal Wyszynski, primate of Poland, the last of the communist states has put its Catholic hierarchy behind bars, or in forced detention in monasteries, or banished them into exile. In none of them does the normal church structure any longer exist, as far as the state can prevent it from existing by acts of force.

The list of the martyrs is long and still growing. It includes parish priests, nuns, vicars, bishops, archbishops, cardinals, and laymen. The state has attempted to interfere with dogmatic formulations and liturgical prayers hallowed by centuries-old tradition, substituting atheistic censors for ecclesiastical authorities. It has removed the imprimatur from Catholic books, since the state itself claims to be the exclusive authority in deciding what is to be printed in the field of religion, as in the field of science, of politics, of art, of belles lettres. Its decrees on registration of monastic orders and clergy and its decrees on the filling of ecclesiastical offices are intended to lay down a legal basis for the continuous intrusion of the state, captained as it is by men who do not believe in God, into the affairs of the church.

As late as May 1950, the Polish government concluded a new agreement with the Catholic church in which the state solemnly promised to "recognize the jurisdictional authority of the Pope" in the church. The very constitution written by the communist rulers provides for a separation of church and state which is now violated. When that constitution was promulgated, President Beirut stated in express words, which we quote: "The constitution means that the church has its own autonomous organization and organizational character."

Now the same irreligious and antireligious authorities have set aside both the ancient government of the church and their own constitution.

The communist countries make war on all religions, a war which they wage unceasingly for a variety of reasons. If they have been slower with the Catholic church in Poland than with the Catholic church elsewhere and with other religions, it is merely because their step-at-a-time tactics recognized the peculiar position of the Roman Catholic Church in the history of Poland. Now Stefan Cardinal Wyszynski, primate of Poland, joins Josef Cardinal Mindzenty, primate of Hungary, Archbishop Joseph Beran of Prague, Czechoslovakia, Aloysius Cardinal Stepinac, primate of Yugoslavia, and Thomas Cardinal Tien, archbishop of Peiping, in the roster of leaders of the Catholic church that are jailed, interned, exiled, or otherwise prevented from carrying out their duties.

In the Gospel of St. Luke there is a parable which portrays Jesus as being tested by spies. The spies asked him, "Is it lawful for us to give tribute unto Caesar or no?" And he answered them, "Render unto Caesar the things which be Caesar's, and unto God the things which be God's" (Luke 21:22–25, King James Version).

Through the ages, though men have differed as to which things be Caesar's and which God's, this dictum has served as a guide in affairs of Christian conscience and in deciding the always difficult question of the relations between church and state. But it is the nature of totalitarianism that it attempts to secure total dominion over the body and spirit, over thoughts, feelings, actions, beliefs, and conscience. The total state is total in that for it all things are Caesar's. Therefore, it attempts to coordinate even the churches of God and the consciences of men into instruments and possessions of the state.

Totalitarianism is a philosophy of government which believes that the state is coextensive with the whole of society. The total state recognizes no nonstate organizations, no nonstate activities, no nonstate hopes, aspirations, dreams. Wherever it moves in, it seeks to regiment men's ideas about everything, men's feelings, men's words, men's thoughts.

As soon as totalitarians take over a given country, their first effort is to get hold of all nonstate organizations, all churches, trade unions, political parties, cooperatives, and voluntary associations, and turn them into organs and instruments of the state. *Gleichschalten* was Hitler's word for this process. Lenin and Stalin called it "turning mass organizations into *transmission belts* of the communist party."

In the case of the church, this unlimited thirst for power is reinforced by other motives. For the masters of the total state, the state itself is god. The rulers of the total state claim to be keepers of the individual conscience. Moreover, they are atheists and materialists in their philosophy, which makes it particularly intolerable that they should assume authority in matters of religion and church administration.

The particular charges made against churchmen, like those against union leaders and party leaders, have no importance. The church, the party, the union, must be coordinated, turned into a transmission belt or instrument of the state. Those who resist this process of conquest of man's spirit must be removed, framed up, "confessed," liquidated. The punishment is decided first, and then a crime fabricated to fit the punishment. Those who consent to become state agents are called "patriot priests." Those who remain faithful to their vows are deposed by impious hands, prevented from following their calling, charged with absurd charges of "espionage, dissoluteness, blackmarketing, treason."

Finally, this war of the men in the Kremlin upon a subjugated peoples is also a war on their national independence and national memory. The same motives which lead the Kremlin to put Soviet marshal [Konstantin K.] Rokossovsky at the head of the Polish army as commander in chief and proconsul, make them seek to put some pliable puppet priests at the head of a so-called Polish patriot church and turn it from the church of the Polish people into a transmission belt of the Kremlin and its Polish puppets.

But the terrible tenacity of Poland's national memory and the depths of the religious devotion of her people have been demonstrated again and again in her history. As in other lands, in this one too the spirit of man can never be permanently subdued by the straitjacket of the total state. Neither puppet generals nor puppet union and party leaders nor puppet police nor puppet priests can forge chains which can forever chain the human spirit.

November 19, 1953

The Voice of the Silent

Today, November 30 [1953], the Congress of the United States opened hearings on the fate of the Baltic republics of Lithuania, Latvia, and Estonia. The first witness before a congressional committee of seven members was John Foster Dulles, secretary of state. He testified that the United States had not withdrawn recognition from these republics and did not intend to. Though the American government welcomes opportunities to settle specific disputes with the Soviet government, he said, the United States looks upon the conference table "as a place for making our principles prevail—not as a place to surrender them." This declaration set the tone for the hearings.

If the Soviet government kept its plighted word, it too would be recognizing the independence of the three republics which it so solemnly pledged to respect in so many treaties. The seven-man congressional commission has already held hearings in Europe and gathered a mass of relevant documentation which makes this crystal clear.

Thus, on July 12, 1920, the Soviet government signed a document which read: "Russia unreservedly recognizes the independence, self-rule, and sovereignty of the Latvian state and voluntarily and forever renounces all rights over the Latvian people and territory." It accompanied this by similarly worded treaties with Estonia and Lithuania.

On September 28 [1920], it signed solemn non-aggression pacts with the same republics. On April 4, 1934, it renewed those pacts. At that time, Foreign Commissar [Maxim] Litvinov declared:

> It should be clear to the whole world that our proposal is not of a temporary nature nor inspired by a casual conjunction of circumstances, but is an expression of our constant and permanent policy of peace and an essential element in the preservation of the independence of the young states you represent.

"The Soviet state," Mr. Litvinov added, "is a stranger to chauvinism and nationalism . . . and perceives its state duties to lie not in conquest, nor in expansion of its territory."

On June 14, 1940, in violation of these solemn promises, ultimatums were dispatched to Lithuania, Latvia, and Estonia, followed by Soviet occupation two days later. These invasions followed by exactly nine months a new series of "mutual assistance and nonaggression pacts" in which the Soviet government pledged itself once more to "respect the economic and governmental organizations" of the respective countries.

The spirit of the invasion of June 1940 is made terrifyingly clear by another document in the hands of the congressional committee, a document which is a photostat of an original filed with the International Red Cross in Geneva. The document is NKVD order No. 0054, dated November 28, 1940, directing the NKVD head, or nominal head, for invaded Lithuania, Guzevicius, to list "all suspect persons, all enemies of the people." The list of suspect persons is not based upon individual actions or individual crimes as would be the case in a free country. In the total state, suspect persons are listed by category. The individual person may have done nothing; he may even have been pro-Soviet or procommunist, but if he happens to fall into one of the suspect categories, he must be listed in the NKVD list. Here are the main categories as set down verbatim in the NKVD instruction:

a. All former members of the anti-Soviet political parties, organizations and groups: Trotskyists, Rightists, S.R.s [Social Revolutionaries], Mensheviks, Social Democrats, Anarchists.

b. All former members of the anti-Soviet political parties, organizations and groups: Nationalists, Young Lithuanians, Voldemarists, Populists, Christian Democrats . . . Active members of student fraternities, riflemen's organizations.

c. Former gendarmes, policemen, employees of political and criminal police and of the prisons.

g. Persons expelled from the communist party and Communist Youth.

i. All citizens of foreign countries, representatives of foreign firms, employees of foreign firm offices, former citizens of foreign countries.

j. Persons having personal contacts and maintaining correspondence abroad, with foreign legations and consulates, Esperantists, and philatelists.

k. All former employees of Ministries of the rank of Referent (writer of reports) or above.

l. Former workers of the Red Cross.

m. Religionists, priests, pastors, members of sects, and active religionists of religious communities.

n. Former noblemen, estate owners, merchants, bankers, business men, shop owners of hotels and restaurants.

Thus it is only in the fourteenth place that this terroristic brand of "socialization" places businessmen and landowners. The other categories make patriotism into a crime, religion into a crime, foreign correspondence into a crime, even if it is so innocent as stamp collecting or correspondence in Esperanto. Thus the Iron Curtain shut down on Lithuania, and in similar fashion on Latvia and Estonia. Under these sweeping orders some 10,000 Lithuanians were slain and over 40,000 banished to Siberia during the short time between the Stalin-Hitler pact and Hitler's invasion of the Soviet Union. Other reports in the hands of the congressional committee show that of 2,000 Catholic priests in dominantly Catholic Lithuania, only 200 survive, and these, like the philatelists and Esperantists, have been cut off from their connections abroad.

It is this Iron Curtain that has descended upon the Lithuanians, Latvians, and Estonians that the congressional inquiry is intended to lift. From exiles scattered all over Europe and North and South America, from thousands of such exiles in the United States, from the voiceless slaves in camps from Karaganda to Dal'stroy, from diplomatic representatives of the three republics, from documents, from eyewitnesses of other nationalities, the seven-man committee will build up a picture of how Soviet imperialism operates: what the total state does to a land which it claims to have "liberated"; what the fraudulent electoral system is like by which citizens are forced to appear to vote for their own enslavement; what secret agreements were made between the Nazis and the men in the Kremlin; and what life is like in sovietized Lithuania, Latvia, and Estonia.

In opening his testimony, Secretary of State Dulles recalled other nations which were supposed to have fallen and vanished forever from the face of the earth. But their national memory remained alive and they rose again. The witnesses before the congressional committee will speak for the silent, give voice to the suffering of the voiceless, record the broken words, the treacherous conquest, permit a tortured people to preserve its history and national memory. Secretary Dulles recalled that some of the earliest peoples mentioned in the old testament were from Israel, Arabia, Egypt, and Lebanon. "How many times," he asked, "have these peoples been submerged, only to rise again?"

"The Baltic peoples," he concluded, "maintain their will to be free . . . Their martyrdom keeps patriotism alive." The United States recognizes their right to exist as independent governments.

December 1, 1953

The New Course in the Soviet Union and Satellites

For the past six months the world has been watching the series of programmatic pronouncements and structural changes in the Soviet Union and its satellites, collectively called the New Course. Will they continue? Are they connected with Stalin's death? With Beria's arrest? Or are there deeper causes? These are some of the questions that the world has been asking. And here are some of the answers that leading experts on Soviet affairs in England, France, Germany, and the United States have been coming up with.

1. Despite hesitancies, zigzags, fearful retreats, despite large slogans and small deeds, there has been a trend toward concessions to the needs of the consumers and worker and peasant producers, both in the Soviet Union and the satellites, which may properly be called New.

   In East Germany and Hungary, it has been admitted that unwilling peasants have been forced into collective farms. Some peasants have been allowed to leave. Delivery quotas and taxes have been somewhat reduced and arrears canceled.

   Furthermore, there have been some concessions to consumers. So far these are mostly in the realm of promises, but some food prices have been lowered. In some places the government-hoarded war reserves of food have been dipped into. Some gold, currency, and goods have been expended on emergency imports of food, textiles, leather. The five-year plans for investment in capital goods and heavy industry have been slowed up, and more consumers' goods have been promised.

   As such promises have been made so many times before and not fulfilled, both the people of the Soviet Union and satellites, and the expert observers, are waiting to see how promise squares with performance.

2. The death of Stalin, and the fact that the struggle for a successor remains still unresolved, is offered by many as a cause of the con-

cessions and promises. Restlessness in the Soviet Empire as mani-
fested in East Germany on June 17, and in Pilsen and other places
earlier, is offered as a second explanation.

3. The major explanation offered, however, is neither the power
   struggle nor the mass discontent, but a severe agricultural and
   economic crisis that has gripped both Soviet Union and satellites.
   It is this crisis that is expressed in the startling satellites. It is
   this crisis that is expressed in the startling cattle figures of Khrushchev, in the admissions of error of the East German, Hungarian,
   and other satellite governments, in the cessation of canal building
   in Central Asia (the Great Turkmen Canal) and in Romania, in
   the unaccustomed import of consumers' goods, instead of capital
   goods, in the great agricultural discussion now going on in the
   Soviet press, in communist China's acknowledgment that its
   heavy industry plans had been "overambitious," and in a score of
   other symptomatic admissions of disequilibrium between the war
   goods and capital goods industries on the one hand and consumers' goods production on the other.

The analysis of the crisis that has attracted the most attention is
that of Richard Lowenthal, Soviet expert of the *London Observer.*
His "The Crisis Behind Russia's Slowdown" has been reprinted in
Der Monat, Berlin, and *Commentary,* New York. Lowenthal begins
by agreeing with one of Stalin's last statements that "there are objective laws" governing a planned, controlled, directed totalitarian economy as well as a free market economy. Modern industry, Lowenthal
points out, can only be expanded as fast as the capital on hand (accumulated wealth), the supply of manpower, the productivity of labor
and agriculture, and the supply of raw materials permit.

The total state, however, has gone on the illusion that "planners,"
using enough force, can do anything. The men in the Kremlin for
years have gone on the assumption that all they needed to do is set
down control figures, order men to obey them, raise them again and
again, and they would expand the production of capital goods and
heavy industry as fast as they pleased.

Ever since the attack on Korea in June 1950, the Kremlin has
constantly and stubbornly raised its production targets for heavy industry and the war industries, both in the Soviet Union and in the
satellites. From 1950 through 1952 the targets laid down for heavy
industry in Czechoslovakia, Poland, Hungary, and East Germany
were raised again and again. Labor reserves were exhausted. Raw materials grew short. Consumers' goods failed to keep pace. The workers were worked beyond their strength. Labor productivity dimin-

ished. The fantastic annual increases of 15 to 18 and even 20 percent beat against the absolute limits of capital goods, labor supply, labor productivity, agricultural productivity, raw material supplies. This peculiar type of crisis set can occur only in a total state where there are no natural correctives of the free market to check an excessive capital increase by means of rising costs.

Those who warned that the arbitrary figures were excessive were simply purged. The harshest slave-driving methods were used to get still more out of the overworked labor force. But an ill-fed miner will produce less coal after a while, no matter how much he is threatened. Illness will take its toll no matter what the denunciations of "absenteeism." A factory worker living in a cold home, poorly fed and clad, will turn out less and less no matter what the figures of the plan.

The crisis has reached a point where the further use of force decreased rather than increased the economic yield.

In Poland and Czechoslovakia coal was finally mined by forced-labor "batallions." Then Russia took an increasing share—20 million tons from Poland this year as against 14 million last year—leaving less than ever for Poland to trade for Swedish steel. At the same time, the heavy armament buildup caused a steel shortage in Russia. The utopian thesis, as Lowenthal rightly called it, that an all-out armament drive and progress toward "communism," or even toward more consumer goods, could proceed simultaneously, ended in a profound crisis for the whole Soviet-satellite economy. This is the real reason for the talk of error, for the promise to cut down producers' goods allocations and increase consumers' goods, for the emergency import of food, textiles, raw materials.

Having reached the limits of agriculture, of raw materials, labor supply, productivity, and new capital goods, the Soviet and satellite economies can only get out of their present profound and deepening crisis if they make good on the New Course promises. And they can only make good on those promises if the men in the Kremlin will enter into real agreements concerning the world's trouble spots, and a real agreement for reduction of armaments, including atomic weapons, under proper inspection and control. Then the excessive investment of men, money, materials, supplies in the arms industry can be turned at least in part to consumers' goods, higher real wages, higher farm prices, and the fulfillment of the contradictory and hazy promises that have so far made up the so-called New Course.

December 11, 1953

Freedom for Soviet Music?

All who care about freedom will find cause to rejoice in the latest issue of the magazine *Soviet Music*. In it, Aram Khachaturian, composer, writes against bureaucratic interference with artistic creation and condemns the impoverished works composed during the last few years with: "a glance over the shoulder expressing fear that something untoward might happen."

The very title of the article, "On Creative Boldness," will cause a shiver of surprise to run down the spines of hard-pressed Soviet artists, for Mr. Khachaturian himself has been one of the victims of bureaucratic attack on creative boldness. For many years now, the Central Committee of the communist party, mistaking power over everything for *expertise* on everything, has constituted itself a supreme committee of music critics, painting, sculpture, drama, cinema, novel, and poetry critics, as well as supreme authority on all the sciences. In 1948, Soviet genetics, one of the most notable examples of genetic research in the world, was wiped out by a single act of the Politburo. Russia's greatest humorist, Zoshchenko, was silenced and the lot of the Soviet people made harder for lack of his healing laughter. The gentle lyric poet Anna Akhmatova was forced to lay down her pen. Russia, which all through the nineteenth century produced a literature of giants which stirred the hearts of men everywhere, was reduced to turning out versified, novelized, and dramatized versions of Central Committee directives. Most startling of all was the attack on symphonic music of February 11, 1948. Its chief victims were Sergei Prokofiev, Dmitri Shostakovich, and Aram Khachaturian, each of them a composer of worldwide repute.

Prokofiev, the oldest and best known, tried to placate the critics of the Politburo by entitling his further compositions with such "ideological" names as "On Guard for Peace."

The case of Shostakovich was more disturbing. Younger than Prokofiev, he had not yet reached his full stature. The attack of February 1948 was not the first upon him, but one of a series of blows that had cramped his growth, extorted him from humiliating confessions of musical "sin," and substituted a reluctant servility for the "creative boldness" which Khachaturian's article now calls for. Typical was the treatment of Shostakovich's opera *Lady Macbeth*. First hailed by *Pravda* on January 20, 1936, as a "most brilliant production of Soviet music," and one which "had won the love of the mass spectator," eight days later it was buried by *Pravda* in a bucket of epithets. (He was called "enemy of melody and harmony, inaccessible to the masses, leftist emphasizer of ugliness!") Shostakovich learned to curb his inspiration and worked his way back into favor as best he could. Yet even a decade and more of submission did not save Shostakovich from attack on February 11, 1948.

("I am deeply grateful," he responded in *Soviet Music*, "for this end for every criticism . . . All the instructions, and particularly those which refer to me personally, I accept as evidence of a severe but fatherly concern . . . I call upon all composers to devote all their strength to the fulfillment of this remarkable resolution.") In his effort to satisfy, he wrote works whose very titles betray his plight, such as "Over Our Motherland Shines the Sun" and "Cantato to Stalin's Reforestation Program."

When the 1948 bomb burst on the Society of Composers, Khachaturian was its general secretary. He was unceremoniously deposed and replaced by a mediocre musical politician named [Tikhon] Khrennikov. The new "commissar for music" called for more and more *ideinost* (ideology) in musical composition. Khachaturian responded by announcing in his plan for 1953 such pieces as "Spartakus," "Admiral Ushakov," and the hope of beginning work on "The Life and Struggles of the Peoples of Transcaucasia."

Now, like a breath of fresh air in a dungeon cell, Khachaturian's article condemns these "time-serving, monumental compositions of recent years" which employ such safe themes as "Love for Our Country, Struggle for Peace, Friendship of Peoples." He points out that "ideological correctness" and "musical literacy" do not make up for the "lack of creative élan" which comes from command performance and "the glance of fear over the shoulder. The time has come," writes Khachaturian, "to revise our established system of institutional control of composers . . . Let the artist be trusted more fully and he will, with even greater responsibility and freedom, approach the solution of the creative problems of our time . . . No tutelage! Let us take the risks of creation."

In the choking atmosphere of the Soviet dictatorship, these are brave words. But there are phrases in the article that remind us that

Khachaturian is treading on thin ice: respectful tributes to past Soviet criticism; an obeisance to the late bullying culture commissar [Andrei A.] Zhdanov [1896–1948]; phrases about the "true Soviet artist" giving expression to "the spiritual world of Soviet man."

For after all, the party bosses still possess a total monopoly of power, including all the means of publishing or performing music. They still claim to be authorities on everything and the total state still claims total control in every field. They are still determined to treat man himself as a mere malleable material to be molded according to plan into something called the new Soviet man.

But for the moment, there is a little weakening of power in the Kremlin. Stalin is dead. The men who struggle silently with each other—not so silently in the case of Beria—need to seek support in the populace and in all layers of society. Moreover, the attack of 1948 was principally Zhdanov's work, and Malenkov was Zhdanov's rival. Even Beria, in his reach for power, found it necessary to advocate a more benign penal code for the moment, as Khrushchev, boss of agriculture, finds it necessary to appear as the advocate of gentler agricultural laws.

What is really significant is that the moment the screws are loosened even a little, the indestructible human spirit springs back into shape. Khachaturian's article is undoubtedly permitted, even directed. But for one who has been through what he has been through to use such words gives them an unexpected charge of energy. In any case, our good wishes go with those devoted Soviet artists and scientists who have continued to produce as best they could under such restrictions.

December 21, 1953

And So Died Lavrenti Beria

Yagoda, Yezhov, Beria!

Three high chiefs of the secret police. Three great executioners. Three heroes of labor, three recipients of the Order of the Red Banner, three decorated with the Order of Lenin. Three great constructors of canals, clearers of swamps, miners of gold in the Far North, fellers of timber—with the forced labor of millions of Soviet citizens. Three who between them ruled over the great Russian land and all the Soviet peoples with the aid of gun and dog, barbed wire and knout. And each of them died a miserable death. According to the Soviet organs, a traitor's death. Each of them died with a bullet in the base of the brain, in the cellars of the Lubyanka, just as they had executed so many other Bolsheviks, and so many ordinary Soviet citizens.

Lavrenti Beria is charged with "using his position in the organs of the Ministries of Internal Affairs and State Security, committing a number of serious crimes with the aim of destroying honest personnel loyal to the cause of the communist party and the Soviet cause."

The same charge was leveled by Stalin, Malenkov, Molotov, and Beria against the police chief who preceded him, Nikolai Yezhov, who killed hundreds of thousands and jailed millions of innocent human beings.

The same charge was leveled by Stalin, Malenkov, Molotov, Beria, and Yezhov against Genrikh Yagoda, the police chief who preceded Yezhov. It was Yagoda who conducted the first great purge trials. With the help of Yezhov, Malenkov, Molotov, and Beria, under the orders of Joseph Stalin, Yagoda conducted the first two great show trials of old Bolsheviks in 1936, and 1937, including Zinoviev, Kamenev, Bukharin, Rykov, Tomsky, Radek, Piatakov, the whole generation of Lenin's closest associates. They were great trials, complete with "mad dogs, enemies of the people," confessions, proofs that they had always been traitors to the revolution, even before they helped Lenin to make it and while they helped Lenin to make it.

But in the last of these trials, in 1938, Yagoda, the old fox, changed roles, changed places. Yezhov, helped by Malenkov, Molotov, and Beria—and of course, Prosecutor Vyshinsky—liquidated Yagoda! Now Yagoda was confessing that all along he too had been a diversionist-wrecker-saboteur, spy mad dog, and murderer of innocent Soviet citizens.

And in 1939, Stalin, Malenkov, Molotov, and Beria arranged for Yezhov's execution for having, under their orders, murdered so many innocent people. Beria was now "the shining sword of the revolution."

Beria had risen fast. First he had tormented Georgia, Azerbaijan, Armenia, and the other peoples of Transcaucasia. He was made boss of all Transcaucasia.

Then his reputation became nationwide when he showed that a Chekist [member of Cheka, first Soviet political police (1917–1922)] can rewrite the history of the past with the aid of a pistol in place of a pen. His first masterpiece thus written with a pistol was *Stalin's Early Activities in Transcaucasia.* Stalin was so pleased that he promoted Beria to all-union police chief, and employed the same methods in writing the *Short Course in the History of the Communist Party.*

Beria was made a marshal by Stalin. He was put in charge of international espionage on atomic weapons and domestic experiment with and production of atomic energy. He promised amnesties. Gentler nationalities' treatment. A more benign penal code. A spot remover for the bloodstains on his shirt.

And now? Now it turns out that Beria was an enemy of the people, an agent of a foreign power, a foul traitor, a murderer of innocent people. Not only now, but all along when he was helping Yagoda and Yezhov, Malenkov and Molotov, and Stalin to build the forced-labor camps, to construct the great slave-labor canals, to confess and imprison and execute innocent people.

Thus for over a quarter of a century, a great nation of 200,000,000 people has been at the mercy of three brutal apostles of terror, three men with the mark of Cain on their foreheads, three bloody, brutal, criminal, unscrupulous adventurers. Their own government proclaims it.

Malenkov, who was nominated by Beria as premier, and who nominated Beria as first deputy premier, himself proclaims it. Malenkov, who in Stalin's secretariat, behind the scenes, helped to plan the trials, the purges, the enslavements—now proclaims the eternal guilt of his close associate and comrade in arms, Lavrenti Beria.

What shall we think of a government that for three decades has been terrorizing with the aid of three criminal executioners of the innocent? And is now ruled by their closest associates?

Is this the wave of the future? Is this the image of the "higher democracy?" Is this the peace that prevails at home in the "camp of peace?" Is this the glorious dream of socialism and the road to "full communism?"

Beria has died ignominiously, in the same cellar by the same pistol, the same charges, and confessions as he used on so many. None will shed a tear. Yagoda is dead. Yezhov is dead. Beria is dead. But Malenkov, Molotov, Khrushchev, the men who worked so closely with him, and Kruglov, the man who carried out the great slave canal constructions under him will carry on his work.

How long will a great people continue to be at the mercy of this tyranny that in its official acts and communiqués depicts itself as so ruthless and unjust and bloody? How soon will the day come of which it has been written: They That Take the Sword Shall Perish by the Sword? Already in this amazing "collective leadership" each man's hand is against his brother's. Surely the day must come at last when the great Russian people and all the peoples of the Soviet Union shall once more get control of their destinies and create a government that is severely limited in its powers and responsible to the will of a great and free people.

December 24, 1953

Free Elections in the Soviet Empire

As the year 1953 comes to an end, the government of West Berlin has announced the number of East Germans who have "voted with their feet" during the past year, and fled from East Germany to the haven of West Berlin. The figures are eloquent of the strange times in which we live. Three hundred forty thousand East Germans have abandoned the homes of a lifetime, left their worldly goods behind, since even a suitcase would arouse suspicion, and have elected the uncertainties of a refugee's existence rather than remain in the communistic paradise of East Germany.

Each of the 340,000 has an individual tale to tell, but personal stories, personal sufferings, personal motives are submerged when the statistics run into the hundreds of thousands. Nor can statistics show the number who tried to escape and were caught by the police, snagged in barbed wire, shot crossing a wasteland belt.

The 340,000 East Germans who escaped in 1953 are more than double the 148,000 who escaped the year before. Two hundred eighty thousand of those who escaped during the past year did so prior to the insurrections of June 17. And even though the police measures and barbed wire were multiplied after June 17, each month still saw some 10,000 East Germans who managed to "vote with their feet" against communist tyranny and oppression.

Strangest of all the figures in the cold statistical report is the news that 4,700 members of the East German People's Police were among those who escaped to freedom! This helps to explain why barbed wire, watchtowers, guns, dogs, inspection and check points, and border guards are not enough to keep people imprisoned in the vast prison that the Soviet occupation and its communist puppets have been making of East Germany. How often have the police looked the other way—feeling a glow of sympathy in their hearts as they watched men and women trying to escape—thinking of the time when they too would renounce their supposedly privileged positions and flee?

All around the vast perimeter of the Soviet Empire, each day the same type of election takes place. In no other place is it as easy as Germany. In East Germany, if you have once broken through the iron ring around East Berlin, the trip to the West is comparatively simple. But all around the rest of the Soviet Empire, the Soviet and satellite police have created an artificial wasteland to prevent ingress into or egress from the Soviet paradise.

The wasteland is a belt of soil from which all inhabitants have been ousted, all trees uprooted, the soil ploughed up fresh so that every footprint will show, the whole surrounded by barbed wire entanglements, with, at fixed intervals, watchtower redoubts; in some places land mines, in others, electrified wire; along the whole frontier guards, guns, fierce dogs.

Thus the whole of the Soviet Empire is converted into a vast concentration camp from which none may leave except on an official mission with an official pass. Yet, somehow, between the mines and the wires men crawl. Under the earth men tunnel. Through the roadblocks they break with trucks going at full speed. Locomotives are driven with throttle wide open past the barrier at the end of the line. Men tunnel under. Men fly over. Men put to the open sea in tiny skiffs; leap from Soviet or satellite ships in foreign harbors. Every known means of locomotion, and every feat of human daring and human ingenuity have been put to use in this effort to escape.

Thus the Soviet Union and its satellites know two kinds of elections. There is the rigged election in which there is only one party and everyone is driven to the polls and compelled to vote although there is nothing to vote about, no choice of candidates, parties, or platforms.

Then there is the real election, dangerous, illegal, punishable by concentration camp or death, yet a genuine election to which men sometimes are able to choose between communist slavery and the uncertain freedom of the refugee. On every frontier, in every communist land, wherever men can, they have chosen freedom. They have voted, as Lenin so well said of the Russian peasants during World War I—"they have voted with their feet."

On November 14, 1946, Andrei Vyshinsky told Committee III of the General Assembly of the United Nations that his government was demanding the return of "more than 1,200,000 refugees and displaced persons."

Since that date over 5,000,000 additional persons have escaped from Iron Curtain countries. Over two million have escaped from East Germany, where the chance to "vote" in this fashion is greatest. Over 760,000 have escaped from other subjugated satellites of the Soviet Empire in Europe. Over 1,300,000 from communist China through Shanghai and Hong Kong. From North Korea, since the Soviet occupation troops split Korea in two, more than two million have escaped to South Korea. Is this not a plebiscite as to which kind of government and what kind of world the Korean people prefer?

Finally, as in the case of the 4,000 German People's Police, there is the strange case of the Chinese "volunteers" in Korea. Here, too, the year 1953 saw the greatest free election in the history of communist China. Out of 20,720 Chinese prisoners of war held in United Nations camps when fighting ceased, 14,500 have refused to be repatriated. More than two out of every three Chinese "volunteers" have chosen freedom. When suddenly the subject of the communist total state finds the screws released, the frontier open, a chance to escape, a haven in the outside world, even if that haven be no more than a prison camp followed by the uncertainties of a refugee's fate, he "votes with his feet," and chooses freedom. Such were the great free elections of the year 1953 in the Soviet Union and its satellites.

December 31, 1953

The Arts Under Totalitarianism

I should like to distinguish between the fate of the arts under an ordinary dictatorship and under a totalitarian dictatorship. The old-style dictator limited the sphere of his interests primarily to that of political life. The arts were forbidden to attack him, and rewarded generously for flattering, serving, or pleasing him. But, for the most part, art, like other nonpolitical social activities, remained outside of the dictator's interest.

The total state, however, is distinguished by its determination to be total. It believes that the state is coextensive with society and that all social activities should be state activities.

The total state aims to infuse an overall style not only into political life, but into cultural, intellectual, emotional, aesthetic, and private life. The Soviet state concentrates in its hands not only all the means of production and distribution of material goods, but no less the means of production of spiritual goods—all presses, newspapers, magazines, books, all paper and ink, all loudspeakers, microphones, meeting halls, street corners, clubhouses, walls, all movie cameras, cinemas, montage and cutting rooms, theaters, concert halls, theatrical troupes, directors, critics, all caricatures, art galleries, all chairs, lecterns, pulpits, and, so far as it can, all love and hate, all thought and feeling, all gestation and creation, import and export of, and traffic in ideas.

It is not the artist's right to accept or reject. There is no resignation from the state's service or the calling of artist or writer, no chance to live in the interstices of society. Even the right of silence is denied. A quest for remote and neutral subjects is suspect and condemned as desertion, "internal migration," or treason. The inquisitor, himself a past master of Aesopian language, is driven by the morbid distrust of all the independent, creative, uncontrollable, unplannable and indictable, or simply incomprehensible aspects of life, to ferret out and destroy anything which may sow the tiniest seedcorn of independence or doubt. He thrusts a bayonet into the suspected mattress, looks for a false bottom in the trunk, rips up the flooring in search of the hidden, unpublishable manuscript. He is so sure that it is he which represents "posterity" that he feels justified in searching the hidden recesses of the soul for a lurking doubt, a hidden reluctance, a wayward emotion, or he puts a bullet in the base of the brain as a sure end to all refractory thoughts and moods.

There have been many zigzags in Soviet policy toward the arts, periods of severity being followed by periods of relative untightening of the screws, but the long-range trend has been toward ever-greater control and ever-greater dictation of content, mood, theme, and style.

Literature and the arts were freest in the early days of revolution, civil war, and NEP [New Economic Policy]. With the triumph of Stalinism and its forced industrialization and forced collectivization, the first drive for total dictation in the arts began with the writers geared into the class struggle and the plan and designated as "engineers of the soul."

During the great blood purges writers disappeared in droves never to reappear again. To mention only a handful of the hundreds I have recorded among the poets Erdman, Kluyev, Mayakovsky (suicide), Kornilov, Mandel'shtam, Tsvetayeva (who voluntarily returned to Russia in 1937 and hanged herself in 1941); among the novelists— Babel, Pilniak, Makarov, Tarasov-Rodionov, Tretiakov; in the theater the great director-innovator Meyerhold and his actress wife.

During the war, the fetters were loosened, and the spirit which is indestructible sprang back into more human shape. But after the war came the terrible Zhdanov drive [a campaign of ideological purification]. By the end of 1952 the rulers themselves had to recognize that all the arts, and many of the sciences, were in a profound slump. Now there is a new lurch in the zigzags, but no liberalization has ever reached the high point of the previous one.

All these zigzags have proved two things: First, that no system which aims to dominate, coordinate, predict, prescribe everything, no system which claims to know everything, to be infallible, omnipotent, and omnicompetent can tolerate the unpredictability which arises from difference, creativeness, spontaneity, that unique tension between the inner self and the outer world out of which springs something new that nobody can foresee, command, predict, and control.

And second, that man, being man, will continue under the most unfavorable circumstances to suffer, to dream, to surprise, to create, to stake his life on his conscience and his vision. Every time the screws have been relaxed even a little, the indestructible human spirit springs back into human shape.

February 11, 1954

The Wonders of a Soviet Election

Once more, the Soviet Union is going through an election campaign. The election will not take place until March 14 [1954], but since early January the press has been full of nominating meetings, committees to bring out and count the votes, names of candidates, meetings, and campaign speeches. There are no competing issues, no rival platforms, only a single list of candidates, no possible doubt about the results except whether the vote for the single list of candidates will be 99.2 percent or 99.88 percent of the total of eligible voters.

Though news may be sparse—the Soviet paper is normally only four pages—endless columns are taken up with lists of election committees from Kamchatka to Kalinin, and from Murmansk to Yerevan.

Though there is a shortage of other "consumer's goods," the country is being blanketed with millions of pamphlets. Though there is a shortage of agricultural labor, hundreds of thousands of political agitators are giving full time to the grinding out of millions of spoken and written words to inform Soviet citizens that they must vote.

Though nobody is running against anybody else, and nobody is given an opportunity to choose between alternative issues, platforms, or parties, every home is being visited and checked on, every citizen being told why he must choose the candidate which has been chosen for him and why he must go to the polls.

Though the factory workers need nothing so much as rest after a hard day's work, they are being kept in after hours to listen to agitators and campaign speeches. Though there is nothing more boring and humiliating than for grown-ups to have to pretend that there are issues when there aren't any, that there is an election when the candidates have already been elected elsewhere, though there is nothing more humiliating than that officials in power should mock men's natural longing to choose their own representatives and decide their own fate, millions of tired and bored workingmen and peasants and intellectuals and officials are compelled to go through this strange simulacrum of an election campaign for two full months of days and nights and Sundays and holidays.

Another strange feature of this strange electoral process, a feature unheard of in any democratic country, is that *Pravda* instructs its citizens that they are to speed up even more and work even harder to show their gratitude for this mockery of an election. All during the campaign, workingmen are apprised that they must joyfully double or triple their output, overfulfill their quotas, and up their norms in gratitude for being given the right to vote for the candidates selected for them.

Another object of the electoral campaign is to explain how wonderful is this system of having your candidates chosen for you and your party chosen for you, and having to listen to speeches and go to the polls even though there is no contest. Said the Crimean *Pravda:* "Deputies to the Supreme Soviet are elected on the basis of the most democratic electoral system in the world by means of general, equal, and secret balloting."

The balloting is certainly "general" since every citizen over eighteen, except those in prison, concentration camp, or insane asylum, is permitted to go, even accompanied, marshaled, and driven to the polls. Heaven help the citizen to whom it should occur to speak his mind openly and say: "I don't want to vote where there is no choice, no contest, no issue, no doubt as to the outcome, nothing and no one to choose between."

And the balloting is "equal," for all alike must go through this performance.

But one wonders what they mean when they say such a "vote" is "secret."

Since there is only one candidate, there is no secret if you vote for him. To vote against him, the voter has to go to a special booth where pencils are provided, and has to cross out the only name. He is not allowed to insert another. The only thing secret about it is how many people actually go through this brave, defiant, mortally dangerous, and—so far as results are concerned—futile gesture. The counting of the ballots is indeed secret, and the government, which has reappointed itself and forced the populace to endorse its acts, decides whether it wishes to report the magic 99.2 or 99.8 percent. As early as January 13, one day after *Pravda* issued the election orders, the youth paper, *Komsomolskaya Pravda,* sagely predicted: "There is no doubt at all that the communist party and nonparty bloc will win a new and brilliant victory at the forthcoming elections."

If this is so, and it is so, one may well ask why they trouble to hold elections at all, with its cost of millions of man-hours of the agitators and the passive listeners, and millions of rubles of newsprint, pamphlets, broadcasts, leaflets, and the like. Besides the additional excuse for hammering in the government's slogans and commands and the added excuse for speedup, there is a much deeper reason.

Though it despises the democratic system, the communist dictatorship imitates compulsively many of the processes and the very terms worked out in centuries of struggle for parliamentary democracy: the nominations, the candidates, the mass meetings, the secret ballot. For the dictators know that after centuries of struggle, modern man everywhere is filled with the longing to have the right to pick his own representatives, instruct and recall them, reject policies which he does not approve of, turn out arrogant, dictatorial, and blundering officials from office, determine his own destiny.

A French philosopher once said: "Hypocrisy is the tribute which vice pays to virtue." In the same way, these mock elections are the tribute which dictatorship pays to democracy.

More important still, a totalitarian dictatorship is aware of its perpetual illegitimacy. Deep in its heart it feels the need for some sort of show of approval of the regime and its deeds by its victims. This quest for legitimacy and the show of legality explains the rubberstamp Soviet, the elections and plebiscites that modern dictators feel obliged to stage again and again despite their ubiquitous police, and their monopoly power and their iron control over their people.

And every one must participate in the show. Not only is there no right of opposition, of real choice, of control from below. There is not even the right of abstention or silence. As Stalin himself asserted in his speech "On the Draft Constitution" in 1936: "It may be said that silence is not criticism. But that is not true. The method of keeping silence, as a special method of ignoring things, is also a form of criticism."

Therefore, though every one knows that election means select, that election means choice, that democracy means control of the officials by the people, and not the reverse, though every Soviet citizen knows that he is being mocked and participating in a mockery, still on March 14, all will go to the polls, and 99.2 or 99.8 percent will vote for the dictatorship. But the real "secret ballot" is the

choice that is deep in the heart of man. There the longing for freedom and human dignity burns as an undying flame that no
agitpunkt [the headquarters from which election materials or party
speakers are sent out] propaganda can possibly extinguish.

February 17, 1954

Letters

1953–1976

Replying to an attack by Congressman Fred E. Busbey (R.-Ill.) who accused him of still being a communist sympathizer, Wolfe summarizes his record of anticommunist activities since 1939.

August 22, 1953

To: Fred E. Busbey

Your attack on me, made on the floor of the House on August 3, came to me while on vacation in Provincetown, in the form of a brief and distorted report in the *Chicago Tribune.* I have only now secured that issue of the *Congressional Record.* I find your speech considerably stronger and more plausible seeming than I had expected. Your research worker did everything possible to make a case against me—everything but quote honestly in context, study the real development of my spirit and my work, and try to find out from it and from me what I think and am doing.

And you, following the research worker's leads, delivered a truly effective speech. To be sure, you might have gotten in touch with me first and asked me whether your research worker had painted a true picture of me and what it is I really believe. I am not one who hides behind the Fifth Amendment, or denies his past, or refuses to answer questions. In my books and articles my spirit and my thought is laid bare. Yet, I know that congressmen are busy, and your research worker with his ax carefully sharpened did a very plausible job. I have nothing to reproach you for personally except for not getting in touch with a man you were about to accuse before condemning him in such sharp, and as I shall show you here, such completely unjust and unjustified terms.

A year ago, I was told, you also attacked me. Then I was admonished that as a matter of "protocol" a State Department subordinate does not get directly in touch with a congressman, but only through our congressional liaison officer. Apparently he was incompetent, or did a bad job, or neglected it on the foolish principle of "let sleeping dogs lie," or you would not now have attacked me a second time, for

I provided him with overwhelming evidence that the first attack was unjustified. No question of "channels" or "protocol," indeed, no considerations whatsoever, can stand against a man's right to defend himself when he has been unjustly accused. Moreover, men whose judgment of figures in public life I respect, men like Ray Murphy of the State Department and Benjamin Mandel, director of research for the McCarran committee, have assured me that your anticommunism is genuine, and that you would not knowingly attack a man who is doing more effective work than perhaps any other in America to fight international communism and totalitarianism in all its forms. So I am getting in touch with you directly, with the expectation that when you have read what I write here, and examined even a fraction of the supporting material, you will right a grievous wrong which, mutual friends assure me, you would not knowingly commit.

1. *Am I a Marxian Communist?* I am neither a Marxist nor a Communist, nor have I been in any sense of either term whatsoever, for more than a decade. All my articles of recent years, which your research worker carefully kept from your attention, testify to the contrary.

    a. My article "Totalitarianism and History," delivered as a paper before the American Academy of Arts and Sciences and since published in the *Antioch Review,* is one long polemic against the Marxist certitude concerning the "inevitability" of social revolution and socialism, and a proof that whoever is so cocksure about the future, does not hesitate to violate the present and falsify the past. Thus Marxism, despite the fact that it was in Marx's day not yet implemented with the fearful implements of power, nevertheless by its doctrine of inevitability (and by other features) leads straight to totalitarianism. In that article I write among other things:

        What the totalitarian is sure of is what the rest of us are most unsure of. Historians find it hard enough to determine what really happened in the past, more difficult to apprehend what is happening in the present, and impossible to foretell the future. It is the totalitarian's certainty as to the future which makes him so ruthless in manipulating the present. To make the present conform to the inevitable future, he finds it justifiable to use force and fraud, persuasion and violence, and wage total and unending war on "all existing conditions"

(Marx and Engels: *The Communist Manifesto*), on all
classes of society, on all realms of the spirit.

And the article concludes with these words:

> Thus totalitarianism, which begins by being so sure of
> the future that in its name it declares war on all the
> existing conditions of the present, ends by making war
> on the entire past. Yet the past will not be mocked and
> takes its own peculiar revenge. It is wiser to approach
> the past with the "revolutionary" principle of the Apos-
> tle Paul: "Prove all things, and hold on to that which is
> good," than with all the slogans of Marx, Engels, Lenin,
> and Stalin.

Could any secret Marxian Communist have written that
or thought such thoughts?

b. Or could any secret Marxist or secret Communist have written such scripts as "The Moral Evil in the Communist
Idea," which depicts the international communist movement as "an organized evil which spreads cruelty and terror
throughout the world," as "immune to every form of moral
and political suasion" and which, following Reinhold
Niebuhr's book, discusses the evil of any "monopoly of
power," the evil of class dictatorship, and which contains
such sentences as

> Marxist theory wrongly assumes that economic power
> inheres solely in the *ownership* of property. It fails to
> see the power of the *manager* of property and therefore
> wrongly concludes that the socialization of property
> causes economic power to evaporate, when in actual
> fact it merely gives a single oligarchy a monopoly of
> *both economic and political power.*

Would not this single script have upset the whole tissue of
falsehood which your research worker provided against me?

c. Or could any secret Marxist or secret Communist have written my script called "The Great Blackout?" It ends with this
paragraph:

> One thing is clear, where the people have no control of
> taxation and government expenditure, there is no de-
> mocracy. Where there is no recognized opposition to de-

mand an accounting, to turn out of office, to change
governmental policies, there is no democracy. Where
there is no accounting by public officials to the citizens
on all public matters, the officials are not public ser-
vants but masters, and the citizens not citizens but
subjects or slaves. It took man centuries to fight for parliamentary institutions, for legalized opposition, for control of taxes, government budgets, government plans,
and policies. In three and a half decades the Soviet government has wiped out all of these achievements. It
calls itself a democracy—which means rule of the people, for the people, and by the people. It even calls itself
a "people's democracy," which means a people's rule of
the people. It does not account for its stewardship.
Everything it does, it does in secret. Secrecy is the
breeding ground of tyranny. Secrecy is the opposite of
democracy. Secrecy in government means that every
communist government is neither more nor less than a
conspiracy against its own people. Communism everywhere and always begins as a conspiracy against existing governments. And, wherever it manages to seize
power, it continues as a governmental conspiracy
against the people.

Mr. Busbey, is this the voice of a secret Communist? Or
is this not rather the voice of one who knows the value of
democracy and freedom, knows how to explain and defend
these values, knows how to strike hard blows on behalf of
freedom in a world where it is insidiously and openly challenged? Could you have made that speech if your research
worker had been honest enough to bring you that script? Or
indeed, any of the nearly three hundred scripts put out by
me as chief of the Ideological Advisory Staff, or the hundreds more inspired by me and written by other writers?

2. *Am I an enemy of free society and republic form of government
and a Marxian disciple of proletarian dictatorship?* I am a be-
liever in freedom, recognized wherever men fight to defend their
freedom or to regain it, as one of their most effective champions.
I am opposed to all dictatorships, proletarian or otherwise. My
writings abound in proofs that under modern conditions dictatorships tend to be total, that the proletariat and peasantry and intellectuals and men and women of all classes suffer alike under the
so-called proletarian dictatorship.

. . . Examine for yourself . . . *Three Who Made a Revolution.* Or examine my broadcast scripts for the Voice of America, something which your researcher dared not do, or dared not to report to you on, for every one of them is a blow struck against dictatorship and for the defense of the free world and our own society and institutions. Instead he chose to quote unfairly from articles written when I was in the slow and painful process of breaking with communism, and ignore those that represent my present thought and spirit. . . .

. . . I should like to add that I am not a Socialist, democratic or otherwise, and that I think that the socialization of all industry tends to put political and economic power in the same hands and therefore, even in countries with democratic institutions and traditions and in the hands of men who believe in democracy, contains within it a totalitarian danger. . .

4. *Has my presence in the Voice of America been a help or a hindrance to its work?* . . . Here I want to detail only a few of the campaigns which I initiated and carried through.

   a. *The United Nations investigation on forced labor.* Almost as soon as I entered on duty, I learned that the Soviet bloc, which had been boycotting the Economic and Social Council, had suddenly decided to send its big guns to Santiago, Chile, because they hoped to blast us out of Latin America. To meet this threat, I personally gathered and photostated hundreds of Soviet documents on forced labor in the Soviet Union. I sent to our delegation in Santiago photos showing the seal of the Soviet government, translations, a summary of the high points on which they could base their speeches . . . The neutralists, like India, Burma, Indonesia, who had always thought that "slave labor" was nothing but a propaganda catchword of ours in the Cold War, were so impressed that the vote was unanimous for a worldwide investigation, except for Russia, Poland, and Czechoslovakia . . . [N]ow, after two years, the "workers' paradise" stands convicted before the world as a vast concentration camp behind barbed wire. At this moment we are extending the indictment to China and the Iron Curtain satellites of Europe.

   b. *The Katyn forest murders.* Immediately after entering on duty, I asked my superiors for the right to rectify the grievous wrong we had done on this issue as a result of wartime expediency or grand alliance illusions. I had written the true story of the Katyn forest murders as early as 1944 . . .

c. *Agrarian reform*. The Soviet Union was improperly posing as the apostle of agrarian reform . . . On my entrance on duty, I began a series which argues that the most reactionary agrarian system in the modern world was that of a Soviet Russia with its driving of the peasants into state serfdom and that the country most needing an agrarian revolution was precisely the Soviet Union. Our Yugoslav desk, which was limited in its direct attacks on Tito by considerations of policy, found this series no less useful in encouraging the peasants who were resisting forced collectivization there as elsewhere.

d. *Who's the imperialist?* I found the Soviet Union posing as the champion of antiimperialism and national self-determination, although it had taken freedom away from 800,000,000 people. I began a bombardment on the question: "Who's the imperialist?" which has placed the initiative where it belongs—with us.

Here I must break off, and ask your pardon for having written at such length. But your attack was lengthy . . . and it is always easier to attack than to present a documented defense.

Congressman Busbey, after you have read this far, and looked at even a fraction of the supporting material, you must realize that your research worker did a dishonest job, that you have done me a grave injustice . . .

I am going to ask you, after you have studied this material, to make amends in the *Congressional Record* for the injustice that you did me. I know that it is a lot to ask of a public figure. I know that few men in public life are big enough to acknowledge and correct an error . . . Be that as it may, I am asking you to be big enough to acknowledge that you have struck out at one who is easy to hit because he is a former Communist, but that you have been unjust to his present views and present work. It is a lot to ask, but I have a right to ask it, and I do ask it. I await your reply.

*During the 1950s Wolfe evaluated book manu-
scripts about Soviet Russia for American publishers. Along with his friend Boris Souvarine in Paris,
he played a key role in exposing bogus manuscripts that purported to be accounts of life in the
Soviet Union: for example, the memoirs of Stalin's
ex-bodyguard or the secret diaries of senior Soviet
diplomat Maxim Litvinov that actually were fanci-
ful inventions. In this 1952 memo Wolfe explains
the harm these forgeries produce.*

[undated, 1952]

THE FORGING OF SOVIETICA

The production of false reminiscences and inside stories concerning
the Soviet Union is growing into a big and sinister industry. In the
course of my work I am consistently consulted by publishers who
have been offered a manuscript, already published in France and
sometimes in Germany and England, purporting to be the revelations
of some Soviet escapee, or the memoirs of a deceased Soviet person-
age. I have already convinced a given publisher that he should reject
a particular manuscript, but the vendors are persistent and sooner or
later the manuscript may find a publisher who does not consult experts, or who consults the wrong type of expert who does not recognize the forgery for what it is. On the whole, a small group of us
have managed to keep the American publishing world free from
most of these forgeries, but the French market is flooded and thor-
oughly corrupted by them, and to a lesser extent the German and
English publishers are falling for them, and this serves as a creden-
tial to American publishers as well for many a piece of falsehood. In
the French market so many such works have appeared that by a kind
of Gresham's Law the inferior boulevard revelations are destroying
the market for serious scholarly works and genuine memoirs . . .

It is significant that all of these works . . . contain some impudent
invention which makes it easy for the communist press to carry on a

campaign against all revelations as to what goes on inside the Soviet Union. They are used to show the unreliability of all noncommunist works on these subjects.

Also each of these works shows Stalin or the regime in a favorable light. They contain enough "critical" material to lay a claim to objectivity and then manage to make Stalin appear like a good husband, a good father, a good Georgian, a good bourgeois, a good companion for croquet, a good man to dogs and children, a good gourmet, or something else intended to humanize and normalize the total state and its dictator. Thus they manage both to discredit serious studies and insinuate apologetics at the same time.

———————————◆◆———————————

In the New York Herald-Tribune, *January 25, 1952, Wolfe reviewed* Stalin, *by Nikolaus Basseches, a biography that the publisher, E.P. Dutton, hailed as objective and dispassionate. Many reviewers accepted the book on those terms, but Wolfe attacked it sharply: "Mr. Basseches has written a work of pseudocritical apologetics with just enough of an air of critical independence in secondary matters to facilitate its apologia in all major questions." Apart from disclosing egregious errors, Wolfe quoted from the book: "An inquiry into the facts supplies no evidence that Stalin is more vengeful than other people . . . The proof: He did nothing to interfere with [General Mikhail] Tukhachevsky's career"; Wolfe's retort: "He merely shot him!" His review concluded:*

What troubles me is not that the Basseches book presents a case for Stalinism. On the contrary, reputable publishers would serve a real purpose if they published key works of Stalinism, as they did when they published Hitler's *Mein Kampf.* But the defenseless American

reader is entitled to protection from such care-
less improvisation and concealed apologetics
sailing under the false flag of "objectivity."

*Herbert A. Philbrick, a former Communist, con-
gratulated Wolfe on his incisive review. Wolfe's reply follows:*

February 2, 1953

To: Herbert A. Philbrick

It was good of you to send me your encouraging letter, together with
the copies of your letters to Irita [Van Doren, book review editor for
the *New York Herald-Tribune*] and the publisher. As a matter of fact,
Irita was rather worried about my review because other reviewers
were so feeble in their criticisms that it suggests that they read only
the jacket or that they suffer from the academic notion that all
serious-looking books must be taken seriously. Harry Schwarz [re-
viewer for the *New York Times*] made some mild strictures, and Phil
Mosely [a reviewer from Columbia University] was shamefully con-
ciliatory in his few expressions of difference with the book.

What is particularly shocking is that Dutton has an anti-Bolshevik
Russian as their Russian expert, Nicholas Wreden, who is supposed
to read all books dealing with Russia and who is also a big figure in
the Russian publishing house of the Ford Foundation. I imagine my
review gave them enough of a headache even before you wrote your
letter. I hope they are doing some self-examination as to what they
accept for publication and what they put on their jackets and in
their ads. Both jacket and ads boosted this [book] as "objective."

——————◆•◆——————

Wolfe wrote to the New York Times *to protest Harrison Salisbury's biased reporting about Russia.*

March 10, 1953

To: The Editor

Many of us who admire the *New York Times* as a great newspaper are deeply upset by its violation of its own editorial standards in connection with the Salisbury stories now coming from Moscow. Whatever the pros and cons of the idea of having a man in Moscow sending stories by grace of the censors, surely the *New York Times* does not have to let down its standards so far as to permit him to editorialize in ways which are insulting to the Russian people and to the intelligent reader.

In his report on the funeral orations he wrote: "Mr. Malenkov and his comrades at arms appeared to have the *support* and *enthusiasm* of Soviet citizens of all walks of life . . . The words of Mr. Malenkov seemed to have sent *a surge of hope* through the Soviet listeners" (emphasis mine).

Actually the core of the funeral oration of Mr. Malenkov reads: "We must train the Communists and all working people in the spirit of high political vigilance, of intolerance and firmness in the struggle against internal, inner and the foreign enemies."

That means to the Soviet people that the new government is determined to continue its war on its own people ("struggle against internal, inner enemies") and on other peoples ("the foreign enemies"). What reason for hope can the Soviet people take from such an address? If that is the way Mr. Salisbury wants to speak on behalf of the poor, voiceless Russian people, it is for the *New York Times* to consider whether he is useful as a newspaper correspondent, or at least there should be a blue pencil or a thick lead black pencil available in Times Square to cut out unwarranted editorializing in his stories as the *Times* would in any other reporter's.

———————◆◆———————

*Wolfe was asked by an official of the Museum of
Modern Art if it was true that Stalin, at a meeting
in Moscow of the International, passed the order
along to "create confusion in art and literature,
promote the juvenile, the primitive and the insane, and to further the perverted and the aber-
rant." Wolfe replied:*

December 6, 1955

To: Alfred H. Barr, Jr.

It is obviously one of a series of apocryphal quotations invented by
impudent persons and then quoted and footnoted until it begins to
acquire the air of scholarly authenticity. It is of a piece with the
alleged Lenin quotation "We must force America to spend herself
into exhaustion" about which Herbert Hoover among others queried
me. And the American Medical Association's query when and where
Lenin said "The road to communism is through socialized medicine." Except that it is more impudent, more alien to the spirit of
the author, and has more evil intention than most. I have received
so many queries on such apocrypha that I finally devised a form
letter answer which ended with the affirmation that the quote in
question was manifestly the work of that famous Italian writer
Senone, whose full name is *se non é vero, é ben trovato* (if it is not
true, it is well-founded).

Except that this one isn't even *ben trovato.*

———————◆◆———————

Wolfe gave the following speech in New York before the Tamiment Institute public forum.

IS COEXISTENCE POSSIBLE?

April 14, 1955

Peaceful coexistence is not one word, as one of our speakers suggested, but it is two words in one. As a combination, it has a meaning, a purpose, and a history.

I think I can best contribute to this discussion tonight by questioning the very title which introduced it. The term *peaceful coexistence* comes from the infected lexicon of "Newspeak," that language in which dictatorship is called democracy, permanent purge is called collective leadership, war is called peace, conquest is called liberation, and freedom is called slavery. It was invented and offered to the world as a nostrum, a semantic poison. In it, there is no thought of peace.

The term was coined by men of power and of unending war who have dedicated not their spare moments but their entire lives to the waging of that war and that conquest of power, dedicated themselves to class war, to civil war, to revolutionary war, to colonial war, to imperialist war, to war of conquest, to war of enslavement, all under the name of liberation and carried forward on the bayonets of the Red Army.

Totalitarianism is inseparable from war. And all its days it wages war of two kinds at once. And each of them aims to be total.

The first war is the unremitting war of the Kremlin upon its own people. That war is literal war. A war of nerves, a war of propaganda, a war of closed borders so that none may escape. A war of universal espionage, of systematic detention, of speedup, of purges, of slave camps, of a bullet in the base of the brain. It is a real war, endless and unremitting, that the totalitarian system wages upon its own people.

The other war is a war to extend that system until it has conquered the world. From Lenin to Khrushchev, the canonical writings form a *Mein Kampf* for all our statesmen and our leaders to study, if they care to study. And always it makes clear, despite the occasional peace dove which is launched for a special effect, always it makes clear its nature and its purpose.

The aim of the first of these two wars is the impious one of playing God to man, remaking man's image according to an arbitrary and, I must say having studied it, a miserable plan. It aims to conquer the spirit of man and to make him into something called the new Soviet man; to break his spirit apart and put it together again according to the wisdom and the plan of a Joseph Stalin or a Khrushchev.

The aim of the second war is to conquer the world for Moscow, or, more precisely, for its ruling faction. Both wars are total, both wars are real. Each of them may change in its intensity "according to the calculation of forces"—the words are quoted—"of the moment," may change its tactics, its slogans, its methods, but never its long-range strategy or its purpose.

Both wars, in my humble and hopeful opinion, are doomed to failure in the long run because they mistake the nature of man. But both are serious; both are fraught with mortal danger, and both aim at total conquest and unconditional surrender.

In their war on their own people, it is not enough for the people to give obedience, bow the head, hold the tongue, serve the state. They must cheer when ordered to cheer, love whom they are ordered to love, betray whom they are ordered to betray, and hate whom they are ordered to hate. It is not enough even to have made the revolution—to have been a Communist—to have been an old Bolshevik, as the deaths of Trotsky, Bukharin, Zinoviev, Kamenev have so frighteningly made clear. It is not enough even to have murdered at the behest of your superiors for the greater glory of the state—as the deaths of Yagoda, Yezhov, and Beria make no less clear. And in their war on other peoples, it is not sufficient to accept sincerely the siren song of peaceful coexistence. Ask Lithuania, ask Latvia, ask Estonia, ask Poland, ask Benes, ask Masaryk, Mikolajczyk, Maniu, Dmitrov, Petkov, or Pfeiffer.

It is not enough to have been a devoted Communist, or even to have set up a communist government in your own country. Ask Tito. Unless you are a Moscow puppet, and have guessed right as to who will be the top dog in the perpetual brutal struggle for power inside the Kremlin, you are doomed to destruction. Ask Kostov, ask Slansky, ask Chen Du-hsiu, ask Kao-kang.

No, both these wars are as capricious and as cruel as they are terrible, unremitting, and total. "Peaceful coexistence" then is a nostrum for semantic poisoning, a tactical maneuver conceived as a means of stopping you when you are strong enough to move forward, a means of encouraging you to enter a trap to be sprung later, a means of conquering by infiltration and flank attack, when the defenses are too strong for direct assault, a means of dividing when the intended victims are too united, a Trojan horse for which the walls are to be breached so that it may be taken inside the walls full of armed men.

Peaceful coexistence in short has a history, a history which we can ignore only at our peril.

From the outset, Lenin was a man of war and a man of power. Before 1914 he wanted the Balkan Wars to be extended to embrace his own country, because—and I quote—"It would be useful for the revolution." During the war he detested those who worked for peace, and fought them. He wanted the war to be extended and converted into his kind of war, a civil war which was to continue in all lands until all lands were conquered. He first talked peace only because he could not conquer his own people. He could not take power without it, but he and his successors have given his people no peace.

He next talked peace to a war-weary world appealing to peoples against their governments because he thought that this was the way to protect his own power and spread his revolution. Later he used the term "to sow division" to soften up for future conquest. But always his talk of peace and that of his successors has been double-talk, Newspeak, semantic poison.

The first to invent the term *peaceful coexistence*—the poor devil never gets any credit for anything—was Leon Trotsky. "Our peace program," he said on November 23, 1917, "formulates the burning aspirations of millions. We desire the speediest peace on principles of honorable coexistence" (honorable must have been a Trotskyite deviation because I have never seen it since), "the speediest peace on the principles of honorable coexistence and cooperation of people. We desire the speediest possible overthrow of the domination of capital." Those are two linked sentences. No dots between them.

The year Lenin took up the term and used it on a Hearst correspondent, that same year he told the meeting of cell secretaries that the co-existence of the two systems for any length of time was impossible; that clashes between them were inevitable, terrible clashes ending in the victory of one side over the other.

Stalin, to do him justice, has faithfully continued, developed, and enriched, and made much trickier and if anything more ruthless, this invention of Lenin and Trotsky. Stalin's successors have so far been only faithful disciples; they have made no visible changes or improvements.

The only thing that one can find that is new and distressing about this third of a century of juggling with "peaceful coexistence" is that the leading spokesmen of the free world are beginning to employ the term without an adequate attempt to analyze its history and purify it of the corruption which infects it.

If I were in the Kremlin, I would award a special Stalin prize to that American political leader who first coined the irresponsible and thoughtless phrase—"the alternative is either peaceful coexistence or no existence."

To close, I want to cite a better day for illusions about this term than is the present: the day of Maxim Litvinov. Those days begin with Litvinov offering his neighbors and the world a proposal to scale down armaments. At the same moment, the Reichswehr and the Red Army were in secret agreement to produce inside Russia planes, tanks, shells, poison gas, ships, for the use of both armies. That's the beginning of the Litvinov period. And toward the end, when the world was drunk with Litvinov's rhetoric and slogans, in the League of Nations a delegate, not just any delegate, the delegate of the Republic of Spain, a member of the International Executive Committee of the Congress for Cultural Freedom, Salvador Madariaga, made the following *Animal Farm* description of Litvinov's proposals:

> A conference of beasts once discussed the question of disarmament. The lion spoke first. Looking at the eagle, he suggested the abolition of wings. The eagle, turning to the bull, asked for the suppression of horns. The bull in turn regarded the tiger and demanded the elimination of claws.
>
> It remained only for the bear to speak. He proposed total abolition of every means of attack and defense so that he might take all the animals into his loving embrace.

*Manes Sperber, an old friend and a leading writer
and book editor in Paris, wrote to Wolfe that he
had stopped making predictions about the world
because irrational elements make sound predictions impossible. Wolfe disagreed:*

January 14, 1956

To: Manes Sperber

Your invention of a Jewish way of answering letters is a good one:
thinking what you would say if you wrote, and then wondering why
the recipient doesn't get it . . . how often have I written thus. But
this time I must somehow be more formal.

. . . I do not accept your lamentable alibi that because you have
been arrogant in prediction, or guessed wrong, that it excuses you
from trying to learn from the past, understand the present, and make
the best guesses you can about the immediate future. Just because
you don't want to think à la Hegel is no excuse for giving up thinking. Your example of trying to predict how Hitler would act on the
logistics of moving old people to crematoria is a perfect example of
how not to understand totalitarianism, its dynamics, or the rationale
of its irrationalism. You projected a reasonable man into Hitler's
head, and therefore came to a conclusion which Hitler could not
have come to in a million years of trying to think with a Jewish *kopf*
[head]. But irrational processes can be studied by rational people provided they do not project their rational selves into the situation.
Freudianism is based on that recognition. Any study of Soviet purges
or zigzags must be based on the same recognition. The problem is to
study the irrational rationale of the irrational, to learn its dynamics
from its previous behavior patterns, not to give up trying to understand, foresee, and cope with it. There is a pattern to the lunacy of
the lunatic, and there is a pattern to the dynamics of the totalist
state. Never is there a certainty, but in each zig and zag, the man
who studies attentively the whole previous pattern is able to foresee
better than the man who projects his reason and goodwill into the

situation, or the man who abdicates his reason altogether. The future is always open and always uncertain, nevertheless that is saying so little that it amounts to an easy nothing. It is a mere pride of humility ("look how much I know by knowing enough to know that I don't, can't, know anything"). Our reason is not given to us "to fust in us unused" but to use on the irrational and peer with our myopic eyes as best we can a little way into the past and a little way into the future. Actually you will be pleasantly surprised how much a reasonable man can learn about an unreasonable world and an irrational process if he combines humility with hard work in place of making a nihilistic banner of it.

Hubert H. Humphrey, chairman of the Senate Sub-committee on Disarmament, asked Wolfe for his views on the Soviet attitude toward control and reduction of armaments. Wolfe's reply follows:

December 17, 1956

To: Senator Hubert H. Humphrey

... 1. The leaders of the Soviet Union are set on winning the world for their system, and their dogma teaches them that the ultimate victory of communism is "scientifically demonstrated and inevitable." This does not allow room in their day-to-day thinking for the idea that mankind may destroy itself utterly. Their dogma teaches them that not mankind but capitalism will be destroyed in a future war, or by limited and partial wars and struggles and gradual erosion. As recently as on their visit to England during the past year, they threatened their hosts in public banquet speeches with the few minutes that would elapse between the launching of rockets and supersonic bombers from their bases and the destruction of England. Of all their public utterances on this question the only one that I know of (that of Malenkov) spoke of the possible destruction of mankind without regard to class or system, and that was later specifically repudiated by Molotov, and implied by Khrushchev and [Nikolai] Bulganin. That they are willing to destroy an entire economy and a people in order to make their system prevail is now being demonstrated in Hungary. The "system" has come to mean to them not a certain level of productivity or well-being but a total statification [sic] of industry, agriculture, political power, culture, force, a total control best designated as totalitarianism. This can prevail in a ruined country as well as one with a going economy—at least that is their outlook, and, as far as we can judge by their actions, in the war for the victory of their system they can take economic ruin and mass annihilation in their stride.

2. If they have private second thoughts on this matter, they hide them from their own consciousness, and especially from each other, for it would be a sign of "softness," of unfitness for communist leadership, a sign of a willingness to consider questions "classlessly," involving an agreement to permit the dying capitalist system to live indefinitely in defiance of the "laws of science and history."

3. In their peace campaigns and peace societies in the free world, they are delighted to spread the ideas that the use of atomic weapons, or, indeed, the breakout of a general war, would mean the destruction of mankind. This is a species of valuable blackmail in their eyes, for if the free world lets them cut to pieces first Hungary, then perhaps Poland, or Germany, penetrate and take control of the Middle East, and is afraid to draw the line anywhere lest that might entail all-out war and "the end of civilization as we know it," then they can continue to feel out the weak spots, nibble off piece by piece, conquer and slaughter single peoples, enlarge their controlled area through little wars, civil wars, "punitive expeditions to prevent the recurrence of fascism," etc., and thus further the "historical process" unhindered by nothing more than resolutions and protests. And even these will gradually diminish for neighbors like Finland, knowing that they are unprotected, will prefer to abstain from protest lest they too be locally "rescued from fascism and reaction."

4. They cannot allow free inspection of their world by our inspectors, or of our world by their people, and that for two reasons:

> *1st.* The myth of the superiority of their system is maintained only by not letting the free world get a good look at how it works and not letting their people get a good look at the rest of the world.

> *2nd.* A land which makes even economic facts into state secrets and is dotted with concentration camps and secretive preparations for war cannot permit general inspection.

Yet, if our nerves grow weak, if our negotiators tire of endless repetition of the few elementary things we must forever repeat, then we will settle for pseudoinspection, and be deceived, and deserve to be deceived.

They do not get tired of repetition or of finding new dress for the same old proposals. If we are eager not to prove intractable, they will consider it a sign of the weakness of a doomed order and take advantage of it. Our negotiations from Yalta to Potsdam, and in the tents of Panmunjon, should have taught us that. We have to make up our minds on a few fundamentals: is the insistence on a safe, genuine, enduring peace worth clinging to, no matter if it takes decades and as yet unforeseen occurrences before it is realized? Or shall we settle for a false peace, under the cover of which the drive for world conquest is relentlessly continued? Is "disarmament" without as foolproof an inspection system as can be devised not a snare to be avoided as a plague?

5. To remain forever on guard as long as there is danger may seem intolerable, but its only alternative is to be off guard. It is fashionable to talk of the "lessening of tension," tension being a word with bad connotations of which they are quick to take advantage. But if we translate the word *tension* out of their jargon into its real meaning: "concern"—then it becomes clear that we must cling to our concern (cling to our "tension") as long as there is good reason to be concerned with the fate of peoples and of freedom. What our negotiators need is clear heads, steady nerves, an ability to distinguish between fundamentals and the trivia of protocol and face, and to cling,

for weeks, for months, for years, for decades, if necessary, to those fundamentals.

6. Actually, their system is not as mighty as it looks for it involves unending war on their own people as well as an unending effort to win the world. Even the death of a dictator weakens this inhuman "monolith" as East Germany, Pilsen, Verkuta, Poznán, Warsaw, and Budapest [scenes of uprisings against communist or Soviet rule] have shown. Our task is to make forever clear that we know how to distinguish between the enslaved peoples and their rulers, for they are the first victims of the totalitarian communist system. In our negotiations with the tyrant, it is necessary always to watch that we do not strengthen his hand against his domestic victims.

   You ask what changes are necessary in the Soviet system before we can make genuine agreements to try to avoid war? I can only answer: When the rulers of the totalist state make peace with their own peoples, then and then only will they be able to make peace with other peoples. But that involves a tolerance of man's diversity and right to freedom which is alien to their dogma and their system. Poland and Hungary, no less than Korea and the Berlin airlift, show that they tolerate what they are forced to tolerate, and only as far as they think they are forced to tolerate it.

7. In the proposal to withdraw part and later all of our troops from Western Europe in return for the Russian withdrawal of part, and later all of their troops from their satellites, there is a double trap. On the one hand, our withdrawal would be overseas and theirs only a few hundred land miles. On the other, they have already shown, in their negotiations with Hungary, how swiftly they will ignore any promise if their power is threatened. If the satellites could be held down by puppet armies alone (an impossibility), they would keep out their troops. But if not, they would send them back in a matter of hours, or use auxiliary troops of one satellite against another.

8. Finally . . . I should like to call the attention of the subcommittee . . . to my remarks on peaceful coexistence on pp. 10, 12, 44–58, and 83 of my recent book entitled *Khrushchev and Stalin's Ghost.*

*Writing to historian Karl August Wittfogel in
1959, Wolfe noted his growing pessimism about
the future and his disappointment with Western
leaders:*

March 21, 1959

To: Karl August Wittfogel

I am not in a cheerful mood about the state of the world. I push
against the current, with a few other determined swimmers like
yourself but have an inescapable feeling of being swept downstream,
in good company. I write my "The Enemy We Face." I even get it
published [*The New Leader*, January 26, 1959]. I get scores of letters
and telephone calls. The *Saturday Evening Post* quotes from it in its
main editorial (March 21, 6,000,000 paid circulation), but the traces
are washed away with the first tide (there are tides every day) like
writing on the sand. [Harold] Macmillan presses [Dwight D.]
Eisenhower—as if he needs pressing! [Erich] Ollenhauer presses [Kon-
rad] Adenauer. Khrushchev presses them all, and even metastatic can-
cer is on his side. What kind of leader of the world is it who tells a
press conference (his latest): "Whether I *like it or not*, the Constitution makes me responsible for the conduct of our foreign policy"
([Eisenhower], quoted by Richard Rovere in his article on the press
conference in the *New Yorker*).

—————————◆•◆—————————

*A reader in Canada observed, "Since the commu-
nist party not only controls pretty effectively the
output of historical studies but I imagine has
pretty well cleared the records of the past of
sources that do not confirm their interpretation of
events of the past 40 years, it seems a somewhat
discouraging prospect for any one who tries to get
at the other side of the picture . . . I was wondering whether you have any thoughts on how a person would go about correcting this one-sided
view." Wolfe replied:*

March 21, 1959

To: Stuart R. Tompkins

The question you raise is an extremely serious one. Already I find
that the clichés of communist analysis because of their insistent and
uncontested reiteration are accepted as analytical tools by countless
writers who do not agree with their aims. There are historians for
whom a document which provides a footnote is "documentation." I
found a professor who teaches Soviet economy at one of our great
universities who did not even know that there was a rapid period of
industrialization in the 90s and first decade and a half of the twentieth century which ought to be compared with the tempo of the first
five-year plans to get a perspective on the latter. Most teachers and
almost all students in Russian-area studies speak of Lenin's and Stalin's and Khrushchev's views as "Marxism" without knowing what
Marx himself thought and said. Lenin's theory of imperialism is
called *the Marxist theory* although Marx used the word *imperialism*
only once, to describe the empire of Napoleon III, and thought of the
colonial penetration of Asia by Europe as an enormous "progressive"
process waking them from their "millennial slumber." In short, for
most specialists and their students now in this field, history begins
in 1917.

The odds against the presentation and acceptance of a truer picture are great, but the task is not altogether impossible. The official truths, published in millions of copies, can be compared with yesterday's official truths so that Bolshevik historiography itself may thus throw some light. Then there are the truths of the defeated, hard to come by (the victors write history) in obscure books and pamphlets and journals, scattered over the earth—Mensheviks, Social Revolutionaries, liberals like [Paul] Miliukov and [Michael] Karpovich [historians]. They, too, must be discounted by virtue of their partisanship, but less so, and by collating all the successive and contradictory versions one can often get at the truth, or at least demonstrate the possibilities and keep one's own and the reader's mind open. That is what I meant by saying in my *Three Who Made a Revolution* that one has to use the "archaeological method on a living civilization which is nevertheless buried under successive layers of falsification." There is material, in the Hoover Library, in the Slavonic Division of the Fifth Avenue Library in New York, in the Library of Congress, in certain great European libraries, but one has to spend endless time and energy searching for and stumbling over it, and then evaluating it. That is why I took ten years on *Three Who Made a Revolution* and am taking longer still on the second volume. I have been busy with the work of excavating, restoring, and trying to determine which of the seven Troys is the Homeric one.

————————◆•◆————————

Junius Irving Scales, indicted under the Smith Act
of conspiracy to overthrow the U.S. government,
broke with communism after Khrushchev's de-
Stalinization speech in 1956. Wolfe wrote to Ar-
thur M. Schlesinger, Jr., an aide to President John
F. Kennedy, urging a presidential pardon for
Scales.

February 21, 1962

To: Arthur M. Schlesinger, Jr.

I am sending you a copy of the letter I just sent to President Kennedy. I do not have to tell you personally how important it is to greet openheartedly and with rejoicing any Communist who has reconsidered his views and, having become aware of the brutality of totalitarian communism, rejects it. I hope you will do whatever is in your power to see that the judicial absurdities of the Scales case are rectified as speedily as possible—and in the most generous and dramatic form.

————————◆•◆————————

February 19, 1962

To: President John F. Kennedy

The purpose of this letter is to urge a speedy, full, and ungrudging pardon for Junius Irving Scales, a former official of the Communist Party of the United States in North Carolina, indicted under the membership clause of the Smith Act in 1954. He was subsequently convicted in 1955, but in 1956, while out on appeal, he was deeply shocked by the revelations made by Nikita Khrushchev concerning Stalin's terror and further by Khrushchev's own brutal act of suppression of the Hungarian uprising. He broke with international communism at that point, as an act of conscience, as he had enlisted in its ranks earlier, also, no doubt, as an act of conscience. The Supreme Court subsequently reversed his conviction on the grounds of error in October 1957, but the Department of Justice moved for a new trial and secured a new conviction in 1958 which was upheld by five to four, on technical grounds, as the earlier conviction had been reversed on technical grounds, neither decision taking into account the all-important fact that America should welcome all who break with communism and who show that they are not insensitive to its despotic and brutal practices once they become aware of them.

The Scales case is the more shocking to anyone who considers its human implications and its meaning for our country, since the other membership clause case of the same year, that of John F. Moto, has been reversed and he is free, although he has made no open break with communism. And it is rendered more shocking by the fact that our Department of Justice has decided that it is practically impossible to prosecute further membership cases (e.g., Claude Lightfoot). And still further does the jail sentence of six years seem unjust when it is considered that, under the "active leadership" clause, so prominent a leader as Eugene Dennis was given a lighter sentence.

I am urging upon you, Mr. President, that the pardon be swift and its language generous and stirring, so that Americans and people everywhere may know we welcome and gladly give full measure of citizenship to those who break with international communism and that we do not permit legal technicalities to keep in prison the only man who broke with communism while other technicalities or defects in the Smith Act itself cause the Department of Justice to let others, who are both more prominent in their activities and who continue in the service of our enemy, free to engage in the same activities and acts which Junius Scales now rejects and abhors.

May I ask, Mr. President, that your action be speedy, just, and generous?

When Wolfe learned that Time *was planning to produce a paperback edition of* Three Who Made a Revolution *with an introduction by Allen Dulles, director of the Central Intelligence Agency, he suggested that Dulles focus on Lenin's ideas about violence.*

October 26, 1962

To: Max Gissen, *Time* Reading Programs

. . . I am enclosing for you to send to Mr. Dulles a special study I have made of the brutality and ruthlessness of Lenin's ideas concerning the class war. The ideas are all contained in the book, scattered through its pages, but the impact is simply overwhelming when they are all brought together in a single study. His injunctions include casing banks for holdups, putting tacks under the hoofs of the mounted police, dropping boiling water (to be done by old people and little children) from the roofs of apartment houses, carrying rags caked in kerosene to start fires, etc. I am sure the study will interest Mr. Dulles . . . and think it would be desirable for him to quote the most startling sections of it in the final draft of his introduction.

Wolfe received a despairing letter from his friend
Bogdan Raditsa, a teacher of history in Ulivello,
Italy, about the seemingly losing battle of counter-
ing communist influence in Western Europe. He
replied:

February 23, 1965

To: Bogdan Raditsa

Thanks for your extremely interesting, warm, and gloomy letter. It is
always a joy to hear from you or to see you, which happens too
seldom, and the joy is not diminished by the gloom Bogdan radiates.
As a matter of fact, I have long shared your gloomy view of what we
are accomplishing by our efforts to swim against the current. I too
have been moved to something close to despair by the ignorance of
our leaders, the softening of the brain in their advisers and counsel-
ors, and the state of affairs in France and especially in Italy. The
communist world disintegrates ideologically and organizationally
and economically but our will to understand and to take advantage
of that disintegration dissolves faster. I can offer only crumbs of
comfort.

First of these is that we know which way we want to swim, and if
the stream should prove too powerful, we shall at least have the
satisfaction of keeping our heads turned upstream and being swept
away less quickly because of our effort. That, I fancy, is what the
Stoics told themselves when Rome was declining.

And second, I have lived for many years now and done my work
with three images from classic legend possessing my mind. The first
image is that of Sisyphus. I struggle and toil to push the stone up the
hill, and just as I reach the summit, Khrushchev smiles or Walter
Lippmann or whoever pronounces some orphic idiocy, and whang!
the stone rolls down again. The second image is that of Cassandra,
who had the double misfortune of foreseeing and foretelling the
truth, and not being believed by any one. The third image, Bogdan, is
Tantalus, and I identify neither you nor myself with him. When he

bends down to drink of the waters of peace, they recede leaving him as thirsty and tantalized as ever. Then we start pushing the stone again.

In any case, history is always open, so keep talking with bishops, arguing with Ulivello Communists, teaching young history students, and writing what you have to write. Whatever happens the world will be somewhat less bad for our having striven to keep it from getting worse. In the meanwhile those of us who strive have each other.

When Joseph Stalin's daughter, Svetlana Alliluyeva, sought asylum in the United States in 1967, the Palo Alto (California) Times, *Wolfe's local newspaper, published an editorial opposing her bid for asylum, in part because it came at an "awkward time [when] President [Lyndon B.] Johnson is mending fences with the Kremlin, and presumably does not want to embarrass Moscow before the eyes of the world." In protest to the editorial, Wolfe wrote:*

March 16, 1967

To: The Editor, *Palo Alto Times*

I am deeply disturbed by your editorial proposing that we should refuse the right of refuge to Svetlana Alliluyeva (Stalin).

We will not win the respect of the Soviet Union or of the world by destroying our democratic traditions. America is known in the world as a land of refuge for all who escape from tyranny. We have welcomed those who escaped from Nazi Germany, Franco Spain, Fascist Italy, communist Russia, and many other lands. We will be "mending the fences" to use your editorial's language, mending the fences of tyranny, the Berlin Wall, the wasteland belt around Russia with its border guards and watchtowers. What a field day all tyrants will have if this woman who trusted our democratic tradition is forced to return to her country. Hope will die in the breast of millions in every Iron Curtain country. Svetlana will not be punished, she will be paraded as proof that there is no longer any refuge in the world for those who escape.

You argue that she should and could have escaped while Stalin lived. Do you know that her mother died under mysterious circumstances, either at Stalin's hand or by committing suicide before his eyes? Do you think it would have been easy for Alliluyeva's daughter to escape after that unless she found some pretext for going abroad for some purpose—in this case, respect for India's sacred rite of burning the dead [Svetlana's dead husband] and casting their ashes into sacred waters—which seemed of use to the men in the Kremlin. No one gets a passport to go abroad unless the government finds it useful.

You argue that it would cost money and effort to protect her. We have received many refugees and, with the exception of [General Walter] Krivitsky, most of them are living yet or have managed to live out their days in peace and freedom and die a natural death. Even [Igor] Gouzenko, who broke the atomic spy ring for Canada and England, is living in safe anonymity.

In any case, we cannot sell what is most precious in America's heritage to placate dictatorships or save a little trouble. I beg you to reconsider your editorial stand. While we are "mending fences," let us not mend the walls of tyrants.

———————◆—◆———————

*Wolfe explains to a Jesuit priest why he regarded
the attempt by Marxist psychologist Erich Fromm
to create a humanistic "young Marx" to be spe-
cious and why the prospect of a dialogue between
Marxists and the Catholic church fills him with
gloom.*

March 7, 1967

To: William J. Monihan, S.J.

Your letter of March 4 has plunged me into gloom, and given me a
sense of the hopelessness of trying to explain why.

As a prophet, an economic or a political scientist, an interpreter
and forecaster of historical events, one hundred years of history and
economic, social and political development have left Marx's dogmas
a shambles.

Moreover, if not by his analyses and prophecies, by his fruits shall
ye know him, and the terrible experiences of the fulfillment of his
call to take power in the name of the proletariat have disillusioned
the intellectuals and humanitarians. When Fromm and Marcuse and
Horkheimer and Adorno, etc. came to America it was from the Insti-
tut für Sozialforschung, a communist institute in Frankfurt founded
by the young communist millionaire Felix Weil, who inherited his
father's millions from wheat speculation in Argentina and Germany.
When they got to America, finding the climate unfavorable for selling their product, they cast about for new devices. The first of these
was to encourage those who wanted the luxury of being anti-Fascist
without being antitotalitarian by their famous dual-standard study of
the "authoritarian personality," in which they made it seem that the
authoritarian personality might lead to Nazism or fascism, but
avoided a study of communist authoritarianism. It fitted in with the
Grand Alliance illusions of World War II. But with the war over,
Stalin's use of his occupation forces to crush democracy and set up
his puppets in all countries his armies occupied and in the eastern
half of Germany, the northern half of Korea, etc. ended that era.

The latest selling device of Fromm and his friends is to make Marx acceptable to humanists and those with whom, particularly in America, psychoanalysis is so fashionable by turning to a youthful notebook of Marx which Marx himself chose not to publish, and the very ideas of which he ridiculed so fiercely and mercilessly in attacks on Proudhon, Moses Hess, the teacher of Engels, Weitling, and the "German ideologists" and "true German socialism," and "French socialism."

One has to read and study Marx to get the feeling of *Die Geist der stets verneint,* the "annihilation by labels," the scorn for humanitarian socialism, and for the very words *justice, truth, mercy, humanity.* True, Marx is vast, amorphous, and ambiguous, so that careful selection of a few quotations, particularly from a single work or a single year, enables Lenin to quarry out his Marx, Kautsky his, Jaurès his, Stalin and Mao theirs. Erich Fromm's Marx is at best only Erich Fromm with a big bush of beard. The mature Marx, the "scientific" Marx, the Marx of 1846 to 1851, and of 1870, do not enter into his picture. Still less the Marxism of the epigones.

But to know what Marx really meant, one has to go not to the repackagers, but to the original, difficult, but in the end, clarifying, writings of Marx himself.

This brings me to the subject of my gloom. Your church is now preparing to enter into a "dialogue" with the Marxists and the Communists. As men of goodwill, you are peculiarly eager to deceive yourselves as to those with whom you discourse and concerning what the real subject of discourse is. . . . They meet your will to be deceived by their ardent will to deceive. Hence to me it seems that the outcome of the dialogue can only be an increase in confusion and loss of many of your best in the battle for men's spirits.

Since you, personally, make it clear that you are prepared to accept Fromm's repackaged damaged goods for the original article, I know I am at best wasting words and at worst offending by my frankness and my teasing remarks on the lack in your catalog of the very titles of many of Marx's works and the best of the Marxicologists.

I hope you will forgive me for this frankness, recognize that my words are well meant and not altogether ill informed, and accept this at least as my small if intrusive attempt to take part in the difficult dialogue which the church is ill prepared, and the Marxists of several varieties well prepared, to take advantage of.

And I ask you to believe that I wish your church well as one of the bulwarks of sanity in the half-mad contemporary world, as you must have felt when I defended Thomas More and Erasmus against some of your own theologians. . . .

I hope I am wrong in my idea of the way that your church and its spokesmen are preparing for this difficult dialogue with a wily and a skillful opponent.

Writing to a publisher, Wolfe explains the relationship between V. I. Lenin and Maxim Gorky as revealed in his newly completed manuscript.

March 17, 1967

To: Dan Lacy, McGraw-Hill Book Co.

. . . I have just finished *The Bridge and the Abyss: The Troubled Friendship of Maxim Gorky and V. I. Lenin.* Your inquiry comes at a good time because I am eager for early publication for several reasons.

First, 1967 is the year of the 50th anniversary of the Revolution of 1917 and November 7, the anniversary of Lenin's seizure of power. My manuscript contains Gorky's sharp attacks on Lenin's seizure of power, attacks virtually unknown in this country or elsewhere, because the Soviet government has chosen to conceal them. These attacks are very powerful and will be startling in their impact on those who have been led to believe that Gorky was a Bolshevik and little more than Lenin's official minstrel and favored literary artist. Hence, this brief book is intended as my contribution to the celebration of Lenin's seizure of power.

Second, and no less important, next year marks the 100th anniversary of the birthday of Maxim Gorky. The Soviet propaganda machine will deafen us with false accounts of what he was, what he thought and felt, and what his relations with Lenin were. I should like to even the balance somewhat by contributing a true picture of

Gorky's best years as a writer (he wrote nothing of importance after 1924) and the real nature of his warm but stormy friendship with V. I. Lenin.

The book is rather small as books go, but I have no desire to portray the pitiful spectacle of Gorky in his years of decay and of the ruthless and inhuman attempt of Joseph Stalin to utilize his declining powers for Stalin's propaganda. The friendship of Gorky and Lenin is a human one, for each valued the other, and a fascinating one because of their differences in their attitude toward the Russian people, toward Lenin's ruthless experiment, toward literature, and toward religion.

———————————◆———————————

Writing to a friend at the New York Times, *Wolfe explains why he was happy to be vilified in the Soviet press for his revelations about Gorky and Lenin.*

January 23, 1968

To: Harry Schwarz

I am enclosing a copy of a letter by a Gorky specialist on my new book which I hope you will show to your book review department in order to remind them of the important peg that March 28 represents, the centenary of Gorky's birthday, and that the Soviet presses are already crashing out a flood of unstudies concerning him. However, I planned my book to beat them by a month or so and I think it will not be lost in the flood. Incidentally, after some 40 years or so of being an unwriter, never mentioned, attacked, ridiculed, or footnoted in their journals, while everyone else from you to Sidney Hook and Fred Schuman were given at least the honor of an insult now and again, they are celebrating the 50th anniversary of the seizure of power by the silent act of rehabilitating me.

The silence concerning me was a kind of death sentence in absentia, but since for 40 years I have refused to stay dead, they have now promoted me from an unwriter to a bourgeois falsifier, a "reactionary Sovietologist who has sold his historical conscience in order to throw dirt on the 50th anniversary of the October Revolution," and as a "renegade who left the communist movement along with the CIA [Central Intelligence Agency] agent Jay Lovestone in 1929." Eight mentions of my dishonorable person have been called to my attention in as many journals during 1967. It's good to be alive again and to have been thus rehabilitated. Since you never have died, you will find it hard to appreciate the joy of resurrection.

———————————◆———————————

Professor Robert C. Tucker of Princeton University was writing a biography of Stalin and sent Wolfe an essay-review about Svetlana Alliluyeva. Wolfe disagreed with a passage on the relationship between Stalin and Lavrenti P. Beria, chief of the Soviet secret police, and whether Stalin was planning to purge Beria before Stalin died in 1953.

October 11, 1968

To: Robert C. Tucker

I have read with admiration your *Svetlana Alliluyeva as Witness of Stalin.* You have made the most of even casual remarks of hers to deepen our understanding of the psychology and temperament of Joseph Stalin. It suggests that your book will be a fine one.

I have only one disagreement and a suggestion. It seems to me that your closing section makes a little too much of Beria's influence on Stalin. Beria first insinuated himself into Stalin's graces by undertaking in earnest the great "operation rewrite" with his rewriting of the history of the Bolshevik movement in Transcaucasia. This was the beginning of the great transformation of the past. The remark of Svetlana's mother to the effect that she would never let "that evil man" into her house was not a political remark. Naturally, Svetlana did not know it, being then a very young girl, but her mother knew, and it was common gossip both in Transcaucasia, from where her mother came, and in Moscow, that Beria was a notorious molester of little girls. I imagine Ed Smith [U.S. diplomat in Moscow] must have told you this, for he had occasion to observe the frequent stops of Beria's car before a girls' school to take young girls away from the school.

More important, your very final passage, which makes magnificent drama, contains observations which are subject to a different interpretation. I have good reason to believe that Beria was slated for liquidation by Stalin in connection with the purges that were following the Jewish Doctors Plot, and Beria knew this. Stalin had already given signs of his irritation and suspicion concerning Beria. This might explain Beria's relief and exultation as he stood at Stalin's deathbed. Naturally, Khrushchev, after he and his associates had shot Beria and somewhat later tried him, had every reason to conceal the fact that Beria was slated for execution along with Molotov, Mikoyan, and Kaganovich. . . .

As to the suggestion, if you have another reprint to spare, send it to me and I will forward it to Alexander Orlov [a Soviet defector], who knew intimately Beria, Redens, and many other of the characters who appear in your article. . .

He knows a great deal and is full of fairly authentic gossip which reached him from highly placed officials while he himself was a highly placed official in the NKVD. You will also find it profitable to reread his *Secret Crimes of Joseph Stalin*. . . .

---

*Wolfe replies to questions from a biographer of Jo-
seph Stalin.*

November 12, 1968

To: Professor Robert C. Tucker

This is to answer your letter of October 12, in which you asked
three questions. As to the first question, I do not now remember the
"nameless source" of my information that Beria directed the preliminary gathering of the material for Stalin's collected works. I have a
superb "forgettory," and what little memory I can make use of is
always concentrated on remembering the future—that is, materials
for my next book.

As for Stalin's article on the national question, I know that he
was briefed by both Lenin and Bukharin. Bukharin was then in Vi-
enna, as my memory serves me, and Lenin told Stalin to go to Bukharin for briefing. Thus Bukharin spent more time grooming Stalin for
his "big article" than Lenin did.

As for John Reed's *Ten Days*, I cannot now remember when it was
suppressed in Russia although I have a note about it in my files in
New York, but it was suppressed because Trotsky was suppressed.
Like all contemporary accounts of the October *coup d'état*, Lenin-
Trotsky was treated as almost a single person and, increasingly as
Stalin suppressed Trotsky's role and arrogated the position of number two man to himself, *Ten Days That Shook the World* became
more and more embarrassing. However, John Reed's was still a name
to conjure with—hence the John Reed Clubs for American Writers
until that point in the thirties when the popular front began and
John Reed's name was dropped as too revolutionary and the club was
replaced by the League of American Writers.

*Professor Lewis Feuer, one of Wolfe's closest
friends, sent along his recent essay on Karl Marx's
relationship with his mother. Wolfe responded:*

January 31, 1969

To: Professor Lewis Feuer

. . . Having read your recent article on Marx and his mother, I am
aroused once more to admiration by what and how you write, although I cannot swallow the "he hated his mother" theory as a sufficient explanation. You drove me to the remarkable original article in
Historia Judaica and it seems to me that self-detestation comes out
of every page and he doesn't limit his fire to the Jews of Holland. Be
that as it may, you have further convinced me that you should write
a study in book form of Karl Marx: his works, his moods, his carbun-
cles, and the tragedy of his life and that of his children. It would be a
rich and unique contribution and you simply must do it. If I were
younger and Toronto were nearer, I would be tempted to impose myself upon you as coauthor and as occasional anchor against the blowing of the Freudian winds. But since I am not younger and Toronto is
not nearer, I shall bombard you periodically with demands that you
do this work for which you alone are equipped. It would be both a
best-seller and a masterpiece, two things rarely capable of being
reconciled.

---

*Wolfe thanks a friend for forwarding an attack on
Wolfe that appeared in the Soviet press.*

February 19, 1969

To: Max Hayward

Many thanks for sending me the elegant attack upon me and Natalie
Wraga [Grant, American writer on Soviet affairs] in *Zvezda*. I must
beg you to believe that I am flattered. You have to bear in mind that
from 1939 to 1967 I was an unwriter and an unperson. Everyone I
knew was being quoted, damned, praised, or at least impaled in a
footnote, but as for me, it was as if I had never lived and never
written at all. In 1967, however, an order went out from the chief of
Agitprop [Soviet propaganda agency] that I was to be promoted to a
bourgeois falsifier, a hireling of big business, a man with a dangerous
ability to quote correctly and give an air of scholarship to articles
and books circulated to trap the unwary. Believe me, Max, I am
greatly pleased with the promotion and treasure each insult as testimonial to my existence. I have been duly discussed in *Voprosy
Istorii, Voprosy Filosofii, Voprosy Istorii KPSS, Literaturnaya
Gazeta,* and the like, and now you add *Zvezda*. Whatever they heap
upon me, truly my cup runneth over.

Concerning the suspicious death of Maxim Gorky,
Wolfe explained to a friend why understatement
and a cautious use of sources are better than
speculation.

April 21, 1969

To: Boris Souvarine

Concerning Gorky's death, I have many suggestive indications that
it may have been hastened by the tender solicitude of the father of
the peoples and the patron of all engineers of the soul, but it was my
considered policy not to use these suggestive hints. My reasons are
very simple. The case against Stalin and his lieutenants is so monstrous if we stick to the facts which are documented in documents
which all men must accept that I prefer not to use sources that are
less firm and more easy to reject. I might say more by giving these
hints, but I would give more excuse for fellow travelers and mush
heads to doubt everything I am writing if I put in anything which
gives a ready handle for doubt. I am making a Xerox for you of one
of the notes which I did not use in my book, and it is typical of the
many which I preferred to leave unused so that every page of the
book would be more compelling to those reluctant to believe my
picture. If you ask me whether he died a natural death or not, I
would not be sure of my answer. He was old, infirm, tubercular, and
heartbroken, and totally disillusioned in his attempts to soften Joseph Stalin. Stalin had promised to let him go to Italy whenever his
health required it, but in the end refused to let him go. He tried to
send messages out, but he was surrounded by a network of agents
provocateurs. He did get false treatment from his doctors who, at the
very least, were instructed by the secret police to tell him that a
winter in the Crimea was better for his health than a winter in Italy.
Whether anything worse than that happened is a matter of conjecture although I do have evidence that he told intimates that he was
a virtual prisoner (maybe he didn't use the word *virtual*). That writings sharply critical of the Stalin regime were secreted in his room,

as another illustration, is confirmed by Alexander Orlov. In the first couple pages of my book, I told what I thought best to tell, and left the rest to the imagination of the reader. My method in all polemical writings may be summed up by the old Latin tag *fortiter in re, suaviter in modo* [strength in facts, soft in style].

I hope this answers your questions. I assume you are going to publish something on Gorky, and am looking forward with interest to it and to seeing how you treat the problem of his death.

In the following letter Wolfe recalls Whittaker Chambers, an ex-Communist and the author of Witness.

May 12, 1969

To: William A. Reuben

Whittaker Chambers's "memories" of me in *Witness* have nothing to do with reality. I don't understand how even a romantic imagination can so disremember, but the memory and forgettery are tricky things. My actual relations with Whittaker Chambers are as follows.

He was one of three young men, inseparables, who visited me when I was director of the Workers' School and asked me how they could serve the communist movement and learn to write well. The names of the other two were Michael Intrator and Sender Garlin. I answered them that one learns to write by writing, as one learns to swim by swimming, and told them that if they could stand being directed and given orders by a fool, I could get them on *The Daily Worker*, which was then being edited by Robert Minor. They thought they could and I did. Then I saw no more of them for some years. Working under Robert Minor disillusioned all three of them, in spite of my warning. Michael Intrator remained my friend, but dropped his ambition to become a writer, got himself a job as a furrier, which is a seasonal occupation and highly paid, and spent the off-season fishing off the coast of Florida.

Whittaker Chambers decided that the American communist movement was run by inexpert people and buffoons and wanted to serve "real people and real causes," and became a secret agent of the Russian police. The rest of his story as he remembers it is in *Witness*. I learned of his disappearance into the underground through the grapevine and got subsequent reports on him from Michael Intrator. Through Intrator I gave him a bit of advice as to how to prepare himself for the [Alger] Hiss trial, in which Hiss was lying but seemed plausible, and Chambers was telling the truth but to many innocents sounded implausible. Sender Garlin became a cynical middle-level communist party functionary, and for all I know has remained one to this day. Intrator died of a heart attack, and the story of Whittaker Chambers is a matter of public record.

My impression of Chambers can be summed up in two words: he was alienated from the general life of his time, and a romantic. He broke with the secret police when the bloody purges began in Russia, and when another American secret agent, Juliet Stuart Poyntz, was kidnapped from New York onto a Soviet vessel and then murdered. He did not decide to tell his story to American authorities until Stalin signed a pact with Hitler and he knew that whatever Stalin knew concerning America would be available to Hitler. Then he made great efforts to persuade Alger Hiss to break with the spy ring of which they had both been members, but when Priscilla Hiss went to the telephone and attempted to tell a Soviet agent what he was doing, he fled from their house. That is all I know personally about him, except that for awhile he was the chief editor of *Time* and his underlings regarded him as a stern taskmaster. He gave up that job when Hiss tried to frame him instead of making a clean confession and break. I have known about the career of Alger Hiss from the days when he formed part of a secret ring in Washington, working in the Agriculture Department for the naive Henry Wallace [secretary of agriculture, later vice-president during Roosevelt's third term], and when FDR [Roosevelt] asked Wallace to get rid of his Communists, Alger Hiss served as the finger man for all of the other members of his underground circle in the government, thus appearing anticommunist so that the Russian spy ring in America could use him. That antedates the Hiss-Chambers affair by a number of years. That is all I can tell you.

―――――――――◆◆―――――――――

Wolfe urged his friend Edmund Wilson, a literary
critic and historian, to read several chapters of his
recent book before undertaking revisions of his
own book.

August 22, 1969

To: Edmund Wilson

I asked my publisher to send you a review copy of *An Ideology in*
Power—Reflections on the Russian Revolution. I don't know
whether he sent it, but to make sure I am sending you another copy.
In view of the fact that you are writing a new introduction and reis-
suing your *To the Finland Station,* this book containing my reflections of the last quarter of a century may evoke or provoke some
thoughts in you. I particularly commend to your attention the first
three chapters entitled

1. Marxism and the Russian Revolution

2. Backwardness and Industrialization in Russian History and
   Thought

3. *Das Kapital* One Hundred Years Later and Lenin, the Architect of
   20th-Century Totalitarianism [chapter 9]

We can start our talk from there when we get together.

    Incidentally, it would be a great help to me if you would review
this book somewhere. For some mysterious reasons the *New York*
Times has been boycotting my recent books. I don't know whether it
is because I refuse to hunt with the hippies or ride camp with the
campers or whether they are mad at me for refusing to review [Rob-
ert K. Massie's] *Nicholas and Alexandra,* a Book-of-the-Month selection. Anyhow, if you care to, you could help me break through the
wall.

———————◆——————

Wolfe tells a friend in Paris about a recent meet-
ing with Stalin's daughter.

October 7, 1969

To: Manes Sperber [editor in chief, Kalman-Levy Publications, Paris]

Thanks for your good letter of September 15. I did not answer it
earlier because I have been back East and have sent 69 cases of
books and papers from my library in Brooklyn to the Hoover Institution where I need them for my next two books—D. V. [*Deo volente*
(God willing)]—and where the Hoover libraries would like them to
reside permanently. Incidentally, Ella and I went to Provincetown on
Cape Cod while we were in the East, and the Cape was as lovely as
usual with the added interest that Edmund Wilson wanted to consult me on the critical introduction he should write to a reissue of
To the Finland Station and that Stalin's daughter Svetlana came to
meet us. If I had played the game of impossible prophecies in my
youth, two prophecies high on the list would have been that any
child of Karl Kautsky [Austrian-born Marxist writer and political
leader] or any child of Joseph Stalin should ever become my friend,
but live long enough, and everything happens to you. Benedikt
Kautsky and his wife translated my *Three Who Made a Revolution*
into excellent German, and now Karl Kautsky, Jr., has translated my
*The Bridge and the Abyss: The Troubled Friendship of Maxim
Gorky and V. I. Lenin* into excellent German. Actually, Svetlana has
written many very friendly letters to Ella and me and invited us to
be her houseguests in Princeton. We countered with an invitation for
her to come to Cape Cod and spend some time with us there which
she gladly accepted. Knowing what I have done for—or to—her father, she has nevertheless become a warm friend. This says much
about her present attitude and character.

———————————◆◆———————————

*Wolfe asks a former leader of the POUM, a dissi-
dent communist group active during the Spanish
civil war, if he can identify the source of a 1921
quote by Lenin.*

December 19, 1969

To: Joaquin Maurin

I have just shipped 69 cases of books (a little under two tons) from
my apartment in Brooklyn to the Hoover library. Among my notes
and papers were things written before I had schooled myself to tell
exactly where I got them from, one of which reads as follows:

"We never speak of freedom." (Lenin on the peasant opposition to
the Bolsheviks early in 1921.)

"We never speak about liberty, we practice the dictatorship of the
proletariat in the name of a minority because the peasant class has
not yet become proletarian and are not with us. It will continue
until they subject themselves. Presumably the dictatorship will last
about forty years." (Lenin addressing a visiting delegation of Spanish
socialists, January 30, 1921.)

The above has been suppressed from *Lenin's Collected Works* in
all its editions but the date suggests that he was talking to Spaniards
who were concerned about the freedom of Russian anarchists and
anarcho-syndicalists. Do you know who may have spoken to Lenin
or listened to Lenin on January 30, 1921? Could it have been you?
Casanellas? Nin? Or any other person you knew? If you can help me
to pin down the circumstances of this utterance I shall be most
appreciative.

At the request of the assistant counsel to the Regents of the University of California, Wolfe analyzed a speech by Angela Davis, an avowed Communist who was teaching in the California system.

February 25, 1970

To: Donald L. Reidhaar

The quotation from Lenin you are looking for is enclosed. You can find it in the rather poor English translation of the 4th edition of *Lenin's Collected Works*, vol. 26, page 22ff. It is entitled "Marxism and Insurrection," a nice title for Angela Davis.

I have read her address and conclude from it that she is not only unfit to teach philosophy to anyone but unfit to teach anything. It is obvious that one cannot think of a single subject on which she could lecture coherently and teach students to understand and weigh all points of view and come to their own conclusions. It is a series of incoherent and explosive slogans from one who, as Lenin on his deathbed wrote disapprovingly of his disciple Joseph Stalin, "is a cook who can cook only hot dishes." Any classroom would be the worse for having injected into it in the name of teaching such a series of lethal and mind-deadening slogans. As examples of what I mean I select the following quotations from the text of her speech.

On the University and Its Courses
The university is just another part of a whole system of oppression, of a whole system of exploitation.

❖   ❖   ❖

On Pigs and Panthers
We have to realize that the same pigs who are, and who are still on campus I take it, even though they said they

withdrew them, that those same pigs are the pigs who attacked the Black Panther headquarters in Los Angeles.

. . . Once we really organize ourselves, once we really are able to raise the level of consciousness in all the people so we can move in a united fashion to overthrow this whole system, to overthrow, to overthrow the government. That's what I'm not supposed to say, but I'll say it. To overthrow the government—to overthrow the government.

❖   ❖   ❖

I have to admit that I really felt proud standing out there on Central Avenue early on the morning of December 8 and saw that my brothers and sisters were able to hold off three hundred pigs. They were able to hold off three hundred pigs.

❖   ❖   ❖

When people start saying that we are out to subvert, that we are subversive, we should say, "Hell, yes, we are subversive."

Now one word on panthers and pigs. When I first read that an organization of Negroes had adopted the title the Black Panthers, I thought with dismay, "They are resigning from the human race. They intend to stalk their victims in secrecy, to leap from trees and thickets, to shoot at their targets from behind bushes." I came to this conclusion because of my study of the great show trials and blood purges in Russia. One of the techniques of the chief prosecutor, Andrei Vyshinsky, was to call his victims vile animal names in order to dehumanize them, on the principle that if they are less than human, they are easier to kill. He called them "hyenas, foxes, jackals, vultures," and used such forensic eloquence as "a foul-smelling pile of human garbage," "they must be shot like dirty dogs! Our people are demanding one thing: Crush the accursed reptiles . . . the lowest scum and filth of the past."

After telling friends that the self-chosen name Black Panther indicated ferocity and a resignation from the human race, I waited anxiously to see what term they would use to dehumanize their intended victims. It was *pigs!* This is now to become part of the regular vocabulary of the Philosophy Department of one of our university campuses if Angela Davis is to fulfill the duty of teaching the students how to think philosophically. Understandably it has become part of the campus vocabulary of every little group of storm troopers and of misguided innocents who, looking for excitement, "go where the action is" and are infected by its vocabulary. Since man can only think with words, this determines a circumscribed thought in a whole field of human relations.

Re the incredible appointment of Angela Davis to teach philosophy, I must note that the same gentleman who chose to sanction her appointment (where did he pick her up and who suggested it?) also had the basic responsibility for the appointment of [Herbert] Marcuse [a Marxist philosopher]. The fault lies not so much in Angela Davis as in the learned men who have forgotten their learning and their duties and who find such a character to wish on the students who would like to study philosophy.

There is an old folk proverb in many European countries which says "A fish begins to stink first at the head." I can only conclude that it is the head of this department and some of his close associates who are giving a fishy odor to one of our campuses.

*Writing to poet and literary critic Patricia Blake,
Wolfe discussed his forthcoming lecture about Rus-
sian poets who were driven to suicide during the
Lenin and Stalin eras.*

March 25, 1970

To: Patricia Blake

Never fear, your respectful disciple will not disgrace you by oversim-
plification or overpoliticization. I know how complex the human
spirit is and more particularly the spirit of a creative artist.

My topic will be "Servility, Silence, Suicide: Three Schools of Soviet Letters." I have already gathered many names of suicides and
concerning some of them a fair amount of information and even a
good English translation of a poem or an autobiographical outburst.
According to Arkadi Gaiev there were only two literary suicides of
note in the century and a half preceding the Bolshevik period. He
instances Radishchev and Garshin. In both cases there were compli-
cations of health and despair and he contrasts this with "tens" of
suicides under the Soviets.

I intend to call an honor roll only of the most important and examine perhaps three in sufficient depth to give some feeling and perhaps a decent translation or two of some short work or passage from
each of them. I am particularly interested in Esenin, Mayakovsky,
and Tsvetayeva and, as a striking example of another sort, Fadeiev. If
time permits I may take up a few suicides of political protest by
known literary figures such as Stalin's wife, Trotsky's disciple Yoffe,
and the like.

I have many more names and may submit them to you later for a
comment or two if you give me the slightest encouragement. I shall
want to suggest that there are forms of partial suicide like Pasternak's flight into translation under Stalin, like Babel's and
Meyerhold's defiant utterances or like Kuzma Petrov-Vodkin's withdrawal from painting to teaching after he did his Aesopian version of
the Madonna and Child deceptively entitled *Petersburg, 1918.*

From these few remarks you can see where my mind is running. I am picking many flowers on the way and any blossoms you throw at me will be appreciated. Obviously my main problem will be: What can you handle decently before a Rocky Mountain audience in one hour? but then, all art involves selection and what you put in gains strength from what you leave out. I am enclosing a Xerox of Esenin's letter of February 7, 1923, and I also have a striking verse which he wrote in honor of Nicolas Kuznetsov's suicide at the age of 22 in which the young suicide in his last verse "took pleasure in returning my party card" and in which Esenin asks: "Perhaps I too ought to pack my bag and gather my bones for the long voyage?"

I shall also discuss silence as a form of semisuicide and even servility as yet another form.

Any suggestions you may make either to guide or trouble my thought will be gratefully accepted.

The following are Wolfe's translations of two poems by Ivan Elagin, an exiled Russian poet.

AMNESTY

The man is still alive
Who shot my father
In Kiev in the summer of thirty-eight.

Probably, he's pensioned now,
Lives quietly
And has given up his old job.

And if he has died,
Probably that one is still alive
Who just before the shooting
With a stout wire

Bound his arms
Behind his neck.

Probably, he too is pensioned off.

And if he is dead,
Then probably
The one who questioned him still lives.
And that one no doubt
Has an extra good pension.

Perhaps the guard
Who took my father to be shot
Is still alive.

If I should want now
I could return to my native land,
For I have been told
That all these people
Have actually pardoned me.

ALL RIGHTS RESERVED BY THE AUTHOR

Today at breakfast I read the words:
All rights reserved by the author.

In return, I too shall be generous—
All rights reserved for the wind,
For a star, for the ark of Noah,
For the rain, for the snows of yesteryear.

Highly esteemed author,
What rights have you insisted on?
The right to the bullet that killed Pushkin
Or the rope Tsvetayeva used?

Or the right guaranteed to Mandel'shtam
To lie in a mass grave.

The right to be pure and fearless,
Not to renounce one's words;
The right to face the firing squad,
Even as Gumilev did.

As long as the supply of authors lasts
Their rights are as numerous as the sands:
The right to a bullet in your neck
Or a bullet lodged in your temple.

How many subtle variations!
How many chances to choose:
The right to the pit, to the wall,
Or to hang from a projecting hook.

Or the right to a courtroom verdict,
The scaffold, the jail,
Or to stare through the dungeon bars
To the darkness outside,

The right to suffer under the vigilance of the guard,
The right to drink calumny to the dregs,
To live as Solzhenitsyn lives,
Always with a gag in his mouth!

Here they are, down to the last of them,
All our rights as authors.
The right to the bullet of Martynov,
Or Semichastny's insulting verdicts,

The right to suffocate like Blok,
Or to die like Pasternak.
These rights are conferred on us
And reserved forever more.

All rights reserved for the author.
Thrice accused be these words!
There, face upward turned,
Lies Esenin, realizing his rights.

And there, devoured by his colleagues,
Spreading newspapers on the floor,
Mayakovsky reaches for a revolver,
And sends a bullet into his brain.

And there the author whose book earned
The title, enemy of the people,
Stumbles under a watchtower,
And collapses into a snowdrift.

Lord, send us a better fate,
But first let me ask you a favor:
Don't forget, when you get around to it
To free us from the fearful rights
That are reserved for the author.

---

*Wolfe questions Marx's doctrine of the withering
away of the state.*

April 8, 1970

To: Richard Adamiak

Many thanks for sending me your interesting and closely reasoned
article on the withering away of the state. I have only one possible
reservation, namely, that I have come to the conclusion that even
system builders like Marx are not as systematic and consistent as
they would have us believe. It seems to me that he changed his
formulations repeatedly in accord with his changing passions, the
changing complex of his ideas, the intrusions of brute fact, and the
polemical exigencies of various moments and situations. I think he
originally got the formula concerning "the administration of things"
from the young Engels who got it from Saint-Simon. He got a second
dose of anarchism during his brief Paris collaboration with Bakunin.
But you are undoubtedly correct to emphasize that the formula of
"the withering away of the state" (actually the dying out) was only a
cover for what soon became his systematic statism. In fact, in the
"immediate demands" of *The Communist Manifesto* one of them is
the hair-raising demand for "equal forced labor for everyone, building
of industrial armies, especially for agriculture." And the ten transi-
tional demands ooze statism from every pore.

You do a real service in emphasizing this ineradicable statism
since the word *socialization* has the semantic vagueness of a concept
which has dropped from cloud-cuckoo-land. I have never found a so-

cialist of any persuasion who has given a clear definition of socialism. The latest attempt has been made by George Lichtheim in the latest issue of the *New York Review of Books* in an article entitled "What Socialism Is and What It Is Not."

As to the Soviet Union, it is obvious that the state has undertaken to control and to operate everything down to thoughts and dreams. That is what totalitarianism means. They quote the words about the dying out or withering away of the state less and less often and are manifestly uncomfortable in the presence of any reminder that "full communism" would require such a withering away. They have experimented with "the state of all the people"—a piece of nonsense from the standpoint of Marxism—and then seem to have dropped the formula. Their spokesmen have made several attempts to suggest that even under "full communism" there will have to be an administration of persons as well as an administration of things.

Wolfe recalls Anna Louise Strong, an admirer of
Leon Trotsky, Joseph Stalin, and Mao Tse-tung.

June 4, 1970

To: Robert W. Pringle

I do not know very much about the late Anna Louise Strong because for most of my life I watched her at a bemused distance. But whatever I know follows.

I first became aware of the existence of Anna Louise Strong in either 1919 or 1920. She was then a columnist for a Seattle newspaper. I am not sure now but I think it was the *Seattle Post-Intelligencer.* She did her column under the pen name of Anise. The column, as I remember it, was proliberal, prosocialist and pro-Soviet in varying degrees at different times. She was also terribly excited and moved by the Seattle general strike which was a great event in the history of that city and of the American labor movement.

I next became aware of the fact that she, as I, were both contributing as string reporters to the Federated Press. The Federated Press was a press organization founded in imitation of the United Press and the Associated Press but selling its services to labor papers and radical papers of various descriptions. The Communists infiltrated it, took it over, and later it died a natural death.

The key to Anna Louise Strong's spirit is to be found in the title of one of her books, *I Change Worlds.* That is literally what she did. She ceased to feel herself an American and gave her loyalty first to the Soviet Union and then to communist China. In other words, she changed worlds twice and she changed leaders and heroes, to my knowledge, at least three times. She was first a devout admirer of Leon Trotsky, but when the cart of history gave a lurch and he fell off, she fell off with him. Breathless and panting she chased after the cart and climbed on again and found Joseph Stalin in the driver's seat. (When I knew her in the early 1920s she seemed unusually tall for a woman, big-boned, and inclined to be plump.) She followed Joseph Stalin with less undivided admiration than she had followed Leon Trotsky. She was deeply shocked no doubt by some of the things which Stalin did. The reason I know this to be true is that she asked, or pleaded with, a mutual friend of both of us not to let her aged father know about the blood purges and other terrors of the late Stalin regime. Her father was a preacher of a general prosocialist sympathy who had a pulpit in a Protestant church in Seattle, but in the closing years of his life after he had retired he continued to believe in the Soviet regime without knowing too much about it.

Once more the cart of history gave a lurch. She got in trouble with Joseph Stalin, fell off the cart, I believe was under arrest for a while, and then she fell in love with Mao Tse-tung. And she changed worlds once more, spending the closing years of her life in China. It was in China that she died and Chairman Mao personally attended a state funeral given there in her honor.

Writing to journalist Marquis Childs, Wolfe denies that the Weathermen terrorists were inspired by Lenin.

October 27, 1970

To: Marquis Childs

My friend Ewan Clague was kind enough to send me your column in the *Washington Post* of October 9 in which you suggested that my *Three Who Made a Revolution* is "much sought after among the apostles of violence" as a guide to their tactics of "assassinations, bank holdups and terror." You also suggested that the book was out of print.

I wonder whether you will find space in your column so widely syndicated (one friend sent me a copy from Mexico City) for two corrections:

1. The book is still in print in its fourth edition in cloth and its twelfth edition in paper and has sold between three and four hundred thousand to date.

2. The Weathermen give no evidence of having read it for not only I as the author, but Lenin as one of my protagonists were critical of acts of individual terror.

The following quotation from Lenin is sufficient to suggest his notion if not mine. He wrote: "Individual acts of terrorism arouse only a short-lived sensation, but thereafter lead even to apathy, and to the passive waiting for the next individual sensational terrorist act."

I shall be grateful to you for putting this little distance between me and the Weathermen and even between Lenin's tactics and theirs.

———————◆–◆———————

*Wolfe thanks President Nixon for his response to
the Simas Kudirka incident.*

December 2, 1970

To: President Richard M. Nixon

I share your grief and indignation that a man who attempted to escape to freedom on a ship flying the American flag should have been returned to his captors to be beaten, tortured, imprisoned, and possibly executed.

I want to thank you for the promptness and strength of your reaction and its public nature and for sending instructions to all departments to prevent such a shameful occurrence from being repeated.

May I venture to suggest that you take this occasion also to issue a ringing reminder to the American people that this is a land of freedom, that we sympathize with the plight of those under dictatorial and totalitarian governments, that we regard them as supporters of our common effort to make a freer and safer world, and that we in turn pledge them that our doors will ever be open to those who seek freedom.

———————◆◆———————

Wolfe explains why it is premature for him to contact Leszek Kolakowski, a Marxist philosopher recently expelled from Poland.

December 2, 1970

To: Leopold Labedz

... I was also highly pleased to receive from you the review [of Wolfe's *An Ideology in Power*] from the *Spectator.* I was pleased to have such a distinguished reviewer, and I liked the review. But I think I cannot accept your request to enter into a discussion with Kolakowski. Both because I am buried in obligations and am trying to learn to say "no" to everything but work on my next book. Moreover, it seems to me that Kolakowski has not finished his evolution. I understand what he is going through. At this stage, he is upset by the fact that I seem to reduce the ideology of totalitarianism chiefly to its organizational features, features from which he is attempting to salvage an ideology of Marxism which is still precious to him. The hardest thing for a man in his position is not to learn the things which he does not know (he knows an enormous amount), but to come to grips with the things he knows that are not so. Besides, I have really said what I have to say about the fluctuating, compelling force of an ideology in my chapter entitled "Communist Ideology and Soviet Foreign Policy" and in an occasional article on the organizational views of V. I. Lenin.

———————◆◆———————

*Wolfe explains his views to a scholar compiling a
survey of interpretive writings on the causes of the
Russian Revolution.*

February 23, 1971

To: Professor Vergil D. Medlin

Your outline is improved and more interesting in the second version,
but I strongly doubt if I should be put in the category of "a natural
necessitarian." I think that the Russian Revolution was a result of
(1) the root defect in European civilization in the twentieth century
that caused it to stumble into total war; (2) undue strain put upon a
Russian society in state of flux by a war which shook all the European societies engaged in it; (3) the fact that Russia was ruled by a
weak and romantic tsar [Nicholas] and left the capital, in an exces-
sively centralized state, in the hands of his wife [Alexandra]—a petti-
coat government distrustful of all capable officials and guided by a
half-mad holy scoundrel and fool of God [Rasputin]; (4) the fact—by
no means necessary—that the provisional government attempted to
continue the war after the apparatus of command and obedience had
broken down; (5) the genius for taking advantage of the fact that
power lay for the seizing in the barracks and the streets. For my
estimate of Lenin's key importance read again the opening sentence
of "Lenin, the Architect" [in *An Ideology in Power*]. Indeed, I am
now at work on a book to be called *Lenin and the Twentieth Century* which hazards the guess that after I am no longer among the
living and the century is over Lenin may be seen as "the greatest
man of the twentieth century." Naturally, great carries no moral implications for an historian, merely historical ones. Had he not succeeded in crossing through the enemy lines and gotten to Russia
while power was in the streets, the history of our century would be
enormously different.

Hence, I would suggest that you put me back in the multicausa-
tion view and personal will view. I know I can't be in two places at
once, but my view even so briefly outlined is somewhat too complex

for your various categories and perhaps wherever you put me a footnote should suggest that I belong in several of your categories at once.

———————◆·◆———————

The following letters were written to Stephen F. Cohen, a young political scientist at Princeton University who was writing a biography of Nikolai Bukharin. In the first letter Wolfe offers his reflections on Cohen's essay "Bukharin, Lenin, and the Theoretical Foundations of Bolshevism."

March 12, 1971

To: Stephen F. Cohen

. . . I was indeed sorry that I was unable to receive you when you passed through Stanford, for I know that you are at work on something that interests me greatly, namely, a biography of Bukharin. However, I have spent the last couple of days in communion with you reading and meditating on your article in *Soviet Studies* entitled "Bukharin, Lenin, and the Theoretical Foundations of Bolshevism." I want to congratulate you on a remarkable job, well organized, well thought out, well documented, and well expressed. It was a pleasure to read and pleasant to know that you have done so much of what I was working on and thinking about, and thus have saved me the expenditure of energy for the completion of a study of Lenin's indebtedness to Bukharin and of the originality of Bukharin's thought on imperialism and the bureaucratic leviathan state. I have long held that the extreme contradiction between Lenin's *State and Revolution* and his superstate that was "to organize everything, to take everything into our hands," was not merely due to the fact that he wrote *State and Revolution* when he was trying to overthrow a state and developed the contrary doctrine and practice when he was in power and laying the foundation for twentieth-century totalitarianism. A letter he wrote to [Aleksandra] Kollontai acknowledging an indebtedness to Bukharin started my investigation of that indebtedness. Hence, you can understand why I rejoice to see the splendid job you have done.

A few random thoughts, marginal to your thesis, are herewith offered for your consideration before you incorporate this into your life of Bukharin. The random thoughts deal more with Lenin than Bukharin, and I offer them to you for what they are worth.

1. Lenin's formulation concerning the "uneven development of capitalism" was, I think, chiefly formulated to justify a socialist revolution in a single country, and that a backward one, his own. (This, like the other suggestions I offer for your consideration, does not contradict but rather supplements what you have said.)

2. His emphasis on national self-determination came largely because he was bent on breaking up and overthrowing a multinational state, again his own country, and mobilizing the discontented nationalities of "the prison house of peoples" against the tsarist autocracy.

3. His emphasis on the importance of colonial wars becomes central only at the Second Congress of the Comintern when he had begun to realize that Western Europe was not able to make a communist world revolution, and he turned his attention to the overwhelming majority of backward, agrarian, colonial, and national revolutionary lands of Asia and Africa which were to "lay siege to the world's metropolis" (my quotation marks here to give proper credit to Lin Piao and Mao Tse-tung).

4. The self-determination slogan when he first formulated it was aimed chiefly at the dismemberment of the Russian Empire. When he got to power, he assiduously attempted to reconquer everything which the tsars had possessed and which as a revolutionary he had encouraged to secede. He had some hesitancy, to be sure, about Menshevik socialist Georgia, but thankfully accepted the gift when it was put into his hands. On his deathbed, however, when he had time to meditate on how his lieutenants would do without the schoolmaster's guidance, and to meditate again upon the arrogance of new-baked Russian chauvinist zealots like Stalin and [Grigori] Orjonikidze [Georgian ally of Stalin], then mournfully he considered the problem of how to change the right of self-determination from a "paper right" to a meaningful and

genuine one. Alas, nobody listened, and even Trotsky refused to undertake the defense of the Georgian communists both because Trotsky was a great Russian nationalist and because he was hesitant to engage in an all-out fight with the coterie of old Bolsheviks who were already harassing him.

5. There is, as you must have sensed and in fact indicate, ambivalence in Lenin's antistatism—and ultrastatism—in part it is due to reflecting on Bukharin's writings and above all on quotations from Engels which pushed him towards antistatism, very convenient to a man who wants to overthrow a state. His suprastatism flowed from his authoritarian temperament and his unalloyed admiration for the success of German "war socialism" which managed, with German efficiency, to centralize, rationalize, and statize wartime scarcity due to the Allied blockade. The ex-Menshevik [Yuri] Larin brought him glowing tales of the German success and raised in his unconscious and perhaps in his conscious thought the question: Why cannot backward, impoverished Russia do the same? Must socialism be only the socialization of abundance in the most advanced lands or hasn't blockaded Germany proved that we can hope with enough centralization, enough compulsion of everyone to work, and enough rationing, [to] socialize our Russian poverty and then work toward self-industrialization and the socialization of abundance under a dictatorship of our own?

6. It is interesting to note that after Bukharin's masterly demolition of marginal utility economics and Lenin's denunciation of the anarchy of the market, present-day Russia is struggling toward the application of American economic theory and market regulation in its overcentralized planning . . .

7. Of similar interest is the movement from the semianarchism of *State and Revolution* and workers' control of industry to the rejection of the "anarcho-syndicalist deviation."

   And similarly interesting is the evolution from Bukharin's and Lenin's somewhat differing thinking of and putting all their chips on the hope of war, through Lenin's acceptance of the peace slogan to take and consolidate his power, and from that to the prestidigitation with peaceful coexistence, support for just wars of national liberation, and the compulsion to realize that both Bukharin and Lenin were wrong when they imagined that the great powers would collapse if they lost or liberated their colonies . . .

8. It may interest you to know that when Stalin decided on "the great turn" and the reshaping of his party and the country by purge and revolution from above he felt the need of a "war danger" and a consequent ferreting out of agents of foreign powers in the state and the party. At the Sixth Congress of the Comintern, Bukharin accepted and propagated the legend that Russia was in danger of immediate attack and invasion. After the congress was over, there followed a Byzantine discussion of whether "the inner danger" or "the outer danger" was the greatest and whether "internal contradictions" or "external contradictions" were to be given priority. This was the scholastic form in which Stalin and his faction opened the war upon Bukharin . . .

Incidentally, since it has often been declared that I was "a Bukharinite," I might add that I never believed that an American should guide his decisions on American questions as the tail of any Russian faction. In fact, when I got into a fight with Joseph Stalin which lasted for the next six months . . . he accused me not of being a Bukharinite but "an American exceptionalist." At this fearful pronouncement, the floor was supposed to open, and I fall into flames and brimstone somewhere down in the depths. Instead of being snuffed out, on reflection, I concluded that I was "an exceptionalist" for every country in the world. However, if I am not a Bukharinite nor have ever been, I must say that I considered him the most human and attractive of all the Bolshevik leaders I met.

I hope these few remarks may prove of use. If I can help you with any aspect of your work on the Bukharin biography, I shall do so within the limits of my time and knowledge.

Wolfe recalls how Stalin undermined Bukharin in 1928.

July 26, 1971

To: Stephen F. Cohen

It is hard for one who was not part of the Comintern to realize how the Russians played with the words left and right, left danger and right danger, according to which adversary they were gunning for. It took a long time for Stalin to prepare the downfall of Bukharin, for Stalin was unknown in the Comintern and Bukharin was its chairman, its theoretician, and after Trotsky's fall its only truly popular figure. Hence, "a genius of dosing" [Stalin] began to maneuver Bukharin into accepting the thesis that war was imminent and that the "right danger" was becoming the main danger. Stalin took a long time patiently to hollow out a man until he became morally an empty shell, get him to denounce some of his own most zealous and incautious followers, etc., before he finally moved to crush him. As late as the Sixth Congress in mid-1928, Stalin solemnly declared "There are no differences between me and Bukharin, there are no differences in the Politburo or the leadership of the Russian Communist Party." As soon as the Sixth Congress had safely adjourned, he sprung the trap and it took him another five years before he could lump right danger, left danger, inner contradictions and outer contradictions and other scholastic terms into a single amalgam, "agent of a foreign power," "enemy of the people," "traitor." Not for nothing did Bukharin say: "He will kill me by chess moves" and call him a "genius of dosing."

———————◆◆———————

*Wolfe explains why he is optimistic that totalitar-
ian indoctrination can never be fully effective.*

August 20, 1971

To: Stephen F. Cohen

Your letter is most cheering and reassuring. I, too, have always held
that the methods of the inner barbarians to enforce their blueprint
on the human spirit will never succeed. When my colleagues were
cherishing the nightmare that the indoctrination machine might not
work on the older generation but would be 100 percent effective
when they got hold of the youth who would eventually be turned
out as so many identical robots or janissaries, I kept reminding them
that the youth is always born young and plastic and subject not only
to formal indoctrination but to education by life itself and by experiences which contradict the doctrine.

When, during the bloody terror of the thirties, I was told that
everybody would be terrorized and conditioned into the new Soviet
man, I was rejoicing at the cry of young writers and lovers of poetry
when the translator of Shakespeare, Pasternak, stepped into their
theater. The audience shouted "Sonnet 66! Sonnet 66!" The sonnet
is one of Shakespeare's which contains the line "And art made
tongue-tied by authority." What could the police do about "Sonnet
66?"

*Wolfe explains why he thinks it is appropriate to
call Bukharin "the good Bolshevik."*

March 22, 1972

To: Stephen F. Cohen

Don't be shy about calling Bukharin "the good Bolshevik." All good-
ness is relative and certainly he was the most decent and humane of
the Bolshevik leaders. Even during his horrendous ultraleft period his
formulae were always worse than his deeds. At the Sixth Congress, I
remember him sitting on the platform as chairman and zealously
taking notes concerning each speaker. When I got to the platform, I
peeked at his notes and they were amusing caricatures of the speakers. Actually his so-called right opposition was compounded of the
better side of Lenin, whom he worshipped, the gentle side of socialist "production for use," and a desire to ameliorate the lot of the
masses under a system supposedly being built for their welfare and
happiness.

Don't let anybody scold you into finishing your book faster than
the best possible writing requires. The time you took will be for-
given and the quality of your work will speak for itself.

*Wolfe reveals new information about Bukharin's
role in the decision to execute the defendants in
the 1928 purge trial of so-called wreckers in the
town of Shakhty.*

March 23, 1972

To: Stephen F. Cohen

Once more on "the good communist." Today I received a letter from
Boris Souvarine in which he tells me apropos of my article on the
Shakhty trial that Bukharin not only approved of the trial and the
verdict of guilty but told Kamenev (according to a letter of Kamenev
to Zinoviev dated July 11, 1928, and spread by the Trotskyists and
the Cheka): "Stalin proposed that no one should be shot in the
Shakhty trial . . . we voted against his proposal." Whether this means
that Bukharin was more bloodthirsty than Stalin or, what is much
more likely, that he was convinced that this first wrecking trial was
the honest truth, while Stalin was aware of the fact that for his
forced industrialization he needed the German electrical companies
and their engineers and knew more about the fictitious nature of all
the charges—I leave to your judgment. Incidentally, Souvarine found
Bukharin's boast concerning his vote in the Politburo "nauseating."
To make sure that you lose none of the flavor of Souvarine's letter to
me, I am enclosing a Xerox of his letter. My general feeling is that
Bukharin took on faith, as many good people did, the first charges of
wrecking and that Stalin consciously built up the series of show trials using such "old Bolsheviks" as Vyshinsky, a series of wrecking
charges as part of his terror campaign for forced industrialization,
forced collectivization, and forced extermination of all of Lenin's
lieutenants and then of all old Bolsheviks and finally of everybody
that his creeping suspicion could lay tentacles on. In other words, I
think this motion by Stalin not to shoot anybody and Bukharin's
proposal to shoot represent the beginning of the divide in the road
which led finally to Bukharin's own trial, confession, and ignomini-
ous death. If this conjecture is correct you have a real subject for

drama right there in that first show trial and that first divergence in the Politburo. I am enclosing a copy of my own analysis of the Shakhty trial which I may or may not have sent you before.

------◆◆------

When Stephen Cohen responds that the Shakhty defendants may have been guilty, Wolfe explains why he is certain the trial was a frame-up and urges Cohen to interview Jay Lovestone about Bukharin.

April 7, 1972

To: Stephen F. Cohen

I dictated a letter to you which I had to leave in the office without having time to check it and sign it, and this morning when I was about to affix my signature I received a new letter from you dated April 4 which requires some additional comment from me. First, on the Shakhty. I think my article entitled "Dress Rehearsals for the Great Terror" did a complete wrap-up (the first) of that trial . . . The American scholar, whoever he was, who told you inconclusively that there was "at least part of the foreign link charge with some basis in fact," is spreading the kind of self-serving rumor that is spread by pro-Soviet people concerning such falsified events. Your "American scholar" may be a victim of such self-serving rumors planted on him but I examined German sources as well as other sources before I wrote my article and I can assure you that the Shakhty case was a frame-up from the first word to the last.

. . . Finally, do an interview with Jay Lovestone on Bukharin. To secure such an interview will be difficult, for he is trying to live down his past without coming to terms with it, and this requires evasions. However, if you bear this in mind and bear in mind further that Lovestone was for sometime an ardent admirer of Bukharin but has an incurable wound in his spirit because of his last-minute attempt to repudiate and renounce Bukharin in hopes that he could placate Stalin and retain his leadership of the American Communist Party, then the interview might be interesting.

———————◆•◆———————

Wolfe explains to an executive at the University of Michigan Press why a recent book by Angelica Balabanoff about Lenin was not a success.

June 1, 1971

To: John Scott Mahon

I am not surprised that *Impressions of Lenin* didn't sell well. I had an uneasy feeling that it wouldn't sell well as soon as I saw the title you had given it. The title is quite colorless. If you had translated her title more literally and added a touch of proper publicity, it would have read *A Close-Up of Lenin* by Angelica Balabanoff, first secretary of the Communist International. That would have helped the sale whereas *Impressions* is vague and unattractive. I should have made my suggestion as to title earlier, but didn't learn about it until you sent me the printed book. Titles play an important role in the conception and popularization of my own books. I go to work on a title before I do anything else. If you take a look at my titles you will find *Three Who Made a Revolution; Six Keys to the Soviet System; Marxism: 100 Years in the Life of a Doctrine; The Bridge and the Abyss;* etc. We live in a world which is flooded with an endless outpouring of paper representing vast forests felled for no good purpose and to that flood of paper is added the din of the radio and the idiot antics of the television machine. What chance has a good book if it doesn't insist upon attracting the attention of the drowning man? I think I have saved some of my friends' books from oblivion by rechristening them before they went to press. One of my essays insisted in its very title that the world was less likely to perish from atomic fallout than from "Drowning in a Paper Sea." That is one of the dangers that besets you as a publisher of serious books.

———————◆•◆———————

Wolfe gives his recollections of Scott Nearing (1883–1983), a fellow traveler, to a biographer of Nearing.

July 14, 1971

To: Professor Stephen J. Whitfield

There is not much I can tell you about Scott Nearing since I have been only occasionally in contact with him and not at all in recent years. I can tell you, as you no doubt know, that he became a celebrity in radical circles when he was ousted from the Wharton School of Economics of the University of Pennsylvania for his critical attitude toward the profits of certain industries in Pennsylvania. He went into the socialist movement, and I met him when he began to lecture at the Rand School of Social Science of which I was then the publicity director. The Rand School catalogs can probably be found in the section of the New York University Library to which the Rand School Library was eventually donated. He lectured only rarely at the Workers' School (I have deposited all that school's catalogs in the Fifth Avenue Library in New York). He became a fellow traveler and justified all communist actions including purges but so far as I know never joined the communist party, merely followed its line.

My last contact with him was, I think, in 1944 or 1945 or 1946. During or immediately after World War II, we spoke on the same platform. I protested that Stalin was killing all the elite that made up the leadership of the Polish people from the murder of 10,000 plus Polish officers in the Katyn forest to the execution of the Jewish

socialist leaders [Henryk] Alter and [Victor] Ehrlich "as agents of Hitler" (a likely job for a Jewish leader!). Nearing retorted that to kill
the elite of any nation was a great social service. This got a round of
applause from fellow travelers in the audience. But when I said to
him, "You know, Scott, that if the Communists took control in this
country you would be one of the first to be executed," and he answered, "Yes, I do know that," then the audience became silent. I
know his son, John Scott, who was a roving research editor for *Time-
Life-Fortune* who never uses his father's last name. I knew his first
wife, Nellie Seeds Nearing, whom he divorced but never met his
second. They are gathering maple syrup from a stand of maples, I
think in New Hampshire. He lives on "nature foods" and at rare
intervals still issues a horrendous pronouncement supporting some
communist position in a conflict with a neighbor country.

That's all and good luck to you.

Wolfe comments on a New York Times *story
about the daughter of Lenin's friend Inessa
Armand.*

July 19, 1971

To: The Editor, *New York Times*

I get the *Times* out here by mail and it takes me a little time to
catch up with your current news. I hope this will not prevent you
from finding space for a brief comment on your Moscow correspondent's article in the *New York Times* of July 9 dealing with the death
of "little Inessa," the daughter of Lenin's intimate friend and disciple, Inessa Armand. Your correspondent has brought in my name in
the following.

"Bertram D. Wolfe, an American expert on the Soviet Union, in
an article about Inessa Armand, has suggested that she was Lenin's
mistress. But this has received no backing here from Soviet histori-

ans, who have simply noted that she was a close friend." This would imply a repudiation of my documented research on this question which was published both in the *Slavic Review* in the United States and in *Encounter* in England.

What is surprising is that Soviet historians should have said anything about "little Inessa" when she died now at the age of 73.

The Soviet government in various ways has recognized the accuracy of my contention, namely:

1. I did my literary detective work basing myself on 10 letters from Lenin to Inessa published in the fourth edition of *Lenin's Collected Works*. As soon as I broke the secret, the Soviet government published 40 letters of Lenin to Inessa during the same period, which appear in the fifth edition of his *Collected Works*.

2. They published several articles by Inessa's daughter, whom Lenin and Krupskaya [Lenin's wife] adopted; by Madame Stasova, then in her nineties; and some booklets on Inessa Armand.

3. When Israel Shenker, in charge of the *Time* bureau in Moscow, wrote a profile of Lenin for *Time* in which he gave a two-and-a-half sentence decent and discreet summary of my article, they closed the *Time* bureau for six months and deported Israel Shenker. I do not feel repentant at his fate since he has been doing such splendid and so much more important reporting for the *New York Times* in a series of interviews with American intellectuals and the coverage of important scholarly conferences. Some people have said that the deportation of Israel Shenker was my Lenin Prize.

May I add that I published this article in a scholarly journal rather than in a mass circulation journal because I wanted to reach scholars, I wanted to document with adequate footnotes, and I did not want to contemplate an advertisement headed "Read About Lenin's Mistress." Lenin's private life is none of my business as a historian, but since Inessa Armand had the courage to differ with the leader she worshipped and since he was compelled to answer her not with the usual abuse of epithets such as "counterrevolutionist," "agent of the bourgeoisie," and the like but had to explain patiently his real position to her in these letters, I wanted to call the attention of the scholarly world to the special importance of his 10 letters to Inessa which enable scholars to see more deeply into what Lenin really believed. The addition of 40 letters added to this precious deeper insight into his views.

———————◆•◆———————

*Preparing to write his autobiography, Wolfe asked
Max Nomad, an old friend, to help him recall two
people they had known 50 years earlier.*

August 30, 1971

To: Max Nomad

I hope this letter finds you in good health and engaged in doing something interesting. Young writers should keep busy. It keeps their machinery from rusting.

Now this young writer who has begun his autobiography badly
needs your help and you alone have the age, the wisdom, and the
many-sided knowledge that may enable you to help me. I should like
to know all that you can tell me about Bill Shatoff (Shatov). All I
have been able to find about him is that he was a dashing and popular figure in Greenwich Village, and an anarchist of sorts and that he
handled the funds which were supposed to help Russian revolutionary exiles in the United States to go back to Russia after the tsar fell.
(According to David Shub's recently published chapter from his memoirs in the latest number of *Novyi Zhurnal*, Shatoff signed the names
of one or more good revolutionaries in his receipt book and kept the
money.) Further, I have heard that when he got back to Russia he
was welcomed by Lenin and given first some high post in Petrograd
to confound the confusion and then a post in the direction of the
railway system. Anything you can tell me about him will be
appreciated.

My other subject of author interest is Dr. Julius Hammer, whom I
knew personally as a young man, and who if memory serves me was
convicted of what was then the high crime of promoting an abortion
in a patient who had requested it. As I understand, he lost his citizenship, was convicted of committing a felony, and barred from the
future practice of medicine. But all turned out for the best in this
best of all possible worlds (after all it is the only one we've got), for
he went to Russia, started a pencil factory with his son, Armand,
which factory was useful and profitable. I do not know whether he

died in Russia or the United States, or when, but Armand Hammer now gives in his *Who's Who* autobiography himself as director of the pencil factory from 1925–1930. It would appear that in 1930 when Stalin was destroying the NEP [New Economic Policy] he converted his profits into jewels, icons, and other treasures which became the stock-in-trade of the Hammer Galleries in New York. Armand Hammer went on to higher things such as banks, whiskey companies, and oil companies and is now a multimillionaire, which shows what a great thing the Bolshevik Revolution was. I should like to know whatever you can tell me about Julius Hammer, his age, his appearance, what punishment he suffered in the abortion case, when he got to Russia, how he got to know about pencils, and when he died. Julius Hammer is not in *Who's Who* except as the father of Armand but if anybody's mind is a who's who for such matters it will be yours.

———————◆———————

Wolfe's friend Philip Jaffe was writing a book, The Rise and Fall of American Communism, *and sent Wolfe a section of the manuscript for his comments. Wolfe replied that he no longer knew what socialism meant.*

September 20, 1971

To: Philip Jaffe

... As to the word *socialism*, I have a question to raise. What is socialism? Who has ever defined it? What socialism are you talking about? How can you make the same conclusion about socialism which is vague and indefinite as you do about communism which is intimately associated with a definite totalitarian structural organization? The proof that communism has such a definite form lies in the invasion of Hungary and Czechoslovakia just as soon as they attempted to make some type of socialism less totalitarian in structure. When you say socialism, are you thinking of England; are you thinking of Denmark, Norway, and Sweden; are you thinking of a welfare state; are you thinking of a totally planned economy with the abolition of a free market? In short, I have never met anybody who has been able to answer the question: What do you mean by the word *socialism?* This includes many leaders of socialist movements who are completely stumped when I ask them what they mean, or merely say, "I mean a system in which the worker gets a better deal," or some other vague formulation. I, therefore, would suggest that you separate socialism from communism, and that in this Introduction you make your conclusions only concerning communism. Later on, somewhere in your book, you may choose to discuss the indefinite and multiple forms of organizations and countries calling themselves socialists, and you may possibly draw some conclusions that apply to all of them. If you do, you are a better man than I am.

When Nikita Khrushchev died in September 1971, Wolfe wrote the following script for broadcast in Russian on Radio Liberty.

On the Death of Nikita Khrushchev

One cannot help but feel indignation at the shabby treatment of Nikita Khrushchev's death by the present Soviet regime. As in 1967, at the celebration of the 50th anniversary of the October Revolution when Khrushchev was not allowed to appear, so too at the time of his death he is relegated to the place of a mere pensioner.

What shall we now say about a regime which first produced the man whom Stalin portrayed as a foolish old grandpa [Lenin] who allegedly surrounded himself with spies, who was followed by the man [Stalin] who murdered Lenin's closest associates? He in turn was followed by a verbose adventurer [Georgi Malenkov] who resorted to harebrained schemes and who was followed by gray nonentities now puzzled by the problems which confront them as though the regime were new, instead of over half a century old. What can we expect from a regime like this? At least Khrushchev was inventive as a leader. He struggled to solve the unsolvable problems by trying first one approach and then another. But the present rulers do not even have the courage to invent. They just hold on. They terrify other comradely countries by invading Czechoslovakia. At home, they leave no room for even an occasional thaw, jailing writers or sending them to lunatic asylums, and maintaining Russia's world-famous culture in a state of permafrost. I can only protest the low treatment of Khrushchev's death by those gray nobodies who only serve to confirm Wolfe's Law of Diminishing Dictators.

*Wolfe explains to a young historian how America
should have conducted the Korean and Vietnam
wars.*

March 2, 1970

To: Justus D. Doenecke

. . . On the Korean War I gave our government an eighteen-day warning as to the exact date on which the North Koreans, heavily armed by Russia and China, would cross the boundary into South Korea. I said June 25. They paid no attention. On June 25 the troops did cross the line and then they tried to get me into the Department of State to get a secure lock on the stable after the horse had been stolen. I worked for them throughout the Korean War and urged upon the government two things: (a) To continue the [General Douglas] MacArthur pincers' tactics on each Chinese army that entered Korea. Since we controlled the sea, this was easy. We could have taken prisoners indefinitely and eventually unified in freedom all of Korea. It was my contention that if they discovered that when they opened wars they lost some territory instead of at worst returning to status quo, they would stop their probing attempts. Under the pressure of European allies who wanted us to protect Europe and not Asia and under the pressure of some of Truman's advisers, I lost out on that one. (b) My other principal aim was to convince our government not to return the Chinese prisoners by forced repatriation. On this I made many friends in high places and then, with the unexpected help of Syngman Rhee [president of South Korea] who released the majority of the Chinese prisoners, I won that one.
. . . On Vietnam, it would have been proper to intervene had we intervened properly. A great nation doesn't back into a war as if it were walking out and doesn't attempt to free only half of a country if it ever expects any of it to be free. Had we gone in seriously and swiftly from the start, it would have been over before misunderstanding and opposition could develop and the same lesson about not feeling out the weak spots if you know you are going to lose territory

would have been taught. We have never known how to engage in Vietnam and therefore we hardly know how to disengage. As the world's leading great power we must concern ourselves with freedom in Europe *and* in Asia but where we do not know how to engage properly or feel that we are overextended at the moment, we should know enough to indicate our stand, stay out, and bide our time.

After many years of not being in contact, an old friend writes to Wolfe in 1971 urging him to write his autobiography. Wolfe replies:

November 8, 1971

To: Joseph Davis

Being a disciplined comrade, I am obeying your instructions and have begun work on my autobiography. It will be a slow job because of my unbeatable forgettory and the need to look up and pin down every time I try an explicit sentence. But as you know, explicitness, concreteness, the exact detail, and the precise word are things that make writing come alive, and as you have probably guessed, I am my own severest critic as to style and thought.

As to your other instructions, a man who has reached my age is grown-up enough to know that he can't do everything. Actually, as soon as I finished *Three Who Made a Revolution,* being then 52 years of age and just beginning my work in the Russian field, I knew that I had an insoluble problem. That book dealt with life lived in a narrow and deep channel whereas any continuation would involve a number of volumes since the picture widened to include a world war, two revolutions in Russia, the history of a regime, an analysis of its character, attempts at world revolution which would carry the story to many lands, etc., etc. After much thought and inner conflict, I finally decided to undertake larger enterprises as if I might live forever and at the same time to break them into small parts each of which could be published and live a life of its own independently of whether I ever did any further work or not. Thus, I did five chapters for a study on who betrayed the Marxist heritage, Lenin or Kautsky or Plekhanov and then found myself asking, What heritage? So I made it into a book that lives a life of its own, *Marxism: 100 Years in the Life of a Doctrine.* Similarly, I discovered some marvelous quotes from Maxim Gorky in which he denounced Lenin for destroying the freedoms conquered in 1917, and I puzzled over the psychological mysteries of mutual admiration, friendship, and antagonism. The result was *The Bridge and the Abyss.* And I began at once to study the problem of the nature of the regime Lenin set up and Stalin amplified. On this, I worked for a quarter of a century publishing along the way separate studies when I found that they could live alone and be submitted to the judgment of my peers and from time to time gathering collections of them, which explains *Six Keys* at the end of fifteen years, *Communist Totalitarianism* at the end of twenty years, *An Ideology in Power—Reflections on the Russian Revolution* at the end of a quarter of a century. I have a few more studies to do in this series, namely on the perpetual agricultural crisis, on the planless plan, on human resistance, and covert and overt dissent. If the Great Reaper doesn't reap me before that, I may get out a new edition of *Ideology* some five years from now. The materials are there in my files and the reflections in my head; all that is lacking is time which I know is not unlimited . . . In short, I live each day as if I were to live forever or might wake up tomorrow morning to find myself dead. That is why I publish separate pieces and books whenever I am satisfied that they can live by themselves and why they all fall into a general pattern. I am most pleased to read your words "Your ability to see intellectual problems in a new light even after a lifetime of living with them." That's a splendid diagnosis of what ails me . . .

———————◆·◆———————

Wolfe rejects the label of political prisoner *for
someone convicted of possessing marijuana.*

November 15, 1971

To: Leni Sinclair

I am sorry to see from your circular letter of November 8, 1971, that
you have put the case of your husband in too large a framework
which, in my opinion, makes his case more difficult, as it does in
several too-large causes which you invoke in that letter.

At the request of the P.E.N. [international association of Poets,
Playwrights, Editors, Essayists, and Novelists] club, I wrote a letter
to the governor of the state of Michigan, a copy of which I sent to
the P.E.N. club committee formed on behalf of your husband as a
subdivision of our Writers in Prison Committee and received an answer promising most serious consideration of the case. I did so because your husband is a writer, the length of his prison sentence is
outrageous, the law in such cases in the state of Michigan more outrageous still, and I consider the whole question of punishment for
the smoking of marijuana to be dubious. When marijuana grows wild
in our country, when the smokers of the weed are to be found in
such numbers, to me it seems that it falls into a category similar to
alcohol and tobacco, with the sole difference that the present push-
ers are noxious underworld crews whereas the sellers of alcohol and
tobacco are legally recognized and respected vendors.

But it is impossible for me to regard the smoker in prison as a
"political prisoner" as your circular letter suggests or to have any
connection with the slogan peace and power which your letter also
invokes. Such arbitrary linkage makes the case of the sufferers from
the harsh law more difficult. Smoking pot neither makes one a political prisoner, nor does it involve peace and power. Smoking pot is not
a political act in the sense in which the word political prisoner
should be used. It is a harsh law and a harsh sentence, and we have a
better chance of eliminating both if we concentrate our fire on the
matter in hand rather than diffusing it over all sorts of things which

are irrelevant. Moreover, as a conscientious writer and a man interested in a decent world, I can only think that such use of the words *political prisoner, peace,* and *power* debases all three of them and rather than widening narrows the circle of persons who can be rallied to correct an injustice and to force the repeal of an unduly harsh law. Forgive my frankness for it is well meant, and I hope without too much confidence that my remarks may be helpful. In closing, let me assure you that I will continue my efforts to secure your husband's release and the repeal of the law in the ways that it seems to me most effective.

Wolfe clears up a case of mistaken identity.

November 29, 1971

To: Professor Vergil D. Medlin

I must apologize for upsetting you and for my state of confusion at the moment I wrote my last letter to you. It was, as you suspected, a case of mistaken identity, and I herewith retract my last letter and pronounce it unwritten. In Mexico, we have a happy device which does not exist in English; when a man has opened his mouth and put his foot in it at a party and every face registers shock, he says, *"No he dicho nada,"* whereupon the words go back down his throat much as if you were viewing a reversed film at a movie and every face clears up with satisfaction. But there is nothing I can say in English or Russian to match that. I shall not attempt to explain what occurred, for both of us are much too busy and aside from the hurt look on your face which I hope has now cleared up the whole matter is unimportant.

On the eve of the World Psychiatric Association congress in 1971, Wolfe wrote an article attacking the use of psychiatric terror against political dissidents in Russia and urged the editor of the National Review *to print it immediately.*

December 6, 1971

To: William F. Buckley, Jr.

I badly need your help, speedy and unstinted, not for myself personally but for the tormented psychiatrists of the Soviet Union who are being compelled to violate their consciences and their Hippocratic oath under police compulsion and to commit sane men to insane asylums and give them and apply to them psychiatric tortures, of which you already know and details of which are given in my article below.

What I am asking of you is that you publish the article I am submitting herewith in your earliest possible issue, even if you have to tear out something already set up; that you send it to your senator brother [James A. Buckley of New York] with a request that he base a speech upon the article, and read the article into the record. If that seems to you too much of a family affair (personally I think not), he can ask some other senator who enjoys his confidence, perhaps Senator [Henry A.] Jackson [of Washington] to do it . . .

I should also appreciate your sending out an advance release to the press and agencies, and most particularly to the *New York Times* which has at least on this question maintained a decent record.

———————————◆•━━━━

Wolfe urges the American Psychoanalysts' Association to protest the use of psychiatric terror.

December 15, 1971

To: Robert Wallerstein

I am enclosing an article of mine which will appear in the next issue of the *National Review* which goes to press this Friday, December 17, dealing with a subject which I hope will be of interest to you and to the conference which meets in the Waldorf-Astoria beginning December 16. I have chosen the *National Review* because I knew that its editors could act promptly in deciding whether to accept the article and because I thought prompt and widespread dissemination of the material contained in it was desirable both so that our psychiatrists might give some aid and support to their fellow psychiatrists in the Soviet Union who are being subjected to intolerable police pressure to put their science to degrading uses as a means of torment of wise, courageous, and sane men who are being thrown into lunatic asylums as a means of political punishment and suppression. Particularly in view of the failure of the international psychiatric conference just finished in Mexico City to give such needed help to their fellow practitioners and to the victims of a perversion of the science of psychiatry, I hope that our American psychiatrists now assembled in New York will rise to the occasion and give such needed support in the form of resolutions addressed to the Soviet government. That government is already beginning to retreat from this intolerable situation since it has received protests from the psychiatric association of British Columbia, the psychiatric association of Canada, and various organs of public opinion in England, Sweden, Switzerland, and in the *New York Times* here in the United States. It takes only a little effort to get them to release less-celebrated victims and less-known ones as they have already released Jaurès Medvediev [Zhores Medvedev], geneticist and molecular chemist.

*Wolfe challenges the claim that the Soviet prac-
tice of putting political prisoners into lunatic asylums dates back to the tsars.*

January 24, 1972

To: Bernard Noskin

Thanks for your long letter of January 15. I have no time at present
to discuss anything in it except that I want to correct one error that
has been implanted in you, probably by Cyrus L. Sulzberger [writer
for the *New York Times*], who had it implanted in him by an apolo-
gist who is on his research staff. It is absolutely untrue that the tsars
put people in the lunatic asylums merely because they were critical
of the regime. There is literally only one case in which the philosophical writer [Petr] Chaadayev wrote a philosophical letter in
which he said that Russia never contributed anything to human culture or civilization. To offset the impact of this published letter,
Nicholas I sent an alienist to Chaadayev, declared him mad, con-
fined him to his own residence for a year, and had the doctor visit
him once a week. During that time, he continued to write and publish, receive guests, and engage in all normal activities. He remained
a respected writer all his life, and yet all the succeeding generations
of intellectuals execrated Nicholas I for that one stupid but not outra-
geously cruel response to a somewhat one-sided published utterance
concerning Russia's role in civilization. I wrote Sulzberger rebuking
and telling him that he was giving aid and comfort to the present-
day barbarous rulers of Russia and their cruelties. He thanked me
warmly and apologized. But then the staff member in question
searched and searched and searched and came up with [Anton] Che-
khov's famous story *Ward Number Six*, whereupon Sulzberger pulled
the boner again. Don't you repeat it or I will fire you as my research
assistant. It is unjust to the comparatively cultivated tsars, that even
goes for Nicholas I . . .

The fight isn't over yet. During this last week my article was
broadcast in Russian from Munich by Radio Liberty. A number of

comments have been published on my article. And Julius Epstein is now preparing a series of articles for publication in the German press. You cannot make these people ashamed of their cruelties but you can shame them by exposing this evidence that they do not constitute a civilized government but a government of the inner barbarian who has usurped power over a great people which particularly in the nineteenth century produced a truly great culture which astonished the world.

———————◆•◆———————

Wolfe replies to an inquiry about Pablo Neruda, a Nobel Prize–winning Spanish poet who extolled Stalin.

January 4, 1972

To: Patricia Blake

On Pablo Neruda, I did some inquiring of the Spanish department and am told that a poem to Stalin appears in a book of his called *Tercera Residencía*, published in 1947. This is a plausible year since it is the 30th anniversary of the seizure of power by the Bolsheviks in 1917. I have no doubt that Neruda wrote more than one eulogy of Stalin since there were recurring birthdays, anniversaries, and other occasions for him to do his bounden duty. If you need to get hold of Neruda's works, the best place to look for them is in the Hispanic Library of Columbia University where Ella and I got our M.A.s in Spanish literature. I am sure they have everything he wrote, and I am sure he published the bad along with the good in his works . . .

Incidentally, it would be interesting for you to make a comparison of the English translation published by the *New York Times* of a poem of Neruda's on the Spanish civil war which the *Times* published when he received the Nobel Prize with a translation by me of a poem by Leon Felipe on the Spanish civil war which I published in

Tri-Quarterly of fall 1969. Then you can judge who wrote the greater poem on the Spanish civil war and who is more deserving of a Nobel Prize when it comes to writing poetry in the language of the Spanish people. But because Leon Felipe neither hunted with the hounds nor fled with the hares and was always a loner with no claque and no clique, he did not even get an obit notice in the *New York Times* when he died at the age of 84, much less a Nobel Prize.

After learning that his friend Edmund Wilson was in failing health, Wolfe urges him to revise his book To the Finland Station.

March 6, 1972

To: Edmund Wilson

The review of the book by Leonard Kriegel published recently in the *New York Times* spurs me to write you a letter I have long contemplated writing.

It seems to me, Edmund, that it is highly desirable that you return now to a revision of your book *To the Finland Station,* one of the most important books you have written and one which you surely do not want to leave to posterity in its present form. A new introduction telling your readers how they have moved the Finland Station around since the day when you started to write that book and where the station stands now would be of enormous value to all of us. Certainly you are no longer young. I imagine you are as old or perhaps a year older than I am. It is time for you to remember that whatever you touch now is to be in the final form that you are likely to leave it. I should love to see you do your best to put *To the Finland Station* in the form that will be most appropriate to the richness of your thought on Russia over the course of a lifetime. You have thought much since you started that book and thought much since you finished it and released it for publication, and I think there is no more important thing for you to do now than to put that in the final form in which you would like to leave it.

I know perfectly well that each one writes what he feels compelled to write or what the mood of the moment stirs him to write, but I beg of you to give serious consideration to this suggestion. I do that as a friend and an admirer of your work and perhaps a sounder judge than you of what might be most important for you to do at the present moment. At any rate, please think the matter over.

I am sorry to hear from Joan Colebrook [a writer and mutual friend] of the present condition of your health. But that is the way it is with all of us. The only way to avoid the aches and pains and handicaps of old age, the only sure remedy, is one that most of us are reluctant to take, namely to die young. If we do not permit others to read our obit, it becomes our painful duty from time to time to read the obits of our friends. In any case, I am sure that your spirit is as stubborn as ever and that you have still a great deal to say. Please think of saying the full story of your meditations on the Russian Revolution and the consequent state of the world because that revolution took place in the twentieth century.

All the best to you. Please let me hear from you your thoughts on the *Finland Station* and whether and how far you have gotten in doing a new introduction to a new edition of that book. [Wilson died in 1972. A revised edition with a new introduction was published after his death.]

———————◆•◆———————

Writing to the editor of Encounter *in London,*
Wolfe expresses skepticism that détente means the
end of Soviet-U.S. conflict or the need to study
Russia and proposes to launch a countercampaign
to study totalitarianism.

May 16, 1972

To: Melvin J. Lasky

Suddenly, the state of Slavic studies in America is in mortal peril.
All the academic politicians, responsible to no organized body, that
manipulate, withhold, and bestow millions upon institutions and the
contrivers of projects have decided that we no longer need to study
Russia because the president is going to shake hands with [Leonid]
Brezhnev and this means détente and the complete extinguishing of
scholarly and official curiosity concerning the nature of the Soviet
system. As [British prime minister Neville] Chamberlain brought
back an umbrella under his arm and a promise from Hitler from
shaking the bloodstained hands of that dictator and announced to
the world: "I have brought back peace in our time," so President
Nixon has shaken the hand of Mao Tse-tung and now of Brezhnev
and has told us in advance of the handshakes that his mere journeys
have brought the world "twenty years of peace." Hence, all of a sudden the great Harvard Russian Institute is bankrupt and the lesser
ones in miserable condition, the far-famed public library system in
New York is also bankrupt and New York's greatest pride in scholarship, the Slavonic Division of the Fifth Avenue Library, is being shut
down. The very term *totalitarianism* has been condemned to disappear from social studies, and we are inviting the perils that come
from folding one's arms or leading with one's chin when we should
be keeping our guard up.

Hence, as a lone wolf in his 77th year of life, I have begun a
countercampaign. My first step was to persuade the Association for
the Advancement of Slavic Studies to have a panel discussion
opened by me under the title "Totalitarianism Revisited" with a

coreporter, Professor Henry Brompton, to damn and ban the very term in the name of political science and Max Weber. The paper I presented there was received with tremendous enthusiasm and even Professor Brompton retreated in his closing speech. On May 23, I shall deliver a talk of double the length of the paper I presented there to open a discussion at Stanford University. I shall follow that with visits to a number of universities beginning with the University of Colorado where I am always welcome and going on to the Ivy League where I am more coolly received.

------◆·●------

Writing to a Jesuit who was organizing a sympo-
sium on the American Revolution, Wolfe explains
why Jefferson's views on revolution are misunder-
stood and how the notion of a humanistic young
Marx was created.

July 21, 1972

To: William J. Monihan, S.J.

I have just received with interest your announcement of your symposium for July 1972, and I am delighted to find that you are dealing with the American Revolution which brought out nation into being. I am also pleased to note the names of your three protagonists, Thomas Jefferson, Benjamin Franklin, and John Adams. Being an old propagandist, I might have been inclined to include Sam Adams and Thomas Paine, but three is a trinity and five is a crowd.

However, as an admirer of Thomas Jefferson I am not altogether happy with your paragraph which begins with his name and ends with the sentence, "I hold a little rebellion now and then is a good thing . . . it is a medicine of the sound health of government." The quotation is, of course, correct, and more than once he spoke of rebellion as a useful correction for tyranny. Thus he wrote:

The spirit of resistance to government is so valuable on certain
occasions, that I wish it to be always kept alive. It will often be
exercised when wrong, but better so than not to be exercised at
all. I like a little rebellion now and then. It is like a storm in the
atmosphere (letter to Edward Carrington, January 16, 1787).

His ablest biographer, Dumas Malone, comments: "He did not actually *like* rebellion, but he most feared repression and . . . he was putting his trust in the people," and "in such private correspondence he
resorted to hyperbole." Of course, people have forgotten by now that
this was always in private correspondence and never in public utterances, but, for whatever purposes, these utterances have been much
published by many people since. I further observe that he never used
the word *revolution* except for the blessed one you will celebrate. He
did not approve of overthrowing all the existing institutions, the precious along with the outworn or obnoxious, without any sense of
responsibility as to what might take their place.

Even more characteristic of Thomas Jefferson than this one-sided
quote from private correspondence is his profound reflection when in
1801 he found himself with the power of the presidency of the
United States in his hands. As a great reformer, a democrat, and liber-
tarian, he debated with his own spirit as to what use he could properly make of the great power that had thus come into his hands.
This is what he told himself and then wrote to an intimate friend,
Dr. Walter Jones, on March 31, 1801, that is to say, less than a
month after his inauguration: "When we reflect how difficult it is to
move or deflect the great machinery of society, how impossible to
advance the motions of a whole people suddenly to ideal right, we
see the wisdom of Solon's remark, that *no more good must be advanced than the nation can bear.*"

This, I take it, after many years of study of the uses and abuses of
power, is probably the wisest and most self-denying admonition that
a man, finding himself endowed with the awful implements of
power, can bid himself to bear in mind. This is my Jefferson and I
hope he will be properly presented and represented at your symposium in the light of this, his wisest saying.

This thought is particularly important now at a moment when on
the margins of the great Society of Jesus an infection is spreading of
Jesuit Maoism and Jesuit Marxism-Leninism.

The weakening tissues of thought that prove the most frequent
breeding ground for the spread of this infection are the coquetting
that I find fashionable in some Jesuit circles with "the Marxism of the

young Marx," which I take to be a desire to be "with it" and engage in a dialogue with the Marxist-Leninist as some sort of also-Marxist.

As you know, the so-called "Young Marx" is nothing but a notebook he kept when he was reading other and, I think, nobler thinkers than himself, as a young man, noting long passages from their works in the fields of economics, politics, and philosophy and adding a few youthful comments of his own. As you also know, he repudiated the views of these men, and challenged and denounced them, within a year of writing the notes in that notebook. Many times thereafter he made fun of their humane and idealistic phraseology in his subsequent writings. He boasted to Engels that even when he wrote for the British trade unionists the manifesto of the first International, he put in no more of the soft language than he had to, and he reassured Engels in these words: "My proposals accepted . . . only I was obliged to accept in the Preamble of the Statutes two *'duty'* and *'right'* sentences, ditto *'truth, morality, and justice,'* which is placed so that it can do no harm."

As you know also, he never cared to publish that youthful notebook. It was not published until the twentieth century and then only for the sake of completeness in the *Collected Works* and the *Gesamtausgabe* of the two Marxicologists, [Franz] Mehring and [David] Riazanov [editors of Marx's collected works].

However, they have been recently used as bait to make it easier for certain religious participants in this dialogue to assume in some weird fashion the title of Marxist by acceptance of this youthful notebook in order to assume a pseudo-Marxist garb, a common cause of terminology with those who regard the dialogue as a tactical maneuver in their reach for power and who regard all religious feeling as "impeding human progress and dehumanizing man and alienating him from his humanity."

It would be equally proper for a man to call himself an Augustinian because he accepts the young Augustine before the latter had the change of heart which makes him the great church authority that he became. Or to call himself a Gandhian because he accepts the young Gandhi who had not yet acquired his intense revulsion toward sex, which revulsion came when he was in bed with his wife in one room and his father lay dying in the next, and he was too engrossed in his own pursuits to perform the rites for a dying father such as the closing of the eyes and other Hindu ceremonials.

If I have called the legend of the young Marx bait for the unwary, that is not to discount the usefulness of the 1846 notebooks in communist countries where everything bearing Marx's name is part of an equal sacred canon, so that thoughtful dissenters who wish to challenge the brutalities of Marxism-Leninism in practice can often proceed under an umbrella of quotations from those useful notes and thus give their protests a cover of respectability as Kolakowski has done.

But I marvel that no one among the Jesuits with their tradition of learning and their quest for clarity should have examined the original writings from which the youthful pre-Marxist student named Karl Marx made his notes: such men as the humanistic [Ludwig] Feuerbach, the gentle Moses Hess (who converted Engels to socialism), and the youthful Hegel (not to be confused with the cloudy philosopher of Hegel's later period), instead of accepting the assertions that this so swiftly outgrown period is authentic, and even "more authentic" Marxism or Marxism-Leninism than the whole body of his actual views and writings and the practices that they have followed in his name. Can this be the spirit that put energy and confidence and humanistic reform into the Counter-Reformation which in the first confusion of the verbal and physical battles of the period of the Reformation it had lacked? Can this be the heritage of savants and theologians and diffusers of learning that they now permit their bitterest opponents who have exterminated their order wherever they are in power to choose the battleground on which the dialogue (really controversy) shall take place?

Well, Bill, enough, nay too much. Where angels fear to tread I rush in, and who am I to tell the church or the Society of Jesus, to both of which I am at best a well-wishing outsider, anything about how they array themselves in battle or controversy?

Forgive a clumsy intruder. But remember that I am on firmer ground when I say that the American Revolution did not want to overthrow all existing institutions but to preserve and enlarge the rights it possessed so proudly, the rights of freeborn Englishmen. That is why our revolution was not followed by blood purges like the French and the Russian, but permitted the Loyalists to withdraw peacefully to Halifax and both Jefferson and Hamilton and even Daniel Shays to die peacefully in their beds. And that is why the stillness that descended on the battlefield of Appomattox was broken by the kindly voice of General [Ulysses] Grant telling the Confederate cavalry, "Keep your horses boys, they'll be needed for the spring planting." And that is why Jefferson Davis died in his bed and Robert E. Lee in his. And why the revolutionary democrat and reformer could contemplate the awful power that had just been conferred upon him and bid himself remember that "no more good must be advanced than the nation can bear."

———————◆◆———————

Wolfe thanks a British historian for sending him a
Scotland Yard dossier on his activities in Mexico
during the 1920s.

July 26, 1972

To: George Leggett

I am deeply grateful to you for having secured for me a transcript of a part of the mysterious dossier on the mysterious Bertram and Ella Wolfe that reposes in the records of Scotland Yard or some other such agency. I hasten to inform you, however, that the dossier is wrong in nearly every sentence, not to mention in spelling of certain key words. Thus in the second sentence of Telegram No. 52 I find that the Erom is a Mexican labor federation. Actually its name was FROM, meaning Federacion Regional Obrera Mexicana, now defunct. The one correct sentence in the dossier reads, "Ella Goldberg is . . . the wife of Bertram Wolf." She is still the wife of Bertram Wolf, but he has always spelled his name with an *e* at the end. Thus giving a tail to the wolf. Aside from that, it might be of minor interest to you to know that she left Mexico when she got good and ready and was never expelled from that country, although her husband was. Further, she never brought funds from Russia for Mexican railway strikers nor for any other purposes. She never even went to Russia until 1929 (with me) and then returned penniless and brokenhearted because I had waged a six-month-long fight with Joseph Stalin, which upset her more than it did me. Incidentally, though she did not then know it, she should have rejoiced that he had not yet perfected his technique for ending discussion and, therefore, we both returned to the United States alive, as this letter and your own eyes have testified. And, by the way, neither did her husband return from Moscow with Russian gold for Mexican railway strikers. Thus you can judge the value of the sentence concerning the Mexican police which reads "The police have full knowledge of her movements for the last five years."

Now the dossier is most useful for my autobiography since I intend to have a section on deportation from Mexico, which section will be a fearful lesson for historians who think that they can make official government documents into dependable footnotes. When I was deported, the government first declared officially that it was as a *vendedor de drogas heroicas* [drug peddler]. When this first was ridiculed by the then senator from Michoacán in the Mexican senate, the government issued a new statement that I had been deported because I brought $50,000 in Russian gold to foment a railway strike in Mexico. The one story is as false as the other, but I was deported chiefly as a vendor of another type of poisonous drug, namely as director of education for the Mexican Railway Federation: I was trying to teach them to pay their own dues, employ their own labor leaders, and rent their own headquarters instead of accepting from the government soft jobs for their labor leaders, confiscated palaces as their headquarters, and government paper and printing for their journals. I told them that everything would be less elegant, but it would be theirs and not the government's. Can you blame the Mexican government for deporting me and not telling the reason?

---

*Replying to an old friend who had written to
Wolfe after reading a review of his newest book,
Wolfe comments on Leon Trotsky's anti-Semitism.*

July 27, 1972

To: Max Scharf

Yes indeed, I remember well your face peeking out of the wicket at the Brooklyn General Post Office and your discussions with me on various things. However, those discussions were always cut short by the growing line of impatient men and women behind me. Therefore your notion of my views on Leon Trotsky are incomplete and one-sided. I think that Trotsky was deeply influenced in his psychology by his Jewish heritage, but much of the influence was to develop a kind of Jewish anti-Semitism and a rejection of his parents, their outlook on life, his heritage as far as it was conscious, his religion, and religion in general. He put minus signs and antipathies where others might put plus signs, which is not to say, as you do, "that Jewish factors in Trotsky's life were nil and nonexistent." A man can reject his heritage but he cannot root the traces of it out of his soul . . .

As for me, I swim against the current. If I get swept downstream it will be more slowly and at least I will know where I am heading and will hope to leave some landmarks along the stream in the form of books and articles which may speak to a later generation.

———————◆•◆———————

Wolfe explains his views on the Vietnam War.

September 13, 1972

To: Helga Bailey

I should like very much to put my signature on your letter, for I sympathize with the plight of those whose crime was to try to develop an independent government of their own and a socialism more human and humane than the totalitarian brand forced upon them in the name of "liberation," but one sentence in your letter makes it impossible for me to sign it and that is the sentence in which you say, "I feel shame for what our country is doing in Vietnam."

I think that our country is trying to do for South Vietnam what it should be trying to do for Czechoslovakia and Hungary and other European countries, namely, protect the right of the inhabitants of South Vietnam to determine their own destiny and resist conquest and the subsequent slaughter of a million or so of its inhabitants, their magistrates, teachers, and village elders if North Vietnam succeeds in imposing its rule by force. If I feel ashamed, it is not of that general effort but of the bungling way in which our government failed to use its massive power in the first moments of its intervention and failed to declare openly what its motives were. Three successive presidents now bear responsibility for the bungling, but I am proud of the way in which President Nixon is extricating our troops from the bungled war he inherited, is trying to put the South Vietnamese in a military position where they can defend themselves, and is seriously trying to interdict the continuing invasion of South Vietnam by blockading Haiphong harbor and bombing bridges, gasoline and oil pipes, and concentrations of the munitions which the Russians and the Chinese are pouring into North Vietnam. I do not see why Asians should not have the same right to self-determination that Czechoslovaks or Hungarians should have.

Incidentally, I hope these remarks will raise a broader question in your mind. When you try to arouse lovers of freedom, and I count myself as one, to defend the right of self-determination of Czechoslovakia, don't tack onto your appeal other situations of which you know less and which you have not familiarized yourself with as you so manifestly have with the situation in Czechoslovakia.

I wish you all the best in what you are trying to do, but I do hope that you will have the wisdom to strike out the irrelevant sentence on Vietnam from your letter. If you send me the letter thus revised and agree that the revised letter will be the one you will release to the press, I should be most happy to sign and to get many others to sign your appeal.

———————————◆—◆———————————

Professor Richard Pipes of Harvard University sent Wolfe a telegram congratulating him on being attacked as "a henchman of anticommunism" by Titorenko, a Soviet historian. Wolfe replied:

October 20, 1972

To: Richard Pipes

Many thanks for passing on to me the award of *Voprosy Istorii KPSS.* I didn't know how much I was in debt to you until I saw that it was thirteen pages long and all of them directly or indirectly devoted to your friend the henchman. *Henchman* has a more unpleasant sound in English than *oruzhenosets* so I prefer Titorenko's version to yours. I shall call myself *armsbearer* or *swordbearer*. Actually, the occupation is one which provides me with a chariot so that I may follow the great warrior and hand him according to his needs now a battle-ax, now a *poignard*, now a sword. I feel all set up, for previously I never got more than a paragraph or two of agreeable insults from them. I cannot avoid the suspicion that Titorenko is engaged in an Aesopian attempt to call attention to my writings.

———————◆———————

Wolfe recalls V. F. Calverton, a communist literary figure and editor of Modern Monthly *during the 1930s.*

November 2, 1972

To: Leonard Wilcox

I would like to emphasize one aspect of Calverton's life and personality which may not be apparent to you from your study of the documents alone. Calverton was a very gregarious person. He had the ambition of bringing all intellectuals in America together both with each other and around successive magazines in the days when it was easy for writers and intellectuals generally to gather together in good fellowship—that is to say, the days before the blood purges which sowed factional bitterness and hatreds where previously there had been a certain comradeship and good fellowship. Calverton served the role of a catalyst. He liked to write himself, but he had a prehensile rather than an original mind (I used to say that his mind was as prehensile as a monkey's tail). He needed meetings of fellow writers, editors, publishers, artists, and critics, so that he could pick up ideas from them as well as participate in good fellowship. And these ideas used to appear with his own personal stamp upon them in his subsequent writing. I think he would have been much more sterile were it not for these contacts and these nights of talk.

During prohibition he had the skill, the connections, and the ability to bring the most diverse people together who otherwise would have worked in solitary loneliness, one of the diseases from which writers suffer. Calverton arranged a monthly law-breaking session— to violate the Eighteenth Amendment and the Volstead Act prohibiting the purchase and sale and manufacture of any alcoholic beverages with more than one-half of one percent of alcohol, a law which gave us near beer. We used to meet once a month at Teutonia Hall underneath the Third Avenue elevated railway at Third Avenue and, I think, Sixteenth Street where the law breaking began with a huge stein of beer (real beer) and then we ate good Teutonic dinners after which wealthy men whom Calverton managed to enlist would vie with each other to take the whole pack of us in a string of taxicabs to one of their homes, where there would be all conceivable alcoholic beverages secured by each wealthy man from his respective trustworthy bootlegger. It was the custom of ocean liners to bring genuine scotch and aquavit and all the liquors of Europe and the world to twelve miles from America's shores where they would be dropped off to be picked up by speedboats and sold to our wealthy patrons. Said patrons also supplied all conceivable types of tasty tidbits like caviar on sour cream, deviled eggs, etc., etc. And we would pass the night till dawn in what seemed to us brilliant conversation. It was there that I met some of the best writers of our time and many other interesting people of various sorts. Without V. F. Calverton as catalyst these pleasant and exciting gatherings would never have occurred. With the blood purges to sow discord where previously, without jesting, one could speak of "the good love of comrades" among the most various people, each of whom held to his own views, but fought for the right of all the others to express their views also, and with the untimely death of V. F. Calverton from leukemia, the entire New York City and eastern seaboard intelligentsia was dispersed into solitariness once more. That is why I call George (his real name was George Goetz but coming from Baltimore, he adopted the pen name of the town of Lord Calverton, the founder of Maryland, which is how he came to be V. F. Calverton) a catalyst or the catalyst for so indeed he was.

Perhaps I should add one more word about his death. Both of us had opposed America's entrance into the First World War as we had opposed the breakdown of our civilization with its engendering of the first total war of our century. I visited Calverton when he was dying and knew that his end was very near, but both of us were then engrossed in an attempt to keep America out of the second total war of our century, and we both were active in the Keep America Out of War Congress. It was one or two days before he died, but his mind was still clear during the visit and he spoke eagerly to me about our efforts and questioned me on what successes we were having. That was my last meeting with V. F. Calverton and I have never ceased to miss him and the role he played.

Wolfe expresses doubts about détente to a U.S. diplomat in Moscow.

November 5, 1972

To: Franz H. Misch

As always I remain stubborn and recalcitrant in my disbelief in the permanent seriousness of the word *détente.* The Soviet bosses are worried about the present state of their industry and agriculture and when the Devil was sick, the Devil a saint would be, when the Devil got well, the Devil no saint was he.

Moreover, they continue to drip hatred in the *Pravda* cartoons right through the détente, are looking to advance deeper into Europe by negotiation, and to get recognition of the satellites acquired first by their pact with Hitler, then by their violation of the Atlantic Charter at the war's end. They still arm North Vietnam with super sophisticated rockets and other weapons, worried a little—not too much—about cumbersome, slow-moving China and will feel out the weak spots where they can.

Wolfe explains the origins of his essay on totalitarianism to the publisher and editor of the Lugano Review.

November 27, 1972

To: James Fitzsimmons

What with the crusades of revisionist historians, the scholars who forever search for novelty and get weary of using any term or concept for more than a half decade, and those who find fresh warrant for their dislike of recognizing the phenomenon or using the term *totalitarianism* now that the word *détente* acts as a great eraser to wash the slate clean of everything one has known and thought or is struggling to comprehend in this regard, I found it desirable to open a new discussion on the nature of totalitarianism and the opportunity came to me when the program committee of the AASS [Association for the Advancement of Slavic Studies] wrote me asking for suggestions for a special panel of the political science section of the AASS. My answer: "As my friend Arthur Koestler once wrote, 'if God had any purpose in giving man a neck, it was to have him stick it out,' I therefore am sticking mine out to offer you a paper on the nature of totalitarianism to open the political science session."

———————— ◆ ————————

*Wolfe criticizes Senator Henry M. Jackson's pro-
posal to extend diplomatic recognition to the Peoples' Republic of China and sever diplomatic ties
with Taiwan.*

March 7, 1973

To: Senator Henry M. Jackson

I shall ask you to forgive me for taking the liberty of telling you how
deeply I disagree with your recent statement coupling the diplomatic
recognition of the Peoples' Republic of China with a proposal to
sever diplomatic ties with the Republic of China in Taiwan, while
still retaining our treaty commitments to the latter. If I venture to
tell you of this disagreement, it is because of my general admiration
for your stand on virtually every other question as such stands have
come to my notice.

It is not for a democratic state such as ours to deal in the fictions
of uncountries, ungovernments, and the like. The United Nations
has already disgraced itself in the eyes of thoughtful people by omit-
ting Taiwan with a population of 15,000,000 (and a volume of foreign trade approximately equal to the volume of mainland China)
from the *U.N. Demographic Yearbook.* The U.N. has not stopped
with relegating Taiwan to the status of a noncountry or uncountry,
but its officials have even stooped to the communist device of rewriting history and composing unhistory. At the U.N. headquarters in
New York there has long been a plaque identifying the Republic of
China as donor of a marble slab containing a quotation from Confucius. Confucius and the donor have been removed together at the
demand of Peiping.

I beg you to re-examine this question once more. And if on further thought you should come to the conclusion that your proposal
was unwholesome or unsound, you would really electrify our people
by doing something which political figures have almost never been
known to do, namely, making public acknowledgment of an error.
This is the way great political leaders can educate our citizens. My

opinion of you is sufficiently high that I venture to hope that you might do the same.

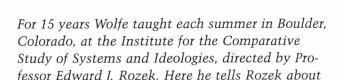

For 15 years Wolfe taught each summer in Boulder, Colorado, at the Institute for the Comparative Study of Systems and Ideologies, directed by Professor Edward J. Rozek. Here he tells Rozek about a new edition of Three Who Made a Revolution.

March 7, 1973

To: Edward J. Rozek

I have really exciting news for you concerning one of the members of your institute faculty. I have just learned from a long and interesting article in the Paris newspaper *Russian Thought* that my *Three Who Made a Revolution,* despite its 650 pages, has been published and is being circulated by samizdat [self-published writings by political dissidents]. When you give this as a textbook to our students this summer, tell them that those who are reading it in Russia risk prison, torture, incarceration in insane asylums. But you needn't promise them the same treatment. I have not felt so proud of any translation or edition since I learned that this 650-page book has been tape-recorded for the blind. To circulate in both these kinds of darkness is a honor for any author.

——————————◆•◆——————————

*Writing to Eliseo Vivas, an old friend and a retired
philosophy professor, Wolfe probes the psychology
of political converts.*

March 16, 1973

To: Eliseo Vivas

As to conversions, I want you to know that I am, as Stalin told me,
"an exceptionalist." He coupled it with the adjective "American"
and I promptly declared that I was guilty as charged and guiltier than
charged for I was an exceptionalist for every country in the world,
believing that each moves toward its own unique future in terms of
its own past and its own traditions. I think the same is true for
individuals. Each converts in a different way and unconverts according to his own nature and resulting from his own accumulation of
doubts and differences, his own immediate and special last straw and
then becomes a distinctive ex-Catholic or ex-Communist, or ex-X. I
said something to this effect in the introduction to *Strange Communists I Have Known.* There is the fanatical Communist who becomes an equally fanatical anti-Communist as so many Catholics do
not become indifferent but bitterly anticlerical or anti-Catholic.
Thus there are ex-Communists who spend all their life, not merely
their spare moments but all their days and nights as Lenin wished,
only devoted not to being Communists but to being anti-
Communists—professionals so to speak. I permanently lost the
friendship of one such by telling him that the Politburo was still
determining his every action, only he put a minus where they put a
plus and he put a plus where they put a minus and waited anxiously
to know what to believe until they declared themselves and vice
versa. If this view doesn't satisfy you, you can join with Stalin in
denouncing me as an incurable exceptionalist. You will at least be in
important company.

———————◆•❚————————

In 1973, when the Soviets discovered a new
weapon for suppressing samizdat, Wolfe tried to
rally opposition to this maneuver.

March 19, 1973

To: David Dempsey

One of the things of which P.E.N. may justly be proud is its long
fight to get all countries to endorse the Geneva Copyright Convention and to respect the right of American authors to a valid use of
their copyright in the Soviet Union and the further right to prevent
tampering with the spirit and letter of their original text when translated into Russian or other languages of the Soviet Union. Now that
we have gained a victory in this long struggle, our laurel wreath
threatens to be turned to dust and ashes by the latest decree of the
Supreme Soviet on this matter, namely, decree no. 138 of the Supreme Soviet passed on February 21 and given public notice in the
Weekly Bulletin of New Legislation dated March 15 and signed by
President Nikolai V. Podgorny. This decree says that "the copyright
pact adopted in Geneva in 1952 will apply to works first published
on the territory of the USSR—or, not published, but found on the
territory of the USSR in any objective form."

This means that the remarkable publication efforts of the free
samizdat publishers are now to be checked by the Soviet censorship
and police since any work which the government publishing house
Gosizdat—Gosudarstvennoe Izdatelstvo—rejects can no longer be
published by the perilous mode of private mimeographing, typewrit-
ing and carbon copy distribution, or other form of samizdat (self-
publishing). If the police in their search and seizure activities lay
hands on a single copy of a samizdat publication, according to decree
no. 138 they can thus prove that the material was "published or
found on the territory of the USSR in an objective form." They will
then call the author to an inquisition and demand to know whether
he authorized any publisher to publish abroad without the state's or
party's permission. If he answers "yes" he has committed a crime by

publishing something which those who have power over everything and therefore knowledge of everything have deemed unfit for publication. As you no doubt know, Solzhenitsyn has denied that he granted authority to publish abroad some of his masterpieces which he could not publish at home. Under this new decree, the Soviet government can then seek an injunction, engage in a lawsuit, and demand punitive damages from any publisher who had published the work abroad "without permission of the author." If the author says that he gave permission, then he is guilty of treason. In short, the Soviet government is joining the community of civilized nations in this regard to increase the barbarity of its publication control and suppression of any literary activities the state and party may disapprove of.

It is hard to know how best to treat this new maneuver. P.E.N. can of course protest in all public bodies including the U.N., UNESCO, etc. that the purpose of copyright is to protect and encourage writing and publishing, not to suppress it. But it seems to me that P.E.N. should also take the initiative to ask writers who belong to it, and publishers, to refuse to permit the publication of any works in the USSR or to accept any works for publication in America until this mischievous decree against the encouragement of writing is repealed. I would, of course, welcome any other action which the collective wisdom of the members and executive committee of P.E.N. and you yourself might devise. Anything we can do is a most proper action in accord with all that P.E.N. has so far done in this field.

*In the early 1970s the United States Senate re-
fused to reduce tariffs on Soviet products until
Russian Jews were allowed to emigrate. President
Nixon, however, demanded the power to reduce
tariffs, regardless of Soviet emigration policy.
Wolfe urged him to reconsider.*

April 16, 1973

To: President Richard M. Nixon

I am writing to you to appeal to you to relax your attempted pressure upon the Congress of the United States in the matter of your
request for authority to grant lower tariffs to communist countries,
including the Soviet Union.

It is understandable to me and laudable that you should desire to
make yourself a place in history as the man who brought about a
strengthening of peace in the world. But it is impossible to secure
peace at the expense of the helpless and voiceless captives that the
Soviet government is holding for pirate's ransom or denying the right
of emigration even at a price. The men who rule the Soviet government have no respect for public opinion in their own country; but
surely it is not the place of our president to attempt to destroy the
effectiveness of public opinion in our own country. The Congress of
the United States, and notably the Senate under truly brilliant leadership, has brought pressure to bear of the only kind the Soviet rulers
can understand, namely, pressure upon their profits. The senators I
am sure will stand firm with the support of the public opinion of all
lovers of freedom in the United States. Moreover, the Soviet government is bound by solemn undertaking of the United Nations Charter
to grant freedom of exit without blackmail or ransom money.

The measure of greatness in a leader of our country lies in his
ability to acknowledge and correct a mistake when he has made one.
This would educate our people and hearten men of goodwill everywhere. I beg of you to send a fresh message to Congress making it

clear that you are not going to bargain away the rights of these people for a trade advantage.

———————◄•►———————

In anticipation of President Nixon's summit meet-
ing with Leonid Brezhnev in 1973, Wolfe sent the
president information about forced-labor camps in
the Soviet Union.

June 14, 1973

To: President Richard M. Nixon

Twice I have ventured to address you by letter, each time in the
cause of freedom, and basing myself on my own special knowledge
of Russian affairs. Each time I have received a courteous response
which I deeply appreciate, but in the second instance, on the matter
of granting the most-favored-nation privilege to the Soviet government at the expense of the freedom of Soviet Jews, your answer, for
all its courtesy, was painfully noncommittal.

Now on the eve of your summit conference with Leonid Ilyich
Brezhnev, I venture to write to you once more on the same general
question of that which is most precious in the tradition of our
country—the question of freedom. I have accumulated as part of my
research and writing duties here as senior research fellow of Russian
studies at the Hoover Institution considerable evidence that the rulers of Russia are repeating once more a maneuver they used in connection with each of three previous détentes, namely, to take advantage of our feeling of goodwill to sharpen their war on their own
people. I do not have to tell you, given your background and your
high position, that this is the dual essence of totalitarianism: a covert and sometimes overt war to conquer another piece of the free
world and a war on their own people.

Thus when Herbert Hoover offered famine relief to Russia in the
early twenties through Maxim Gorky, V. I. Lenin immediately put all

the members of the nonpartisan public famine relief committee in Russia into jail and condemned them to death. He no longer needed these public figures since Hoover had naively made the offer to Maxim Gorky alone, and only the alertness of Herbert Hoover and Fridtjof Nansen saved the lives of such noble people as Ekaterina Kuskova, Sergei Prokopovich, Sergei Bulgakov, and Alexandra Tolstoy. This same type of operation has been repeated each time we have made a friendly gesture to the Soviet government. But our negotiators approach the heads of their government with forgetfulness of the past and an amiable will to be deceived.

I am taking the liberty of sending you the latest report on forced-labor camps in the Soviet Union as prepared by Professor Peter Reddaway of the International Committee for the Defense of Human Rights. His report deliberately omits harrassment by refusal of all employment and then imprisonment as a social parasite, the putting of sane and wise leading Russian figures in lunatic asylums, the use of exile, etc. Yet his report shows that by the beginning of 1973, there were 1,200,000 inmates of forced-labor camps, and as the atmosphere of détente is growing, evidence is coming in to us of an increase of the camp population. I can send you material on the tormenting of people, scientists, artists, dancers, and others of Russia's best for having applied for a visa to go to Israel, and this at the very moment when the Soviet government informs you that they have "suspended" (note: not abolished) the prohibition against visas for Jewish intellectuals and the ransom charge.

Naturally, I have no intention of embarrassing my president, and hence no desire to make this growing mass of material public at this time. But I would be glad to make it available for you as a help in the difficult ordeal you are facing. Indeed, I hope I shall never have to make public material I gather, and beseech you to remember that America's one claim to the allegiance of other peoples is our continued devotion to freedom.

It has been said that such freedom in the Soviet Union is an *internal matter*. The same was said in the heyday of Hitler. But when you are planning to enter into arms agreements, if we violate them there is a free press and a free people to make it known and voice protest. If there is no such freedom in the Soviet Union, we cannot trust one word which they sign, for no one will let the world know if they do not keep their promises. We live in an age, as you know, when the freedom of any great power is a concern of all great powers and of the entire world.

I am sure I am breaking into an open door in telling you all this, and that really this question of winning some freedoms in Russia to make peace stronger and the world safer must be your deepest concern as you approach this difficult summit meeting. Forgive me if I belabor the obvious, but at times like this it is better to say too much than not to speak up.

———————◆•◆———————

Paul Kurtz, editor of The Humanist, *sent Wolfe a draft of* Humanist Manifesto II, *asking for his comments.*

July 17, 1973

To: Paul Kurtz

I have a few specific suggestions to make for changes:

1. I cannot accept your first sentence to the effect that the century of Hitler and Stalin and Mao Tse-tung and of the brutal war against innocents in Northern Ireland can possibly be called "the humanist century." Personally, I am convinced that the century of two total wars and two periods of false peace and massacres of every description is the most brutal century in modern times, certainly more brutal than the nineteenth. I would begin the manifesto with a totally new approach and drop the first sentence altogether.

2. I object to your proposal to put foreign aid into the hands of some single international body and let such body decide allocation and use of the funds. We have already had the dreadful experience of UNRRA to which the United States contributed virtually all the funds and on which the countries behind the Iron Curtain together with new and unexperienced lands that had just been admitted to the U.N. made a series of "collective decisions" allocating the funds chiefly to countries behind the Iron Curtain in such fashion that they could use them to oppress their own people and

in some cases their neighbors. In principle the idea that the better-off nations should give aid to the needier ones is a good one. But India has repeatedly complained that Russia refuses to permit their aid to go to the development of agriculture in the 500,000 villages of India, and insists on projects which involve huge industries that India can neither man nor provide resources for nor use for the well-being of her people. I have documentation on this as I have on the monstrous misuse of "aid" granted by Russia to Indonesia. If you are interested I can send you such material. At any rate, until a world body exists that we can trust as Americans or as humanists, America should continue (with some improvements) to grant funds in her own way for proper purposes.

3. I note that you trace the roots of humanism "from classical Greece, Rome, and China." China has many things to commend it but a land which accepted as natural the exposure of unwanted girl babies can hardly be called humanist. Moreover, no matter what your prejudices against religious beliefs, I think we must acknowledge some indebtedness to Judeo-Christian morality . . .

7. Under Humanity as a Whole you optimistically declare that "the ideological differences between communism, capitalism, social-ism, conservatism, liberalism, and radicalism can be overcome." I am tempted to say: "Nice work if you can get it." In any case, I should like to see added after the word "overcome" the words "if there is free expression and free movement of men and ideas across frontiers."

———————◆◆———————

Journalist Eugene Lyons asked Wolfe about the decision to embalm Lenin's body.

July 23, 1973

To: Eugene Lyons

I know from Boris Souvarine, who was very close to the Bolsheviks even after his break in the early 1920s and kept in touch with Trotsky for some time, that the chief advocate of the embalming of Lenin was General Secretary Stalin, closely supported by the then head of Leningrad, Zinoviev, and by all their unconditional supporters on the Politburo. I further learned from Souvarine that Kamenev disagreed with Zinoviev on this matter, for Kamenev loved Lenin personally so deeply that he even came to imitate Lenin's handwriting and he expressed indignation at the idea of creating a saintly icon of the dead body. So did Trotsky himself and more emotionally, Krupskaya.

I personally reached Moscow in the late spring of 1924 and my first act as a delegate from the Mexican communist party to the Fifth Congress of the Comintern was arranged for me and for all of your delegates by Zinoviev as the chief of the Leningrad district. He demanded that the entire congress hold its first session in Petrograd where Lenin made his coup d'état, and the whole congress entrained to Petrograd (shortly to be named after Lenin) to file solemnly into the wooden tomb, and in the hushed silence of underground Red Square each of them made obeisance in his fashion to the newly mummified corpse. From Bukharin personally I then learned that he was shocked and outraged by the whole procedure. He spoke of a corpse as a corpse and said with feeling, "When I am dead I don't care what they do with the rubbish of my remains." I suppose others opposed the mummification for more abstract "Marxist" reasons, but the deep feeling of Krupskaya, Kamenev, and Bukharin was more than a matter of abstract principles.

But they could not prevail against the political calculations of Stalin and Zinoviev, each of whom hoped to be Lenin's successor, and each of whom wrote a book on Leninism as part of the embalming fluid. Moreover, on their side they had the mood of great numbers of members of the orphaned Bolshevik party, and the orphaned Russian people.

———————•◆•———————

The president of the Earhart Foundation, Richard M. Ware, asked Wolfe if it was true that Lenin said he would abolish capitalism by debauching the currency.

July 23, 1973

To: Richard M. Ware

I can indeed supply some of Lenin's remarks on this matter. There is probably a good deal more on this question in his still unpublished work kept under ball and chain by the Cheka, but there is enough for your purposes already at my disposal.

Lenin began by accepting literally the general view of many Marxist socialists that money and trade through an open market would disappear in favor of a barter system where all goods will be kept in central warehouses and people would turn in certificates of labor time spent in return for objects embodying like quantities of labor time. Lenin spoke of money in contemptuous language. He preferred to call it "symbols" or "money-signs" (Russian, *znak*). When he was reluctantly returning to the use of money, having tried to abolish it altogether and thus destroy all capitalists in Russia and all capitalism, he wrote an article on "The Importance of Gold Now and After the Complete Victory of Socialism." In it he said,

> When we conquer on a world scale I think we shall use gold for the purpose of building public lavatories in the streets of several of the large cities of the world. This would be the most "just" and educational way of utilizing gold for the benefit of those gen-

erations which have not forgotten how, for the sake of gold, ten
million men were killed and thirty million were maimed in the
"great war for freedom," in the war of 1914–18 . . .

But however "just," useful, or humane it would be to utilize
gold for this purpose, we nevertheless say: Let us work for another decade or so with the same intensity and with the same
success as we have been working in 1917–21 only on a wider
field, in order to reach the stage when we can put gold to this
use. Meanwhile, we must save the gold in the R.S.F.S.R. [Russian
Soviet Federative Socialist Republic], sell it at the highest price,
buy goods with it at the lowest price. "When living among
wolves, howl like the wolves." As for exterminating all the
wolves, as would be done in sensible human society, we shall act
up to the wise Russian proverb: "Don't boast when going to war,
boast when returning from war."

You can find this quotation and article in convenient form in English in volume 9 of V. I. Lenin, *Selected Works*, published by International Publishers, and in Moscow in English by the Cooperative
Publishing Society of Foreign Workers in the USSR.

As soon as Lenin found power in his hands and took literally the
view that he could abolish capitalism and capitalists by debasing the
currency to the point of extinction, he solemnly wrote this into the
program of the Bolshevik party in March 1919, where he said in part:

In the sphere of distribution, the present task of Soviet power is
to continue steadily replacing trade by the planned, organized,
and nationwide distribution of goods. The goal is the organization of the entire population in producers' and consumers' com-
munes that can distribute all essential products most rapidly, sys-
tematically, economically, and with the least expenditure of labor
by strictly centralizing the entire distribution machinery . . .

It is impossible to abolish money at one stroke in the first
period of transition from capitalism to communism. As a conse-
quence the bourgeois elements of the population continue to use
privately owned currency notes—those tokens by which the ex-
ploiters obtain the right to receive public wealth—for the purpose of speculation, profit-making, and robbing the working population. The nationalization of the banks is insufficient in itself to
combat this survival of bourgeois robbery. The R.C.P. will strive
as speedily as possible to introduce the most radical measures to
pave the way for the abolition of money, first and foremost to
replace it by savings-bank books, checks, short-term notes entitling the holders to receive goods from the public stores, and so
forth, to make it compulsory for money to be deposited in the

banks, etc. Practical experience in paving the way for, and carrying out, these and similar measures will show which of them are the most expedient.

You can find this in the fourth English edition of Lenin's *Collected Works*, vol. 29, pp. 115–16.

Lenin's government began at once to establish unpaid, nonmonetary issues of certificates to the population to secure provisions, consumers' goods, and to abolish payment for postal and telegraph services, for housing fuel, and communal services. All these broke down almost as fast as they were established. Finally, when the liberation from "the power of money" became intolerable, production in commerce came to a virtual standstill, and the population was perishing from cold and hunger.

During this same period Lenin issued summary decrees prohibiting trade and providing for shooting at sight the "bagmen" or "speculators," poor peasants who came to the starving cities with bags of potatoes, turnips, or grain, and tried to exchange them for hammers, nails, and plowshares. But he found that workers and peasants continued the trade under cover of darkness and by stealth. He next attempted to get grain to the cities by sending detachments of Young Communists for the peasants' "excess grain." This frequently included even the seed grain for the following planting. The peasant responded by producing no excess and tilling only tiny patches for his family. These mad measures far more than the drought in one region of Russia produced the great famine of 1921 when the Hoover Relief Administration saved the lives of some twenty million Russians and incidentally, as Lenin acknowledged in confidence, saved his regime. The last straw was the peasant revolts, from the great revolt of the Kronstadt garrison and fortress to the Green Peasant uprisings in the provinces. By October 1921 Lenin acknowledged,

> Now we can no longer speak of exchange of goods, for that is like a field of battle that has been taken from our hands. This fact is indubitable, however unpleasant this may be. A direct exchange of goods (barter) as a system has shown itself not to correspond to the reality which presents itself to us—exchange of goods through recourse to money, purchase and sale for money. The economic structure has brought us to this: That it is necessary to have recourse to such an unpleasant device as trade.

The above was the beginning of Lenin's move from "full Communist" to the New Economic Policy. At the Fourth Congress of the Communist International he announced the next step, namely, the

restoration of a solid, gold-backed ruble currency, and the stabilization of the ruble forever . . . The stabilized ruble was backed by 25
percent gold, by foreign exchange *valuta*, by short-term obligations,
and liquid assets. Lenin used for this stabilization the services of the
former Constitutional Democratic leader, N.N. Kutler, as his financial expert and followed his instructions in detail. However, after
Lenin's death "forever" didn't last very long. As you know the Soviet ruble lost its stability completely under Stalin and his
successors.

———————————◆◆———————————

On behalf of President Nixon an assistant secre-
tary of state answered Wolfe's letter about inter-
nal Soviet repressive policies and U.S. relations.
Here Wolfe describes three earlier periods when
the United States aided Russia and disputes the
notion of Soviet internal affairs being immune to
U.S. criticism.

October 16, 1973

To: President Richard M. Nixon

Thank you for the courtesy you show me in asking John Richardson
of the Department of State to reply to my recent letter to you on
internal Soviet repressive policies and U.S. relations with that country. As one who has served in the State Department under two presidents, I venture to conclude that if you direct the assistant secretary
for public affairs to answer me, it suggests that you are receiving
many comments similar to mine and you yourself have worked out
with Mr. Richardson the general line of response. If I write directly
again to you, sir, it is because the matters raised are of supreme
importance and Mr. Richardson's letter to me does not contain a
satisfactory answer to the questions which trouble us all.

The gist of Mr. Richardson's letter lies in its two concluding sentences, containing the following assurance: "As closer ties are established between our two countries, we believe the Soviets will realize that it is not in their interest to undertake actions which may cause legitimate public concern in the United States. Closer relations between us should benefit all the people of both countries."

Mr. President, I am moved to ask two questions. What in the recent behavior of the Soviet government toward its own citizens can possibly lead to those conclusions? And what in their whole past behavior each time we have tried closer ties and even liberal generosity, can possibly lead to those conclusions?

During the 56 years of the existence of the present Soviet regime, we have tried a half dozen times closer relations and the granting of generous aid to the Soviet government when it was in distress. Let me recall three such efforts and their consequences.

1. In 1921, Lenin's policies of suppressing trade between town and country, plus a drought in the lower Volga region, produced a famine so severe that Lenin said, "If the peasants plant this spring, we will survive; if not our regime will fall." Knowing that his attacks on all the governments of the West made it impossible for him to appeal for aid, he authorized Maxim Gorky to set up a Russian famine relief committee of reputable, noncommunist public figures. Thereupon Herbert Hoover cabled to Maxim Gorky offering massive relief. Since the cable was addressed to Gorky personally, Lenin took that as a license to dissolve Gorky's committee and condemn all of its public figures to death. Only the personal intervention of Herbert Hoover and Fridtjof Nansen, and the angry protest of Gorky himself, saved their lives. Lenin commuted their sentence to perpetual exile and loss of citizenship in the land of their birth.

2. In the period of Stalin's forced industrialization, we again were generous with technicians, engineers, industrialists, and capital loans. While our Hugh Cooper was directing the construction of the famous Dnieper Dam, Henry Ford constructing their first auto plant, and German engineers reconstructing the coal mines which Russians had let fall into ruin, Stalin took that as license to stage his famous show purge trials: the Shakhty coal mine wrecking trial framing up German and Russian mining engineers; the trials of the nonexistent Industrial party and the likewise nonexistent Peasant party and finally his own party members by the hundreds of thousands.

3. During the infamous Stalin-Hitler pact, when Hitler double-crossed his accomplice and invaded Russia, our president sent Harry Hopkins to offer Stalin tanks, trucks, planes, guns, munitions, and food, absolutely without any conditions. After Pearl Harbor we gave unstinting aid to Stalin as our ally, again without conditions. The period of the Hopkins visit opens with the murders in the Katyn forest, continues with the framing up of the Jewish Anti-Fascist Committee, and continues with the crushing of all Jewish communal cultural life and the deportation of entire tribes and nationalities from their millennial homelands, all this while Stalin was an ally of our democracy.

Thus the whole history of the past half century and more cries aloud its warning that we must not now try a new period of rapprochement and of providing credits, know-how, advanced computerization, installation of entire factories, including huge truck and auto plants that may easily be converted into tank factories to overrun Western Europe, not to mention the most-favored-nation privilege, without first exacting some guarantees of sufficient freedom in public life so those of their citizens concerned with peace may give warning if their government secretly violates arms agreements, as our citizens can give warning. The names of Sakharov, Solzhenitsyn, Amalrik, and hundreds of others of the best of their public-spirited citizens who are being savagely persecuted, sent to prison, camp, or insane asylum, for the sole crime of trying to warn us and their own leaders that détente must be genuine and not a fraudulent and dangerous deception. No sooner had you, Mr. President, held your meetings with General Secretary Brezhnev than this campaign against these noble and public-spirited citizens was stepped up.

My career for the last four decades, Mr. President, as writer, as professor of Russian history, and as senior research fellow, has caused me to keep close and continuous track of these matters. I shall be glad indeed to supply documentation and lists of victims, accounts of how samizdat publications are crushed, sane men sent to lunatic asylums under the direction of police psychiatrists who strap their victims to their beds with wet thongs and give men like the brilliant mathematician Plyushkin massive injections of Halperidol, on which drug I have secured detailed accounts from the American Medical Association's drug evaluation reports. We cannot go into a dubious détente with Soviet rulers who will commit such barbarisms on the best of their scholars and intellectuals without ourselves beginning to bear some responsibility.

Spokesmen of your administration, Mr. President, have reassured our people that "quiet diplomacy" is more effective than open statement to remedy such evils. But you yourself must know, as I do, that there are over 600 cases of *American* citizens and the wives and children of American citizens, some of them for as long as twenty years and in at least one case, twenty-five years, trying in vain to get a permit to go to America. Our representatives have pressed these cases by "quiet diplomacy" for decades with high Soviet officials and gotten nowhere. This is not a case of Jews wanting to migrate to Israel, though I believe they are entitled to this right. These 600 or so American citizens, their wives, children, and other close relatives, have been growing old while we have been trying "quiet diplomacy" with a government that seems to yield only to public outcry and open protest.

As you know, even after the visits and détente talks began, we once more presented their names and circumstances to a deputy foreign minister and to Ambassador Dobrynin in Washington, yet to date there are 570 of them on which we have not even been given the courtesy of an answer. And this has happened before we have thrown away our few trump cards such as generous credits and most-favored-nation treatment. What satisfaction will these Americans and their families be likely to get if we give up all the Russians want without getting in return even common diplomatic courtesy?

Mr. President, it has been said that we cannot make conditions on their "internal affairs." But are these internal affairs? Are we safe in arms reduction agreements if no one in the Soviet Union may speak up and warn us when in his opinion these agreements are being secretly violated, as in our country men may speak up? Is it not true that in the age of totalitarian regimes, such matters are not internal affairs? Have we forgotten our experiences with the treatment of Jews in Germany, and the German invasion of Czechoslovakia, because there was a German minority there, were both treated as "internal affairs"? When the Russians in turn invade and occupy Czechoslovakia because there was a minority of Soviet puppet Communists there, and we did nothing, were we not condoning a similar dangerous international tragedy disguised as an "internal communist affair"? Are we forgetting that those who will not learn from history are condemned to repeat their mistakes?

Forgive me, Mr. President, for having written at such length, but the issues are grave and the danger increasingly clear. We have now heard public protest and public warning from the representatives of many lands. Chancellor Brandt of Germany warned that freedom of movement of persons and ideas comes first, if peace is to be secure in a time of danger. This was followed by a flat refusal from Gromyko, then protests from Foreign Minister Van Der Stoel of the Netherlands, Foreign Minister Andersen of Denmark, from Sir Alec Douglas-Home of Great Britain, from spokesmen of country after country of Western Europe, and from all the great organs of opinion of those lands. Why is it that we alone are silent? Will not our silence make us into accomplices of the acts of tyranny on some of the best and most public-spirited citizens in the modern world?

Indeed, whatever our official spokesmen will now do, our record is not one of silence. The American P.E.N. and international P.E.N., to which I have the honor to belong, have spoken clearly and strongly. So has the American Publishers' Association. So have the psychiatrists of this and other lands. Most important of all, our Academy of Sciences has sent a solemn warning to the Russian academy that no matter what governments may sign, if the Soviet rulers crush such men as Sakharov, they will make cooperation of our scientists and theirs impossible. And both the Houses of our Congress have spoken clearly on the connection between freer trade and greater human freedom. The honor roll is long! I will not enlarge it farther.

But reluctantly and with heavy heart, I must close by asking: Why does not your voice ring out more clearly, along with that of our secretary of state? How will we face the year 1976 if the word freedom loses its supreme place in America's lexicon? In the age of totalitarian regimes, the world needs our voice as the greatest democracy. I pray that it may not falter.

*When President Gerald Ford and Secretary of
State Henry Kissinger refused to attend a dinner
honoring Alekssandr Solzhenitsyn to avoid offending Leonid Brezhnev, Wolfe urged the president to
reconsider his decision.*

July 11, 1975

To: President Gerald Ford

I could not believe my eyes when on July Fourth of all days of the
year, the *Denver Post* carried on the first page a statement attributed
to you by some unthinking White House "aide" to declare that you
did not accept George Meany's [president of the AFL-CIO] invitation
to honor Alekssandr Solzhenitsyn, the most distinguished fighter for
freedom and the greatest literary artist that has been given refuge on
our shores in many generations, because of "questions of Solzhenitsyn's mental stability."

"Can this be the Fourth of July message that our president has
given to us on the opening of the 200th anniversary year of our own
declaration of freedom?" I asked myself. I ran hastily through the
paper (I teach every summer in the University of Colorado) and
found on page 11 that you had tried out a new swimming pool donated to you by admirers. I went back to the story on page 1 and
found that it was from the syndicated service of the *New York
Times.* I turned on the radio and on ABC heard Howard K. Smith, a
reputable columnist, repeating the monstrous story and explaining,
rightly or wrongly, that our secretary of state, Henry Kissinger, had
told you, or said busybody White House "aide," to find an excuse for
your not going to the AFL-CIO dinner "because Brezhnev wouldn't
like it if you went to it."

Mr. President, I can only believe that some unthinking aide with
no sense of the meaning of our history as the prototype of freedom,
the refuge for all who struggle for liberty in their own lands, and the
moral and physical support of all who struggle for freedom, could
possibly have suggested to you, or rather used your name, to back up

the barbarous charge made by Yurii Andropov, head of the G.P.U. and of its special section of police psychiatrists, or could have said in your name that those who fight for freedom in a land of totalitarian despotism are "mentally unsound" or "lack mental stability" and belong in lunatic asylums. Because of his worldwide fame, they dared not put Solzhenitsyn in a lunatic asylum, so they expelled him from his own native land to which he has brought so much honor. Nothing in the world should permit a White House "aide" to back up this vilest of practices of putting the wisest, bravest, and noblest of Russians into lunatic asylums where they are subject to such "treatments" as being bound to prison cots by wet thongs which contract as they dry, injected intramuscularly with sulfazine, aminazine, and other dangerous drugs in massive doses such as are known to unhinge the mind. I have written on this question briefly in the *National Review* of December 31, 1971, of which article I enclose a copy. Should there be any need for more ample documentation, I will be happy to make this entire dossier available to you, your secretary of state, or your busybody "aide," as well as to any reputable psychiatrist or psychoanalyst. A number of their organizations have adopted resolutions concerning this misuse of psychiatry and have sought to give aid and support to fellow psychiatrists in the Soviet Union. I have in my files a letter from Dr. Robert Wallerstein of the Executive Committee of the American Psychoanalysts' Association and copies of letters of protest to the Soviet government from the psychiatric associations of British Columbia, of Canada, and various organs of public and professional opinion of England, Sweden, Switzerland, etc. In short, your "aide," Mr. President, seems to be backing you into a hornet's nest.

I can only think that this scurrilous statement was issued in your name on July the Fourth of the year when we are opening the 200th anniversary of our own struggle for freedom without your approval of its implications. Nothing can so greatly damage our reputation in the free world and your own reputation as to let this statement stand when nothing in White House investigations of the sanity of Alekssandr Solzhenitsyn exists to justify it.

I beg you, Mr. President, for the honor of our country, and for your own honor among all those who believe America stands for aid to ever greater freedom in the world to repudiate this "White House" statement and give a more decent explanation of why you were unable to accept George Meany's courteous invitation. I also urge that you take some early occasion to recognize that in Alekssandr Solzhenitsyn America has received the honor of a stay in our land that has no equal in that of any refugee in a number of generations.

Since I know, Mr. President, that your letters are sifted before they reach you by White House aides, and since the aide or aides who decided on that statement in your name may intercept this letter and keep you from seeing it, I hope you will understand that if there is no evidence in any form that you have received it, I shall have to make this an open letter. I hope you will understand then that I attach so much importance to this issue for you and for our country that I will have no other choice, for such uncalled-for wrongs must be righted, especially when they come from our president and in his name and reach the press on that all-important Fourth of July that opens our 200th anniversary of the Declaration of Independence. I know you yourself cannot doubt that the central word that must stand out in this anniversary year must be the word *freedom!*

Wolfe urges Ronald Reagan to seek the presidency and put an end to the Ford-Kissinger policies.

July 17, 1975

To: Ronald Reagan

I am pleased to see that you are showing less and less hesitancy about announcing your candidacy for the Republican nomination for the presidency. The last letter from your supporters suggested that the main prerequisite for your running is proper grass roots financial support. I take the liberty of suggesting that you have yet another reason for campaigning for the nomination, namely, the need to free the country from the baleful influence of Henry Kissinger upon our foreign policy. If President Ford gets nominated, there is no escape from that influence. As one who has been touring the universities of our country speaking on the détente illusion and watching the reaction of professors and students (students have the vote now too), I get an instant, warm, and virtually unanimous favorable reaction to what I have been saying about the damage which the false image of détente has done to our country's standing in the world. I venture to suggest that you make that issue the central target of your interviews and striking oratorical powers.

———————◆·◆———————

*When a Swedish newspaper criticized awarding
the Nobel Peace Prize to Andrei Sakharov, Wolfe
wrote in Sakharov's defense.*

October 23, 1975

To: The Editor, *Dagens Nyheter*, Stockholm

I wonder whether you can find space in your eminent journal for a brief letter from far-off California? I note that you express a negative view on the Nobel committee's awarding of a peace prize to Andrei Sakharov on the ground that since he was critical of the recent Helsinki agreements "he does not belong to those groups that actively work for peace between nations." Actually, when he decided in his moral and scientific judgment that further testing of the hydrogen bomb was a "crime" for his or any other nation, he was actively working for peace not *between* his own nation and any other single nation, but working for peace *among* all nations that might have the capacity to develop the atomic and hydrogen bombs and test them. He became a "dissenter" on the lack of free speech for public opinion in his own country only when its rulers suppressed his right to give his scientific and moral judgment to them and to his country, as well as to the rest of the world. I should like to tell your readers and the Nobel committee that I think their award of the peace prize to Sakharov was a splendid decision. What other scientist is there who had played so large a part in the perfecting of the hydrogen bomb, then made so courageous a moral judgment on his own work and with rare consistency has accepted all the consequences of persecution for his effort to make all great nations aware of the fact that their further testing of these bombs would be a crime against humanity?

Did Lenin really say, "When we get ready to hang the capitalists, they will compete with each other to sell us the rope"? Here is Wolfe's answer.

November 5, 1975

To: Boris Souvarine

The rope story concerning Lenin I think is more genuine than the rope trick as supposedly practiced in India. Of course, it has never been published in his works but I have heard it from various persons both in Russia and from Russians in exile. The commonest form in which it has been told to me is as follows: During that early period after Lenin took power when he still expected an imminent world revolution, and the Russian people were going hungry with the world revolution as a pacifier, Lenin was addressing a group of activists in one of the two capitals. He said something like, "When our revolution triumphs throughout Europe, we will hang the entire bourgeoisie."

At this point [Karl] Radek, who was standing by, quite properly asked, "But Comrade Lenin, where will we get so much rope?" And Lenin shot back, "It will be sold to us by the bourgeoisie."

I of course do not know whether the wording is exact, but it does accord both with Radek's wit and Lenin's view. At any rate, I heard it from too many people to think that the author is that famous Italian Senone, whose full name is *se non é vero, é ben trovato* [if it is not true, it is well-founded].

———◆–◆———

Wolfe offers his views on Israel and Zionism.

December 16, 1975

To: Professor Philip Siegelman

I should like to add my name to your statement on Zionism and racism, but there are two difficulties for me. A minor one, I have always felt that a true Zionist should want to go to live and work and become a citizen in Israel, and I have no such desire or intention. The second is more important to me. I should not normally want to appear as one who endorses the entire constitutional structure of Israel. I understand that in a period of state of siege it would be difficult to implement a different structure with relation to the Arabs who live and work in Israel (particularly ticklish is the question of service in the armed forces), but I have the hope that someday Israel will be able to become a completely secular and completely pluralistic state, even though its main objective should be to afford protection and a home to Jews everywhere. I hope the day will not be too far off when all citizens of Israel, regardless of religion, national origin, or race, will have equal status in the country. And this makes me hesitant to sign a statement which in its definition of Zionism in paragraph two would seem to commit the signer to Israel's present constitutional structure.

If you would care to make my second point clear in a footnote, I would be happy to have my signature affixed to your declaration, but I realize how that would complicate the problem of your getting signatures and perhaps the effectiveness of your statement. In any case, I shall be referring to Israel and the U.N. resolution in the spirit of your statement in various of my writings including my autobiography on which I am now at work, and I shall always be urging support by our democratic and free country for Israel's right to exist without constant harassment. As for the U.N., when and if I finish my present book, I shall be considering the question of whether I should write a work entitled *The Life and Death of the United Nations.*

When Luis Echeverría, Mexico's president, became a candidate for a high office in the United Nations, his public statements seemed to Wolfe to equate Zionism and racism. Here Wolfe urges the Mexican leader to reconsider his views.

January 5, 1976

To: Luis Echeverría

I hope you will not consider it an impertinence on my part to make some remarks on present Mexican foreign policy. I have a feeling that certain aspects of that policy are determined by a legitimate hope on your part that you may be elected president of the United Nations. I venture to say that at present I cannot think of a better candidate.

But several of your recent public statements seem to me to have been dictated by a desire to win the votes of the so-called Third World. One of these statements was a vote in favor of the nonsensical declaration that Zionism is racism. I am not personally a Zionist, but it is cruel and false to say that Zionism is racism when it is merely one of the many forms of nationalism existing in our variegated world. I note with pleasure that your foreign minister has just resigned and that you yourself and your wife have shown great friendliness toward Israel and its right to exist. Hence, I venture to conclude that the mistake might not have been yours, but that of your foreign minister.

My other remark concerns your recent declaration to the effect that it is very uncomfortable to be the neighbor of a great power like the United States. If you do, as I hope, get elected to the presidency of the United Nations, you will, I am sure, find that the United States is a constructive force in the United Nations and its economic support and its general proposals are beneficial to the wholesome existence of that body.

Be that as it may, for the present I wish only to remind you that if

Czechoslovakia or Poland felt as safe as a near neighbor of the Soviet Union as Mexico can feel safe as a near neighbor of the United States of today, then we would have a much more peaceful and safer world.

I hope you will not think these remarks impertinent, for I assure you that they arise from profound goodwill toward yourself and toward Mexico.

Writing to the former editor of the AFL-CIO Free Trade News, *Wolfe explains how he manages to keep optimistic in the face of discouraging news.*

February 7, 1976

To: Elly Borochowicz

You are right when you say that we are living in an age when our leaders are prey to widespread illusions, confusion, and ignorance. In fact, I am saddened to think that I spend so much of my life trying to get the men who make our policies to understand something about the real nature of totalitarianism and the Soviet Union, and I feel that I have labored in vain. So on my wall I have put up a new photograph of myself taken from the top of Notre Dame. It is a gargoyle with his head in his hands looking deeply dejected at how little effect he has had. But I must add that he sticks his tongue out, which shows he hasn't given up trying.

*Writing to Joseph Coors, a prominent Colorado
conservative and a supporter of Ronald Reagan for
president, Wolfe reflects on the 1976 Republican
convention, which nominated Gerald Ford.*

August 24, 1976

To: Joseph Coors

I can understand the Slough of Despond in which you are, after you
gave so much of yourself, so much devotion, energy, time, and
money in an effort to get the better of the two candidates nominated
by the Republican party. Actually, with the connivance of a few
party machine bosses in the huge states with the big electoral vote,
they have selected two party hacks, one the Republican whip in the
Senate and the other in the House. I could see it coming because
Reagan, not a very experienced politician, let himself be taken in by
the fact that one by one Ford adopted the planks of his rival, and
instead of hitting harder by showing that in his entire practice as
president he did the opposite, Reagan just tried winning by his pleasant personality. He came exasperatingly close, but lost his way in
the matter of principle and forgot that there are still powerful bosses
in some of the states with the big electoral vote.

I have learned that you did not even attend the closing session of
the convention, and I don't blame you. But now there is nothing to
do, as so often in political life, but to select the lesser evil. [Jimmy]
Carter seems to have no platform at all on foreign policy, and when
he speaks on it he speaks ignorantly and dangerously.

There is no point to a write-in of the name of the man you prefer
on election day, for the write-ins are never really counted. One
seems to save one's soul, but one loses one's vote.

I have also heard it said that a number of prominent Republicans
are thinking of forming a third "Conservative" party. As a historian,
I must remind you and suggest that you remind others that third
parties have no future in American politics. They cannot even keep
alive, with the most popular man as their leader, from one election

to the next, because they have no appointments to give out, and no appropriations to hand to one state or another, and no organization or machine. The highly popular Theodore Roosevelt, for example, named [William Howard] Taft as his successor, then became angry with Taft's policies, started the Bull Moose or Progressive party, and it got a vote of millions (4,200,000 out of a total vote case of fourteen million). Yet, with all of Roosevelt's popularity, the party was dead and forgotten by the time the next presidential election rolled around. The same thing happened with the highly popular [Robert] La Follette, who got nearly 5 million out of 28 million votes and had behind him many trade union organizations, yet his third party disappeared before the next election and his son [Philip] after one term as senator, was finally defeated by [Joseph R.] McCarthy and committed suicide. The same story can be told of William Randolph Hearst who tried to fight Tammany [Hall] with a third party in New York City and State, got so many votes that he could plausibly claim that the election was stolen from him by ballot stuffing and throwing of ballot boxes into the East River. Yet despite his possession of the most powerful morning and evening journal in New York City at that time, his party did not outlast another mayoralty election. In the whole history of third parties in the United States, only one ever succeeded and that was the Republican party, which was born as a third party shortly before the Civil War. The only reason it survived is that the slavery issue would not die down and the states' rights issue threatened the unity of the Republic. And, at that, the Republican party succeeded only because the Whig party disappeared, and the Republican party became the second or first party in the United States. In short, write-in means waste and third party means death of the organization that started it. I cannot expect you or any of us to be enthusiastic at voting for the lesser evil in the present circumstances, but that is for the most part all you get in politics.

Be of good cheer, for man does not live by politics alone . . . [I]n the field of politics all we can do, most of the time, is write decent histories and hope to teach the rising generation that its duties are to try to lead our people in the right direction and not idiotically to follow the Gallup polls in order not to lose a few votes at a given moment. Surely the founding fathers of our country would have had contempt for that kind of politics. All of them were genuine leaders of man and they did much to make our country what it is.

*Wolfe explains why voting for Gerald Ford instead
of Jimmy Carter is the lesser of two evils.*

September 7, 1976

To: Joseph Coors

There was one thing I didn't include in my last letter on political
possibilities and that is that out of sheer anger or disgust Ed Rozek,
and for all I know you too, might vote the Democratic ticket. In
fact, Ed told me over the phone that he gives Ford an ultimatum: if
he doesn't fire Kissinger before November 2, Ed will vote for Carter.
Of course, he has no way of telling Ford about his ultimatum. Moreover, it's terribly hard to fire Kissinger because he is a wily fellow
who keeps traveling around and starting negotiations now in this
place and now in that place, and giving Ford and the country the
impression that only he can carry said negotiations to a successful
conclusion. Moreover, it is difficult to ask the head of the State Department for his resignation if he never comes home long enough to
stick his nose into the State Department building. Perhaps you,
whom Ford recognizes as having blocked him from getting the votes
of the Rocky Mountain tier of states, may have more influence upon
Ford than Ed would have. Anyhow, someone has to tell him that he
should ask Kissinger to stay home in the State Department for a
week before November 2 in order to extract from him a tactful
resignation.
    What Ed doesn't realize in his anger is that Carter has no foreign
policy and is a total ignoramus in foreign affairs who speaks out of
one side of his mouth to one set of reporters and out of the other
side to the next set of interviewers. In addition to that, the Democratic Congress is at present slightly like a madhouse that has been
trying to give away more and more government money regardless of
tax rate or budget deficit and has only been prevented at times by
Ford's vetoes. If Carter gets in and the Democratic party in its present state has both president and Congress, they will hand out money
to anybody who holds his hand out and will give so much to so

many layers of the population that they will automatically be voted in at election after election at least until some grave crisis uproots them. You and Ed and Chuck and all the good people in Colorado who have been keeping the Republican party on top in that state are likely to find out that the giveaways will have the same effect in Colorado as anywhere else. I for my part would be keenly disappointed because I have been quietly hoping for the miracle that you would run for the Senate and that we would have your voice and your judgment heard there. Is that too wild a dream?

To save time and trouble, I am venturing to send copies of this letter to Ed and Chuck and I shall ask Chuck to write directly to President Ford and tell him what Ed's mood is at this moment and that Ed was a delegate to the Republican convention but will surely vote for Carter if the president does not manage to make Kissinger stop negotiating everywhere at once and stay for a week in the State Department building which he is supposed to be running while a tactful *public* resignation can be extracted from him.

I hope you realize that all this is none of my business except for my experience in Colorado and my admiration of you three stalwarts and my interest in foreign policy and the good of the country.

Incidentally, this letter and the preceding one are the first I have written you on the important questions facing us now that Reagan has been defeated, and we have no choice but that of the lesser evil.

Wolfe recounts his experience at Stanford University with H. Bruce Franklin, a self-styled Stalinist-Maoist who led demonstrations against the Hoover Institution.

October 19, 1976

To: Professor Irwin Primer

When Bruce Franklin was hired it was largely because of his undeniably interesting work on [Herman] Melville. After he secured tenure at Stanford, his publications notably branched out into quite different fields, largely in magazine articles. He became a lecturer at Venceremos College where his teaching was primarily agitation for a revolution in America and for the disturbance of many of the activities of Stanford University. I sat only a few seats away from him when a large audience of perhaps 800 to 1,000 people came to hear Ambassador [Henry Cabot] Lodge deliver a talk on the difficulties that had developed in the United Nations. A little group seated near and surrounding Dr. Franklin prevented Lodge from speaking, or the people who had come to hear him from hearing him. They did it chiefly by shouting Power to the People, meaning, if it meant anything, the little group of approximately twenty people that sat near Professor Franklin. They did not seem to realize the absurdity of calling themselves the people and reducing the large audience to nothing in the matter of the power or right to hear the speaker they had come to hear. I watched Dr. Franklin closely. He added to the noise when it was safe to do so and remained quiet when his participation would be too noticeable. I offered to testify to this fact at the hearing, but for some reason, those arranging the hearing thought it would be "undignified" for me to involve myself in the case. This was the more unfortunate because my landlady, more nearsighted than I, seems to have observed what I observed, but when she tried to testify, sitting at some distance from the front of the hearing room, Bruce Franklin's defenders asked her to pick him out of a number of people and she was unable to do so, so her testimony was thrown out.

On another occasion I sat among his followers, some of them apparently of high school age from a nearby high school, on the steps in front of the Hoover Library. Those who wanted to make trouble for the Hoover Library sent some scouts to look over manuscripts and other rare holdings a few days before the demonstration against the Hoover Library. They came in barefoot, which attracted the attention of the librarians, and made us change locks, lock doors, and meet the attacking party, well under 200 people, in front of the Hoover Institution. They attacked various employees of that institution and picked me out among the research fellows working at the institution for an attack. When a questioner demanded from our director, Glenn Campbell, why I was permitted to do research in the Hoover Institution, they found to their astonishment that I was sitting among their little group on the steps, using a cane because I had recently injured my leg. It turned out that the questioner did not know me, and when I questioned him as to whether he had read any of my works, he faltered and then said that he was taking a course in western civilization which used my *Three Who Made a Revolution* as one of the texts. I asked him a few questions about the text, and he retreated in confusion. Thereupon Bruce Franklin, who had remained silent in the background, took over to lead the fight. Among his questions addressed to Glenn Campbell was "Why do you have agents in every country stealing documents for your library?" I asked Glenn Campbell to let me answer that question, which he did, and I offered to tell Franklin what piece of paper he was holding in his hand—which was a falsified interview with me. I had given an interview to one of his followers which lasted five hours and was published in the *Wall Street Journal*. I told how we had persuaded the United Nations and the I.L.O. [International Labor Organization] to investigate forced labor in the Soviet Union out of which investigation came a two-volume book published by those two institutions. This was reduced to a statement by me that we had stolen the documents which purported to prove that there were forced-labor camps in the Soviet Union. The next day a number of Franklin's followers visited me to tell me of their disillusionment with him, and their admiration for the book which at that time was part of their course in western civilization.

. . . Finally, I do not have to tell you after the above that I think it would be a grievous mistake at this time to grant him tenure. Perhaps at some future date—sometimes such people grow up and learn to realize what their duties are to the university in which they teach and to their students. I think no man should be condemned forever for such things as you will find in my enclosures. But certainly this is not the time to grant him tenure.

———————◆·◆———————

Wolfe reports to former Congressman Walter H. Judd, an old friend, about his progress on writing his autobiography.

December 17, 1976

To: Walter H. Judd

Our past year has been a tough one . . . But both of us are back in business. Naturally, your medical knowledge will tell you how much time I have to spend in matters other than writing. But I continue to write and am almost two-thirds finished with my book to be called *A Life in Two Centuries* (that's downright impudent!), but the two centuries I speak of are the one which began in 1815 with the fall of Napoleon and ended in 1914 with the beginning of total war. The first sentence of the book says, "I see no reason why anyone should be interested in my personal life," the second tells that I have been at the epicenter of great events that determined the lives of millions and had a chance to observe events at that center freely and close up, and a lifetime to think of their meaning. Since I have a feeling that this may be my last book and that there are many other books within me that I shall never write, I shall try to squeeze my thoughts on them "unnoted" in what pretends to be an autobiography. Since I will be 81 in January, I am realist enough to know that I am in a race with death to finish this book, but have gotten far enough to feel that I may win the race. If I do, I shall of course start another to be called *V. I. Lenin and His Influence on Our Century.* When Death wants me, he will have to grab one foot and pull me away from the typewriter.

❖   ❖   ❖

Bertram D. Wolfe died on February 21, 1977.

Bibliography

Books

Portrait of America (with Diego Rivera). New York: Covici, Friede, 1934.

Portrait of Mexico (with Diego Rivera). New York: Covici, Friede, 1937.

Diego Rivera: His Life and Times. New York: Alfred A. Knopf, 1939.

Keep America Out of War: A Program (with Norman Thomas). New York: Frederick A. Stokes Co., 1939.

Deathless Days. New York: Frederick A. Stokes Co., 1940.

Three Who Made a Revolution. New York: Dial Press, 1948.

Six Keys to the Soviet System. Boston: Beacon Press, 1956.

Khrushchev and Stalin's Ghost. New York: Frederick A. Praeger, 1957.

Communist Totalitarianism: Keys to the Soviet System. Boston: Beacon Press, 1961.

The Fabulous Life of Diego Rivera. New York: Stein and Day, 1963.

Marxism: 100 Years in the Life of a Doctrine. New York: Dial Press, 1965.

Strange Communists I Have Known. New York: Stein and Day, 1965.

The Bridge and the Abyss: The Troubled Friendship of Maxim Gorky and V. I. Lenin. New York: Frederick A. Praeger, 1967.

An Ideology in Power—Reflections on the Russian Revolution. New York: Stein and Day, 1969.

Revolution and Reality: Essays on the Origin and Fate of the Soviet System. Chapel Hill: University of North Carolina Press, 1981.

A Life in Two Centuries: An Autobiography. New York: Stein and Day, 1981.

Lenin and the Twentieth Century: A Bertram D. Wolfe Retrospective, edited by Lennard D. Gerson. Stanford: Hoover Institution Press, 1984.

Pamphlets

How Class Collaboration Works. Chicago: Daily Worker Publishing Co., 1926.

Our Heritage from 1776: A Working-Class View of the First American Revolution (with Jay Lovestone and William F. Dunne), New York: Workers School, 1926.

Revolution in Latin America. New York: Workers Library, 1928.

The Trotsky Opposition: Its Significance for American Workers. New York: Workers Library, 1928.

What Is the Communist Opposition? New York: Workers Age Publishing Co., 1933.

Marx and America. New York: John Day Co., 1934.

Things We Want to Know. New York: Workers Age Publishing Co., 1934.

Civil War in Spain. New York: Workers Age Publishing Co., 1937.

Translation of and introduction to *The Russian Revolution* by Rosa Luxemburg. New York: Workers Age Publishing Co., 1940.

Who Killed Carlo Tresca? New York: n.p., 1945.

Diego Rivera. New York: Pan American Union, 1947.

Essays

"The Balance Sheet of Behaviorism," *Virginia Quarterly Review*, October 1930.

"Leon Felipé: Poet of Spain's Tragedy," *American Scholar*, Summer 1943.

"Lenin and the Agent Provocateur Malinovsky," *Russian Review*, Autumn 1945.

"The Russian Intelligentsia," *Antioch Review*, Winter 1945–46.

"Diego Rivera: People's Artist," *Antioch Review*, Spring 1947.

"Lenin, Stolypin, and the Russian Village," *Russian Review*, Spring 1947.

"Lenin as Philosopher: History of a Text," *Partisan Review*, July–August 1947.

"Science Joins the Party," *Antioch Review*, Spring 1950.

"The Influence of Early Military Decisions upon the National Structure of the Soviet Union," *American Slavic and East European Review*, October 1950.

"Operation Rewrite: The Agony of Soviet Historians," *Foreign Affairs*, October 1952.

"The Struggle for the Soviet Succession," *Foreign Affairs*, July 1953.

"In Defense of *Three Who Made a Revolution*," *American Slavic and East European Review*, February 1956.

Introduction to *Ten Days That Shook the World* by John Reed, 1960.

"Marx, Karl Heinrich," *Collier's Encyclopedia*, 1961.

"Rosa Luxemburg and V. I. Lenin: The Opposite Poles of Revolutionary Socialism," *Antioch Review*, Summer 1961.

"A Century of Marx and Marxism." In Henry L. Plaine, ed., *Darwin, Marx, and Wagner*. 1962.

"French Socialism, German Theory, and the Flaw in the Foundation of the Socialist International." In John Sheldon Curtiss, ed., *Essays in Russian and Soviet History in Honor of Geroid Tanqueray Robinson*. 1963.

"Lenin and Inessa Armand." *Slavic Review*, March 1963.

"War Comes to Russia." *Russian Review*, April 1963.

Introduction to *Impressions of Lenin* by Angelica Balabanoff, 1964.

Introduction to *Stalin: An Appraisal of the Man and His Influence* by Leon Trotsky, 1967.

"Backwardness and Industrialization in Russian History and Thought." *Slavic Review*, June 1967.

"Reflections on the Future of the Soviet System." In Samuel Hendel and Randolph L. Braham, eds., *The USSR After Fifty Years*, 1967.

"Marxism and the Russian Revolution." In Milorad M. Drachkovitch, ed., *Fifty Years of Communism in Russia*, 1968.

"A Historian Looks at the Convergence Theory." In Paul Kurtz, ed., *Sidney Hook and the Contemporary World*, 1968.

Introduction to *The Early Years of Lenin* by Nikolai Valentinov, 1969.

"Krupskaya Purges the People's Libraries," *Survey*, Summer 1969.

"Leon Felipé: Poet of Spain's Exodus and Tears," *Tri-Quarterly*, Fall 1969.

"Dress Rehearsals for the Great Terror," *Studies in Comparative Communism*, April 1970.

Introduction to *Lenin: Notes for a Biographer* by Leon Trotsky, 1971.

"The Influence of Lenin on the History of Our Times: The Question of Totalitarianism." In Bernard W. Eissenstat, ed., *Lenin and Leninism*, 1972.

Introduction to *Operation Keelhaul: The Story of Forced Repatriation from 1944 to the Present* by Julius Epstein, 1973.

Introduction to *The Rise and Fall of American Communism* by Philip Jaffe, 1975.

Introduction to *The Russian Rockefellers: The Saga of the Nobel Family and the Russian Oil Industry* by Robert W. Tolf, 1976.

Articles

"Towards Leninism," *Workers Monthly*, January 1927.
Revolutionary Age series on *The Next War*
1. "What Will It be Like," March 21, 1931.
2. "How It Will Begin," March 28, 1931.
3. "Science Goes to War," April 4, 1931.
4. "The Race with Death," April 18, 1931.
5. "What's to Be Done," April 25, 1931.
6. "What's to Be Done," May 1, 1931.
"Our Heritage from 1776," July 4, 1931.
"On the Agrarian Revolution: Kautsky 'Defends' the Russian Revolution," October 17, 1931.
"The Communists and 'Americanism'—We Are the True Guardians," November 28, 1931.
"Background of Spain's Civil War," *Marxist Quarterly*, October-December 1937.
"The Silent Soviet Revolution," *Harpers Magazine*, June 1941.
"Stalin at the Peace Table," *Common Sense*, May 1943.
" 'Hire a Hall': Some Adventure on a Lecture Tour Through the Land of Free Speech," *New Leader*, October 7, 1944.
"The Battle of San Francisco: Further Adventure on a Lecture Tour Through the Land of Free Speech," *New Leader*, October 14, 1944.
"Poland: Acid Test of a People's Peace," *Common Sense*, March 1945.
"Trotsky on Stalin," *American Mercury*, July 1946.
"China's Fate," *American Mercury*, January 1947.
"The Rise and Fall of the Comintern," *American Mercury*, March 1947.
"Dissenting Opinion on Toynbee," *American Mercury*, June 1947.
"Marx: The Man and His Legacy," *American Mercury*, September 1947.
"Forced Labor in the Soviet Union," *American Mercury*, November 1947.
"Some Wonders of the Russian Tongue," *Modern Review*, November 1947.
"Stalin Worship in Russian Schools," *American Mercury*, January 1948.

"The Individual vs. the State," *American Mercury*, March 1948.

"Politics and Fiction in Mexico," *American Mercury*, June 1948.

"The Case of Harry Hopkins," *American Mercury*, January 1949.

"What Next in China?" *American Mercury*, April 1949.

"American Histories of Russia," *Occidental*, June 1949.

"The Problem of Power," *American Mercury*, September 1949.

"The Swaddled Soul of the Great Russians," *New Leader*, January 29, 1951.

"Russian Jokes Not Passed by the Censor," *New York Times Magazine*, July 22, 1951.

"Names are News in Stalinland," *New Leader*, December 17, 1951.

"Memories of Yusuf Meherally," *Freedom First*, July 1953.

"The Struggle Is On," *New Leader*, July 20, 1953.

"The Fate of Statistics in Communist Russia," *Socialist International Information*, December 26, 1953.

"Drowning in a Paper Sea," *New Leader*, May 2, 1954.

"The Conversion of a Communist [Samuel Putnam]," *New Leader*, June 7, 1954.

"The Strange Case of Diego Rivera," *New Leader*, October 11, 1954.

"A New Look at the Soviet 'New Look,' " *Foreign Affairs*, January 1955.

"This Business of Peaceful Coexistence," *New Leader*, January 10, March 14, 1955.

"Adventures in Forged Sovietica: Some True Literary Detective Stories," *New Leader*, July 25, August 1, 8, 1955.

"The Soviet Slave Labour Reform of 1945–55," *Thought*, November 26, 1955.

"The 'New' Soviet Leaders," *New Leader*, January 23, 1956.

" 'War Is the Womb of Revolution': Lenin 'Consults' Hegel," *Antioch Review*, Summer 1956.

"Stalinism versus Stalin: Exorcising a Stubborn Ghost," *Commentary*, June 1956.

"Why Russia Had to Cut Its Armies," *New Leader*, June 25, 1956.

"Lenin Has Trouble with Engels: A Heretofore Unanalyzed Source of Lenin's Theory of Imperialism," *Russian Review*, July 1956.

"Stalin's Ghost at the Party Congress," *Foreign Affairs*, July 1956.

"The Litvinov 'Diaries': A Literary Detective Story," *Commentary*, August 1956.

"The Hiss Maneuver," *National Review*, May 25, 1957.

"Marxism Yesterday and Today: The Prophet and His Prophecies," *Problems of Communism*, 1958.

"Marxism Today," *Antioch Review*, Winter 1958.

"Nationalism and Internationalism in Marx and Engels," *American Slavic and East European Review*, December 1958.

"The Deadly Enemy We Face," *New Leader*, January 26, 1959.

"Mr. K's Favorite Reporter," *New York Times*, June 5, 1960.

"The New Gospel According to Khrushchev," *Foreign Affairs*, July 1960.

"Leon Trotsky as Historian," *Slavic Review*, October 1961.

"War Comes to Russia-in-Exile," *Russian Review*, October 1961.

"Communist Ideology and Soviet Foreign Policy," *Foreign Affairs*, October 1962.

"Titans Locked in Combat," *Russian Review*, October 1964, January 1965.

"Some Reflections on the Convergence Theory," *Western Politica*, Autumn 1966.

"Das Kapital One Hundred Years Later," *Antioch Review*, Winter 1966–67.

"Lenin, the Architect of Twentieth-Century Totalitarianism," *Russian Revolution*, 1967.

"Stalin, Joseph (1879–1953)," *Grolier's Encyclopedia*, 1967.

"Dictatorship's Lure for Lenin," *Justice*, December 1, 1967.

"The Rehabilitation of an Unwriter: A Fragment of an Autobiography," *Russian Review*, July 1969.

"The Government of Doctor Caligari," *National Review*, December 31, 1971.

"I Learn that Nobody Is Watching Me," *Humanist*, July–August 1973.

Book Reviews

Review of *The Economic Theory of the Leisure Class*, by Nikolai Bukharin. *The Communist*, July-August 1927.

Review of *We Are Many: An Autobiography*, by Ella Reeve Bloor. *New Republic*, February 17, 1941.

Review of *The Hero in History*, by Sidney Hook. *Progressive*, May 24, 1943.

Review of *Ancient Russia*, by George Vernadsky, *New York Herald-Tribune*, September 12, 1943.

Review of *The Conquest of Mexico*, by William H. Prescott. *New York Times*, October 17, 1943.

Review of *The Russian Enigma*, by William Henry Chamberlin. *New York Times*, October 31, 1943.

Review of *Wild River*, by Anna Louise Strong. *New York Times*, November 21, 1943.

Review of *The Real Soviet Russia*, by David J. Dallin. *New Leader*, 1944[?]

Review of *Russian Cavalcade*, by Albert Parry. *New York Herald-Tribune*, February 27, 1944.

Review of *Vladimir I. Lenin: A Political Biography*, *New York Times*, March 5, 1944.

Review of *USSR: The Story of Soviet Russia*, by Walter Duranty. *New York Times*, March 26, 1944.

Review of *What Russia Wants*, by Joachim Joesten. *New York Herald-Tribune*, May 7, 1944.

Review of *The Ukraine: A Submerged Nation*, by William Henry Chamberlin. *New York Times*, December 24, 1944.

Review of *The Ukraine: A Submerged Nation*, by William Henry Chamberlin. *Progressive*, March 12, 1945.

Review of *Russia Is No Riddle*, by Edmund Stevens. *New York Times*, 1945[?]

Review of *Report on the Russians*, by William L. White, and *Russia Is No Riddle*, by Edmund Stevens. *Common Sense*, May 1945.

Review of *Management in Russian Industry and Agriculture*, by Gregory Bienstock, Solomon M. Schwarz, and Aaron Yugow. *New York Times*, May 13, 1945.

Review of *A Picture History of Russia*, by John Stuart Martin, ed. *New York Times*, December 2, 1945.

Review of *Lenin*, by Nina Brown Baker. *New York Times*, December 16, 1945.

Review of *Talk About Russia*, by Pearl S. Buck. *New Leader*, February 9, 1946.

Review of *The Great Retreat* by Nicholas S. Timasheff. *New York Times*, March 17, 1946.

Review of *The Jewish Dilemma*, by Elmer Berger. *New York Times*, March 24, 1946.

Review of *The Peoples of the Soviet Union*, by Corliss Lamont. *New York Times*, April 14, 1946.

Review of *I Chose Freedom*, by Victor Kravchenko. *New Leader*, June 1, 1946.

Review of *Politics Among Nations: The Struggle for Power and Peace*, by Hans J. Morgenthau. *New York Times*, October 24, 1948.

Review of *World Communism Today*, by Martin Ebon, and *American Communism* and 'Ypsilon,' *Pattern for World Revolution*, by James Oneal and G.A. Werner. *Commentary*, February 1949.

Review of *Stalin and German Communism*, by Ruth Fischer. *New York Herald-Tribune*, February 6, 1949.

Review of *Stalin and Company: The Politbureau: The Men Who Run Russia*, by Walter Duranty. *New Leader*, March 26, 1949.

Review of *Lenin*, by David Shub. *Russian Review*, July 1949.

Review of *Stalin: A Political Biography*, by Isaac Deutscher. *New York Herald-Tribune*, October 30, 1949.

Review of *Economic Geography of the USSR*, by S.S. Balzak, V.F. Vasyutin and Ya. G. Feigin. *Saturday Review*, December 17, 1949.

Review of *Journey for Our Time: The Journals of the Marquis de Custine*, Phyllis Penn Kohler, ed. *New York Herald-Tribune*, April 1, 1951.

Review of *Russian Purge and the Extraction of Confession*, by F. Beck and E. Goodin. *Saturday Review*, May 26, 1951.

Review of *The Age of Longing*, by Arthur Koestler. *Partisan Review*, July-August, 1951.

Review of *The Jews in the Soviet Union*, by Solomon M. Schwarz. *Commentary*, September 1951.

Review of *Stalin*, by Nikolaus Basseches. *New York Herald-Tribune*, 1952[?]

Review of *The New Man in Soviet Psychology*, by Raymond A. Bauer. *Saturday Review*, 1952[?]

Review of *Homage to Catalonia*, by George Orwell. *New York Herald-Tribune*, May 18, 1952.

Review of *The Life and Death of Stalin*, by Louis Fischer. *New York Herald-Tribune*, August 24, 1952.

Review of *Labor in the Soviet Union*, by Solomon Schwarz. *New York Herald-Tribune*, October 26, 1952.

Review of *Soviet Policy in the Far East*, by Max Beloff. *Saturday Review*, 1953[?]

Review of *European Communism*, by Franz Borkenau. 1953[?]

Review of *Soviet Empire: The Turks of Central Asia and Stalinism*, by Olaf Caroe. 1953[?]

Review of *The Dynamics of Soviet Society*, by W.W. Rostow and Associates. 1953[?]

Review of *Russian Assignment*, by Leslie C. Stevens. *Saturday Review*, 1953[?]

Review of *The Russian Mind: From Peter the Great through the Enlightenment*, by Stuart Ramsay Tompkins. 1953[?]

Review of *I Dreamt Revolution*, by William Reswick. *Saturday Review*, February 7, 1953.

Review of *Economic Problems of Socialism in the USSR*, by Joseph Stalin. *Saturday Review*, April 9, 1953.

Review of *Russia and Her Colonies*, by Walter Kolarz. *Saturday Review*, April 18, 1953.

Review of *The Shame and Glory of the Intellectuals*, by Peter Viereck. *New Leader*, May 18, 1953.

Review of *The Kremlin vs. the People*, by Robert Magidoff. *New York Herald-Tribune*, June 7, 1953.

Review of *Secret History of Stalin's Crimes*, by Alexander Orlov. *New York Herald-Tribune*, June 7, 1953.

Review of *Through the Glass of Soviet Literature*, Ernest J. Simmons, ed. *New York Herald-Tribune*, August 9, 1953.

Review of *From Lenin To Malenkov: The History of World Communism*, by Hugh Seton-Watson. *New York Herald-Tribune*, September 27, 1953.

Review of *Our Secret Allies: The Peoples of Russia*, by Eugene Lyons. *New York Herald-Tribune*, November 22, 1953.

Review of *In the Workshop of the Revolution*, by I.N. Steinberg. *New York Herald-Tribune*, December 6, 1953.

Review of *Terror and Progress: USSR*, by Barrington Moore, Jr. 1954[?]

Review of *The Prophet Armed: Trotsky, 1879–1921*, by Isaac Deutscher. *Saturday Review*, April 19, 1954.

Review of *Where We Came Out*, by Granville Hicks. *New York Herald-Tribune*, May 2, 1954.

Review of *One Man in His Time*, by N.M. Borodin. *New York Herald-Tribune*, 1955[?]

Review of *The Origin of the Communist Autocracy: Political Opposition in the Soviet State, 1917–1922*, by Leonard Schapiro. 1955[?]

Review of *The Threat of Soviet Imperialism*, C. Grove Haines, ed. *Russian Review*, January 1955.

Review of *The Moscow Kremlin: Its History, Architecture and Art Treasures*, by Arthur Voyce. *New York Times*, January 16, 1955.

Review of *A History of Soviet Russia*, Vols. 1–3, *The Bolshevik Revolution, 1917–1923*, by E.H. Carr. *Commentary*, March 1955.

Review of *The Soviet Regime: Communism in Practice*, by W.W. Kulski. *New York Times*, March 6, 1955.

Review of *The Russian Revolution, 1917: A Personal Record*, by Nikolai Sukhanov. *New York Times*, March 9, 1955.

Review of *Face of a Victim*, by Elizabeth Lermolo. *New York Herald-Tribune*, April 15, 1955.

Review of *The Communist Party of India*, by M.R. Masani. *New York Herald-Tribune*, May 22, 1955.

Review of *Reflections on the Failure of Socialism*, by Max Eastman. *New York Herald-Tribune*, June 5, 1955.

Review of *Portrait of Europe*, by Salvador de Madariaga. *New York Times*, November 13, 1955.

Review of *The Communist Theory of Law*, by Hans Kelsen. *New York Times*, November 20, 1955.

Review of *Les Partis Communistes d'Europe, 1919–1955*, by Branko Lazitch. *American Slavic and East European Review*, 1956[?]

Review of *The Thaw*, by Ilya Ehrenburg. *New York Herald-Tribune*, January 1, 1956.

Review of *The Origin of the Communist Autocracy: Political Opposition in the Soviet State, 1917–1922*, by Leonard Schapiro, and *The Russian Marxists and the Origins of Bolshevism*, by Leopold H. Haimson. *Commentary*, March 1956.

Review of *A History of Socialist Thought*, Vol. 3, *The Second International, 1889–1914*, by G.D.H. Cole. *New York Times*, April 29, 1956.

Review of *The Permanent Purge*, by Zbigniew K. Brzezinski. *New Leader*, May 14, 1956.

Review of *The Changing World of Soviet Russia*, by David J. Dallin. *Saturday Review*, May 19, 1956.

Review of *Soviet Russian Nationalism*, by Frederick C. Barghoorn. *New York Times*, June 17, 1956.

Review of *Soviet-American Relations, 1917–1920*, Vol. 1, *Russia Leaves the War*, by George F. Kennan. *New York Herald-Tribune*, November 25, 1956.

Review of *The White Nights: Pages from a Russian Doctor's Notebook*, by Boris Sokoloff. October, 1956.

Review of *The Big Thaw*, by C.L. Sulzberger. *New York Herald-Tribune*, November 25, 1956.

Review of *The Red Army*, by B.H. Liddell Hart, ed. *New York Herald-Tribune*, December 9, 1956.

Review of *Russia In Transition and Other Essays*, by Isaac Deutscher. 1957[?]

Review of *Oriental Despotism*, by Karl A. Wittfogel. 1957[?]

Review of *The Roots of American Communism*, by Theodore Draper. *New Leader*, May 13, 1957.

Review of *Unholy Alliance: Russian-German Relations from the Treaty of Brest-Litovsk to the Treaty of Berlin*, by Gerald Freund. *New York Herald-Tribune*, December 8, 1957.

Review of *Smolensk Under Soviet Rule*, by Merle Fainsod. 1958[?]

Review of *Russian Liberalism*, by George Fischer. *New York Herald-Tribune*, February 25, 1958.

Review of *Vorkuta*, by Joseph Scholmer. *New York Herald-Tribune*, February 27, 1958.

Review of *Soviet-American Relations, 1917–1920*, Vol. 2, *The Decision to Intervene*, by George F. Kennan. *New York Herald-Tribune*, March 9, 1958.

Review of *Russia, the Atom and the West*, by George F. Kennan. *New Leader*, May 19, 1958.

Review of *Always with Honor*, by Baron Petr N. Vrangel'. *New York Herald-Tribune*, June 15, 1958.

Review of *Stalin's Failure in China*, by Conrad Brandt. *New York Times*, August 28, 1958.

Review of *Doctor Zhivago*, by Boris Pasternak. *New York Herald-Tribune*, September 7, 1958.

Review of *Trotsky's Diary in Exile, 1935*, by Leon Trotsky. *New York Herald-Tribune*, October 19, 1958.

Review of *Trotsky's Diary in Exile, 1935*, by Leon Trotsky. *Encounter*, March 1959.

Review of *A History of Soviet Russia*, Vol. 5, by E.H. Carr. *New York Times*, March 1, 1959.

Review of *Stalin's Correspondence with Churchill, Attlee, Roosevelt and Truman, 1941–45*. *New York Herald-Tribune*, March 29, 1959.

Review of *A History of Socialist Thought*, Vol. 4, *Communism and Social Democracy, 1914–1931*, by G.D.H. Cole. *New York Times*, March 8, 1959.

Review of *Protracted Conflict*, by Robert Strausz-Hupé, William R. Kintner, James E. Dougherty and Alvin J. Cottrell. *New York Herald-Tribune*, July 19, 1959.

Review of *The Prophet Unarmed: Trotsky, 1921–1929*, by Isaac Deutscher. *New York Times*, September 27, 1959.

Review of *The Mind of an Assassin*, by Isaac Don Levine. *New York Herald-Tribune*, November 1, 1959.

Review of *The Red Executive*, by David Granick. *Reporter*, March 3, 1960.

Review of *A History of Soviet Russia*, Vol. 6, by E.H. Carr. *New York Times*, April 17, 1960.

Review of *The Communist Party of the Soviet Union*, by Leonard Schapiro, and *A Concise History of the Communist Party of the Soviet Union*, by John S. Reshetar, Jr. *New York Times*, May 8, 1960.

Review of *Roots of Revolution: A History of the Populist and Social-ist Movements in Nineteenth-Century Russia*, by Franco Venturi. *New York Times*, October 9, 1960.

Review of *The Conscience of the Revolution: Communist Opposi-tion in Soviet Russia*, by Robert Vincent Daniels. *New York Times*, November 20, 1960.

Review of *Civil War in Russia*, by David Footman. *New York Times*, 1961[?]

Review of *Russia and the West under Lenin and Stalin*, by George F. Kennan. *East Europe*, June 1961.

Review of *Alexander Herzen and the Birth of Russian Socialism, 1812–1855*, by Martin Malia. *New York Times*, September 10, 1961.

Review of *The Life of Jean Jaures*, by Harvey Goldberg. *New York Times*, 1962.

Review of *The Taproot of Soviet Society*, by Nicholas Vakar. *New York Times*, February 11, 1962.

Review of *Rebel in Paradise: A Biography of Emma Goldman*, by Richard Drinnon. *New York Times*, February 18, 1962.

Review of *Memoirs of a Revolutionary, 1901–1941*, by Victor Serge. *New York Times*, [1963?]

Review of *The Prophet Outcast: Trotsky, 1929–1940*, by Isaac Deutscher, and *The Basic Writings of Trotsky*, Irving Howe, ed. *New York Times*, November 3, 1963.

Review of *The Life of Lenin: A Biography*, by Louis Fischer; *The Life and Death of Lenin*, by Robert Payne; and *Lenin: The Compulsive Revolutionary*, by Stefan T. Possony. *New York Herald-Tribune*, June 14, 1964.

Review of *A History of Soviet Russia*, Vol. 7, by E.H. Carr. *New York Times*, February 7, 1965.

Review of *A History of the USSR from Lenin to Khrushchev*, by Louis Aragon. *Problems of Communism*, July–August 1965.

Review of *The Great Purge Trial*, Robert C. Tucker and Stephen F. Cohen, eds. *Book Week*, July 4, 1965.

Review of *Stalin's Russia: An Historical Reconsideration*, by Francis B. Randall. *Annals of the American Academy of Political and So-cial Science*, 1966.

Review of *The Merchant of Revolution: The Life of Alexander Israel Helphand (Parvus), 1867–1924*, by Z.A.B. Zeman and W.B. Scharlau. *Slavic Review*, December 1966.

Review of *Russia, 1917: The February Revolution*, by George Kat-kov. *Spectator*, February 24, 1967.

Review of *Twenty Letters to a Friend*, by Svetlana Alliluyeva. *Chicago Daily News*, September 23, 1967.

Review of *Memoirs, 1925–1950*, by George F. Kennan. *Chicago Daily News*, November 4, 1967.

Review of *Untimely Thoughts: Essays on Revolution, Culture, and the Bolsheviks, 1917–1918*, by Maxim Gorky. *Russian Review*, January 1969.

Review of *The Great Terror*, by Robert Conquest. *Slavic Review*, June 1969.

Review of *Only One Year*, by Svetlana Alliluyeva. *Russian Review*, January 1970.

Review of *Lenin: The Exile Returns*, by Kenneth F. and Heloise P. Mailloux. *Slavic Review*, 1971[?]

Review of *Vladimir Il'ich Lenin: Biograficheskaia Khronika, 1870–1924*, Vol. 1, *1870–1905*. *Slavic Review*, September 1972.

Review of *The Young Lenin*, by Leon Trotsky. *Slavic Review*, December 1973.

Review of *Lenin in Zurich*, by Aleksandr Solzhenitsyn. *Lugano Review*, 1976.

Speeches

"Culture and the Total State," Waldorf Conference in Defense of Free Culture, Waldorf Astoria Hotel, New York City, March 29, 1952.

"Totalitarianism and History," Conference on Totalitarianism, American Academy of Arts and Sciences, March 1953.

"Is Co-Existence Possible?" forum with Gerhart Niemeyer, Arthur Schlesinger, Jr., and Harry Schwarz, Tamiment Institute, New York City, April 14, 1955.

Commentary on Peter Wiles's paper on Soviet economic growth, Congress on the Future of Freedom, Milan, Italy, September 1955.

"The Totalitarian Potentials in the Modern Great-State Society," Congress on the Future of Freedom, Milan, Italy, September 14, 1955.

"Durability of Despotism in the Soviet System," Conference on Changes in Soviet Society, St. Antony's College, Oxford University, June 25, 1957.

"Some Reflections on the Origins and Nature of Totalitarianism," Conference of American Association for the Advancement of Slavic Studies, Portland, Oregon, May 5, 1972.

"What Was Wrong with the American Revolution? A Study in Comparative Revolution," American Association for the Advancement of Slavic Studies, St. Louis, Missouri, October 8, 1976.

Translations

Vladimir Maiakovskii, "To His Own Beloved Self, the Author Dedicates These Lines," *Slavic Review,* December 1968.

Borin Slutskii, "God," *Slavic Review,* December 1968.

Ivan Elagin, "All Rights Reserved by the Author," ca. 1973.

Ivan Elagin, "Amnesty," ca. 1973.

Contents of Wolfe's Books

Six Keys to the Soviet System (1956)

1. The Struggle for the Succession
2. A New Look at the Soviet "New Look"
3. Operation Rewrite: The Agony of Soviet Historians
4. Science Joins the Party
5. Moral Education of the Soviet Child
6. Culture and the Total State
7. Some Wonders of the Russian Tongue
8. The Great Blackout
9. The Worker Bound to the Machine
10. The Worker Bound
11. The Most Democratic Elections in the World
12. The Other Election: Men Stake Their Lives
13. Poland: Acid Test of a People's Peace
14. China and the Kremlin
15. Tito and the Kremlin
16. A Note on Colonialism
17. The Nature of Totalitarianism
    Epilogue: The Weapons Are in Our Hands

Communist Totalitarianism (1961) is a new edition of *Six Keys to the Soviet System*, with the following chapters added:

1. Marxism After One Hundred Years
2. The New Gospel According to Khrushchev
3. And One More Note on "Colonialism" Five Years Later
4. Total Power
5. The Durability of Despotism in the Soviet System
6. The Enemy We Face
7. Communist Vulnerability and United States Foreign Policy

Strange Communists I Have Known (1965)

1. The Harvard Man in the Kremlin Wall (John Reed)
2. The Catholic Communist (Jim Larkin)
3. The Conversion (Samuel Putnam)
4. The Red Queen Victoria (Angelica Balabanoff)
5. Gandhi Versus Lenin (Yusuf Meherally)
6. The Last Man in the German Social Democratic Party (Rosa Luxemburg)
7. Inessa Armand
8. The Double Agent (Roman Malinovsky)
9. Trotsky: The History-Maker as Historian
10. The Strange Case of Litvinov's Diary

An Ideology in Power—Reflections on the Russian Revolution (1969)

1. Marxism and the Russian Revolution
2. Backwardness and Industrialization in Russian History and Thought
3. *Das Kapital* One Hundred Years Later
4. War Comes to Russia
5. War Comes to Russia-in-Exile
6. Titans Locked in Combat
7. The Triple Power: The Role of the Barracks and the Street
8. Society and the State

9. Lenin: The Architect of Twentieth-Century Totalitarianism
10. The Durability of Despotism in the Soviet System
11. The Struggle for the Succession
12. The Age of the Diminishing Dictators
13. Prometheus Bound
14. The Dark Side of the Moon
15. The Forced Labor Reform after Stalin's Death
16. Elections under the Dictatorship
17. Party Histories from Lenin to Khrushchev
18. Science Joins the Party
19. Culture and Communist Criticism
20. Some Wonders of the Russian Tongue
21. The Great Blackout
22. Communist Ideology and Soviet Foreign Policy
23. Poland: The Acid Test of a People's Peace
24. The Convergence Theory in Historical Perspective

Revolution and Reality: Essays on the Origin and Fate of the Soviet System (1981)

1. Backwardness and Industrialization in Russian History and Thought
2. The Reign of Alexandra and Rasputin
3. Gapon and Zubatov: An Experiment in "Police Socialism"
4. War Comes to Russia
5. Autocracy Without an Autocrat
6. Lenin and Inessa Armand
7. Krupskaya Purges the People's Libraries
8. Soviet Party Histories from Lenin to Khrushchev
9. A Party of a New Type
10. The Split in the Socialist Parties
11. Tito and Stalin
12. The Struggle for the Soviet Succession
13. A New Look at the Soviet "New Look"
14. Stalin's Ghost at the Party Congress
15. The New Gospel According to Khrushchev

16. The Durability of Despotism: Forty Years of Revolution
17. Reflections on the Future of the Soviet System
18. A Historian Looks at the Convergence Theory
19. The Totalitarian Potentials in the Modern Great-State Society

Lenin and the Twentieth Century: A Bertram D. Wolfe Retrospective, edited by Lennard D. Gerson (1984)

 1. Lenin—The Russian Background
 2. A Party of the New Type
 3. Lenin and the Class War
 4. How Lenin Prepared for August 1914
 5. Lenin-Stalin: How Two Became One
 6. Lenin-Stalin: The Party Machine
 7. V.I. Lenin and Maxim Gorky: A Study of a Stormy Friendship
 8. To the Finland Station
 9. 1921: Lenin's Change of Course
10. Stalin in the Driver's Seat
11. Lenin and the Uses of Power
12. The Influence of Lenin on the History of Our Times: The Question of Totalitarianism

Index

About the Editor

Robert Hessen is a historian educated at Queens College, Harvard University, and Columbia University. He is a senior research fellow at the Hoover Institution and general editor of the Hoover Archival Documentaries series.

HOOVER ARCHIVAL DOCUMENTARIES
General editors: Milorad M. Drachkovitch (1976–83)
Robert Hessen (1983–)

The documents reproduced in this series (unless otherwise indicated) are deposited in the archives of the Hoover Institution on War, Revolution and Peace at Stanford University. The purpose of their publication is to shed new light on some important events concerning the United States or the general history of the twentieth century.